CONTENTS

PREFACE

This volume presents the contents of the second half of a graduate course on Dante's *Divine Comedy* given by Professor Dino Bigongiari, Da Ponte Professor of Italian (and later, a special guest lecturer in the Department of English and Comparative Literature), at Columbia University. In 2005, a volume covering the first half of the course appeared with the title *Backgrounds of the* DIVINE COMEDY (Griffon House Publications).

I noted, in the earlier volume, some of the difficulties encountered in trying to collate and edit notes taken separately by my husband and me in the several years we audited Bigongiari's "Dante and Medieval Culture." The plan to produce a volume for each of the two semesters of the course was virtually abandoned in the intervening years. Not until recently, after my husband's death in 1999, my retirement from active university teaching and two years as Chairwoman of the Board of Trustees of The City University of New York, did I return to the project and bring it to completion.

The major problem I faced in the first volume and again, in the present one, was restructuring, into a fluent text, lecture notes that captured the effective (often dramatic) immediacy of the Socratic exchange of Bigongiari's classroom. The difficulty was compounded, in preparing the present volume, by the very nature of its contents: sharply focused readings of selected passages, readings that Bigongiari often interrupted in the middle of a line in order to enlarge on a phrase or word, or comment on the translation, or for other reasons that would help us better understand and appreciate the poem: *e.g.* "asides" to warn us against misleading interpretations by certain critics, reminders of Dante's terse style, abrupt transitions from one passage to another (at times, skipping over many cantos), contemporary and often personal anecdotes to illustrate a point – an invaluable experience for those of us present, since we could keep up with him easily enough with the text in front of us, but difficult to weave into some kind of continuity, for a book.

In spite of these obstacles, my primary goal was, as in the earlier volume, to structure what seemed a casual, even arbitrary, presentation into a format that would read fluently and yet preserve the substance and, if possible, something of the style of those lectures. The task proved formidable for other reasons besides those already mentioned. In the earlier volume, Bigongiari's vast learning was clearly (and overwhelmingly) evident in the extended discussion of sources, Greek authors and works, philosophical ideas, and much else. In this present volume, his easy familiarity with Greek and Latin texts, the Church Fathers, Church history, Tuscan usage, foreign equivalents of important words and phrases, and etymological sources – as well as his ability to quote from memory relevant passages from a variety of authors and languages – surface only when triggered by a name or reference, when a phrase or a word compelled him to explain and correct. The result is a wealth of precious insights and facts, bits and pieces of scattered treasure falling into place within an implicit design, often with a wry humor and peppered with personal anecdotes. This approach was natural and even necessary, in what was essentially *explication de texte*; but "seaming" together the many interruptions, the abrupt movement from one passage to another, the many asides that gave flavor and immediacy to the readings, proved an even greater challenge than the earlier one. A good deal had to be sacrificed if sentences were to flow easily: repetitions had to be minimized wherever possible, so that the Italian line could move easily into the English version; asides often had to be left out; rhetorical touches, meant to prod students into awareness, had to be deleted; many other adjustments also had to be made if these lectures were to be turned into a readable book. And, of course, the quick references to ancient and modern sources could not be elaborated, as they had been in the first half of the course, where we were introduced to Dante's world in a systematic and comprehensive way.

In spite of the difficulties, what has emerged should prove of interest to Dante scholars and students of the Renaissance. Bigongiari's authoritative voice can still be heard in his references to sources, his explanations, his constant warnings against accepting glib and often unfounded or ignorant interpretations, cautioning even against the use of dictionary definitions. An example of what happens when one relies on dictionaries for meanings of foreign words comes at the very beginning of the poem, with the phrase *mi ritrovai* [*in una selva oscura*], often given in English as "I found myself again [in a dark wood]." Bigongiari was quick to point out that in Florence, the word *ritrovai* meant simply "found [myself]."

Invaluable, still, and indisputable are his many comments on Dante's unorthodox, almost heretical views, especially with respect to the place of Roman history in God's providential design. This kind of discussion was covered in detail in the earlier course (and can be found in *Backgrounds*); here it is reviewed briefly, by way of explaining certain lines: — how, in Dante's view, the legacy of Rome was of equal importance as the legacy of Christianity; how, almost predictably, Dante places the great pagan poets and philosophers in Limbo rather than in Hell proper (contrary to Catholic doctrine of the time); how, on his own authority, he gives Cato, a pagan and a suicide, the prestigious job of guardian of Purgatory instead of placing him in the wood of suicides he himself has created as punishment for those who have sinned against nature and God by taking their own lives — or placing him anywhere else in Hell. In fact, Cato is saved, in Dante's design.

Another departure from orthodoxy and Catholic doctrine (past and present) is his insistence on Free Will, rather than Grace, as the major player in our lives. And, of course, the great instigator, what makes the journey possible, is reconstituted love. As Bigongiari reminds us again and again, the *Divine Comedy* is a love poem, based on a system of love-ethics which applies to all aspects of our lives, including politics. But we are also told, and just as emphatically, that Dante's notion of ethics derives from Plato and has little in common with Christian ethics. All of this comes through unequivocally, clearly (if briefly) articulated in every instance, always supported by Dante's own words.

The plan for the course, as Bigongiari himself tells us, was to focus on selected readings in the *Inferno* and *Purgatorio* only. He hoped that by the end of the course, this representative sampling of key passages would have taught us how to read the rest for ourselves

— how to read the entire poem again, with greater understanding. He taught us what to look for, what to explore, what authors to consult to help us grasp Dante's meaning. We all profited, in some way, from his masterly coaching. He gave us a measure of confidence we would not otherwise have had, especially those of us returning to the text after the course was over. In *Readings in the DIVINE COMEDY* I have tried to capture as much as possible of that unforgettable experience.

No attempt has been made to check Greek spellings or foreign quotations. (I wouldn't know where to start.)

Since Dante's own text often varies from one edition to the next, no large effort was made to check the original lines in Italian or, for that matter, the often archaic English translations (although in some extreme cases, changes have been made to effect an easier, more natural wording).

Long answers to question have been relegated to the end of each chapter. Brief answers have been incorporated into the text.

Chapter titles have been added to give the reader, in each case, some indication of the focus and direction of the discussion.

Whatever errors exist are mine alone.

ANNE PAOLUCCI
February 4, 2006

1. INTRODUCTION: THE MORAL STRUCTURE OF THE POEM; ROME; THE PAGAN WORLD

In the pages that follow, I will focus on the most important cantos of the *Divine Comedy*, and provide a commentary and explanation of certain passages. I will begin with the salient points of the first ten cantos, then discuss the arrangement or classification of the *Inferno* as a whole and move to the most dramatic part of the *Inferno*, the *Malebolge*, the evil pits where some of the most glorious characters are found — glorious not because of their achievements, but for what Dante has done with them. Finally, I will consider perhaps in greater detail, the winding up of Hell, the spectacle of evil at the very bottom [cantos 30-34].

The *Divine Comedy* is a poem with an ethical purpose, which means it's a study of ways and means, you might say, for attaining the state of beatitude: the end toward which all other ends are oriented, as means, but which itself is oriented toward no ulterior end. That is what beatitude, or happiness, is: an end in itself.

For Dante, the happiness which is the goal of ethical activity is described much more along the pagan or Greek lines than along Christian lines; or if it is Christian, it is far from what most of us understand by Christian. The happiness which is the highest good, or God, for Dante is the happiness that appears at the end of philosophic knowledge. It's not the God of the Christians, the merciful father, the one who teaches us to annihilate ourselves for the sake of the absolute

good. It's a God that integrates in Himself all knowledge. In other words, it is the God that connects or
includes all substance and accidents, the source and
cause of all being, the God that explains everything —
not as things are explained in Genesis, but in a way that
only philosophers can attain. And you out there will
tell me, without my having to tell you, that a God that
can be attained only by the philosophically enlight-
ened has no connection with the Christian God. Unfortunately, it is the God of Dante.

At the end of the poem, Dante reaches beatitude
in seeing God; and in seeing God, he controls all sorts
of being and knowing. The *Paradiso*, the third of the
three divisions, shows the process by which this knowledge, which culminates in the intellectual vision of
God, is attained, in connection with what is the source
of all physical phenomena in Dante's astronomical
system, namely, the stars. But in order to have access
to this world where knowledge is acquired, a moral
change must take place. There is, therefore, need of
another section, namely, Purgatory, where Dante describes how the moral condition can be attained, how
man can cleanse himself, morally, so that he is disposed to proceed into the world of knowledge.

But, and this is very Catholic, before you can
begin the process of moral regeneration which is the
Purgatory, you must be properly disposed toward it;
and you are properly disposed only when you have
acquired, when you have developed a repugnance, a
loathing for evil. In order to be regenerated, you have
to take yourself out of your old skin; and you do this
by contemplating what evil does in man; and this —
which is the preparation for the moral transformation
of Purgatory, which is in turn, the necessary prepara-

tion for the ascent into the world of knowledge — is the function of the *Inferno*.

The *Inferno* is not just a gallery of sinners, exemplifying the infamy of sin; it's not just a gallery of criminals more or less graded according to the gravity of their sins. You have that, but you also have an examination of what evil is philosophically, and, if you will, also theologically. That is, after having started off very much as the Catechism starts with the classification of sins — already stable by the time of St. Ambrose though it was worked out earlier in part, having been elaborated by the heathens themselves — Dante realizes he needs something else to tie together the *Inferno* with *Purgatorio* and the *Paradiso*, something to give unity in variety, constancy in development. He gives us a chance to examine the nature of evil, to come to some conclusion as to what evil is. To many, this may seem to be a matter of no importance; but not very late in the development of Greek philosophy it had acquired an eminence and predominance which it was never to lose. From that moment on, we have what since Leibnitz's time has come to be called *theodicy*; and it begins with the realization, on the part of thinking people, that evil is not something that *is*, but something that *is not*, yet should be; it is not an essence, it is not an existing something, but a *privation*.

This will have to be explained from the point of view of the construction of the *Inferno* from time to time. What do we mean when we say that a man is blind? Blindness is not an essence; there is no such essence in nature as blindness. There is such a thing as sight, however, and when this essence is removed, then a thing that should be there is not there. It is not an absence, but a privation; if you say that evil is an

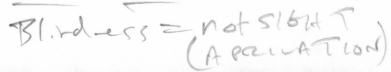

absence of activity, of life — in a stone, for example — you are wrong. There is not supposed to be life in a stone. Privation is different from absence. So that the general predicate under which we can place evil is privation: of something that should be, in the moral sphere, but is not. Dante hammers on that repeatedly, and not only in the *Divine Comedy*.

What gives a peculiar quality to his presentation is that he is going to deal with a privation that is caused by an act of free will in man. Free will is really the great character, the hero of the *Divine Comedy*. If I were to say that Dante is heretical, I could prove it in this: the two great things in Dante are free will, and that something that gives the free will its impulse to act, namely, love. That can't be all, for Christians. If we are going to have God as something more than an examiner and punisher of sinful acts and a rewarder of good works — and for a Christian, God has to be infinitely more than that — you have to have, in addition, *grace*, that something that for Dante has to be more or less sacrificed on the altar of free will. The whole thing can be summed up as the exercise of a free will under the stress of love.

Dante manages things in such a way that evil, moral evil, is not simply a lack of something but a lack of love; that is, love, properly understood, love which operates in all things — in man, in all his varied needs and desires up to the highest human appetite, which is the search for truth. So, in the latter part of the *Inferno* and in the *Paradiso*, as well as in *Purgatorio*, you see the working, the development of love and free will. In the *Inferno* love is pumped out, you have a gradual diminishing of love toward fellow beings, which is indicated pictorially by the ever narrowing circles with less and less room for love, until — when you reach the bottom, the last level, where evil is depicted at its worst, as the greatest deprivation of love — you have what amounts to a paralysis of love, and that, of course, is treason, the worst betrayal of love.

The whole doctrine of the relation of love to ethics is worked out systematically in the middle cantos of Purgatory. *Paradiso* is the acquisition of knowledge through love. Here — I don't know if he was aware of the fact directly — Dante follows very closely, and accurately, the Platonic doctrine of the quest for knowledge, by way of that *eros philosophicus* described in the *Symposium* and the *Phaedrus*. Plato had no difficulty moving into philosophical knowledge, in a process that begins with physical love — desire for beauty in a physical body. We shouldn't be surprised, therefore, in connection with this love of knowledge which Dante satisfies by climbing from one star to another, to discover that in the *Paradiso*, the origin, the means and indeed the end that gives satisfaction at each intermediate stage, is a woman: Beatrice. Anyone who has ever felt passion for the physical beauty of a human body may some day come to feel that same passion for the objects of philosophic knowledge, as Dante did.

The *Paradiso* is simply the manifestation of *eros* — I call it by the Greek word. (We used to speak of philosophic *erotica*, not too long ago, but of course many of us have been overcome by modern psychology and its tendencies, so that the words, no doubt, have a strange meaning.) Very dramatically, throughout the *Divine Comedy*, not so much in the *Inferno*, but increasingly in the other two parts, and especially in the *Paradiso*, this lesson of the fruitfulness of love for attaining beatitude is brought out very much in detail.

The whole thing is made possible by the presence of Beatrice who appears at the close of *Purgatorio* and throughout *Paradiso*.

But there is more to it. The *Inferno* itself, from the very beginning — the whole process of moral transformation — is made possible by love, Beatrice's love. After a hesitant presentiment of some kind of grace, a presentiment which is very dubious, because Dante starts off by being himself horrified by the state of sinfulness in which he finds himself, he then proceeds by a kind of grace that could not possibly satisfy the piety of a Christian soul that wants to be orthodox. This grace, which operates through Beatrice, is, in fact, love. Eventually it will be this love of Beatrice that gives Dante beatitude.

Once before, in life, Beatrice had tried to save Dante by her love. It's the constant reminiscence of this which gives to the *Divine Comedy* its unique quality and which constitutes the point of departure in Hell. Beatrice tried to bring Dante to beatitude, to God — I will not say the Christian God, but the God of Plato — long before the period of the *Divine Comedy*. It isn't so much what he fervently extols in the *Vita Nuova*, nor what he disclaims in the *Convivio*, but that which later on, in writing the *Purgatorio*, he gives as the true account of the meaning of his relation to Beatrice. Reading the lyrical poems for ourselves we are not quite convinced that the situation was as he explains it in *Purgatorio*, but that should not concern us. What should concern us here is the last account he gives of the matter at the close of that second canticle.

What had been the relation between him and Beatrice? It was love, love generated by beauty, the constant efficacy of love — Platonic love stimulated by beauty beginning on a physical level. But if you are a Platonist, or even if you are a Christian of more or less Platonic leanings, at a certain moment this corporeal beauty has to purify itself, ceasing to be material, becoming infinitely greater as a spiritual thing, as a spiritual beauty. The dramatic spectacle of love in connection with beauty is this: Dante fell in love with Beatrice because of her extraordinary physical beauty; but it was a beauty that had moral repercussions on Dante and on others, by gradually operating in the souls of all who saw her. She loves all and everyone loves her. This is a new phase in the literature of love. As he presents it in the closing lines of the *Purgatorio*, Beatrice, in life, purified the longing for physical beauty to the highest point, where you can go no further except by a change that must be, not *quantitative* but *qualitative*. In other words, Beatrice took Dante to the point of passage from the *mundus sensibilis* into the *mundus intelligibilis*, from the sensible to the intelligible world, to use Plato's terms. In order for Dante to see in Beatrice a being of purely spiritual beauty, she had to die.

So Dante interprets the death of Beatrice, in *Purgatorio*, as a necessary phase, a development which was to take place for his salvation and which would be possible only through the passage from this life to death, or from temporal life to eternal life through death. Had he learned what Beatrice had tried to teach him while she still lived, he could have reached beatitude then, and the *Divine Comedy* would not have been necessary. But he did not. He fell back. "Why did you do it?" Beatrice asks. "I could not convince myself that there was true value, true beauty in things not present to the senses," Dante tells her. He could only be drawn by sensory things (not necessarily sex); like the great majority of us, he could not see any beauty in the proper sense of the word unless that beauty was connected with the potency, the faculty of sight, or some other sense. Therefore, Dante lapses from one sin into a greater one — for so it is in the Christian world — and from that into still another which damns him to fall into still another which is graver, and so on, until the only experience left for him is death — not death of the body, not physical death, but the death of the soul.

That does not happen. He wakes up to his plight and struggles to get out of it; but his struggles would have been all in vain had there not come to his assistance a character who, as we shall see, is also activated by love: Virgil. He is sent to help Dante, to guide him through the world of evil, so that he may get through the contemplation of the spectacle of Hell with that *timor Dei* which is necessary for moral reformation. Dante has an attachment for Virgil which is one of the most endearing expressions of love in the entire *Divine Comedy*. The whole thing is conveyed in very few words, but it is very moving.

The transformation of Dante takes place, under the guidance of Virgil and of love, as he contemplates what happens to man, when he forgets that his motive power is love of God — love of God, no doubt, through our fellow beings, yet love of God — and tries to build up for himself a world of self-centered desires, which builds and divides itself viciously, in perpetual conflict. Why was Virgil chosen to do this? One could say that without him the *Inferno* would be very flat. Dante himself never tells us the essential thing that will settle the matter and ease our curiosity. He begins by giving a reason we know can't be the real one. For there is a problem, one we don't worry about much today.

Christianity was from the beginning preoccupied and anxious about it, about the fate of so many good people in the ancient world — by good, I mean morally well-endowed — who, because of the time of their birth, could not know Jesus Christ either by faith or by presence. What happens to those people? At the very beginning we find Justin the Martyr, in the second and third century A.D., saying I cannot believe that such men must suffer. Some Popes were animated by it. And, of course there is Abelard (he was quite a lover too in his own way, though we're not interested in that side of him here). Like some people long before and long after him, Abelard thinks he can discover in the writings of Plato the second person of the trinity, and therefore Christ. But of course for Christians, it's not sufficient to know the second person of the trinity; one must believe that that second person became man: true God and true man. How Abelard imagines he can find the incarnate Christ in Plato, and thus save him for the Christian world, I don't know. Dante does the same sort of thing. He saves many pagans; not only Trajan, who had been looked upon with favor by many popes, but many of his own choosing. Rifeius, to whom Virgil gives one line in the *Aeneid,* is saved. Cato is saved — not only saved, but given charge of Purgatory. These choices have political and moral connections with justice, as we'll see; and that tells us what a State, if it is to be just, must be. The French, the Germans have written dozens of books on the subject.

Dante, who is very often so advanced, so semi-Pelagian, who often takes a position the very opposite of St. Augustine, here takes a position which is very reactionary, outdoing in his pessimism St. Augustine himself. He introduces a whole canto of people who lived either before the coming of the Christ or who lived in lands where He was not preached, and so could not meet the conditions necessary for salvation. These people are not sinners in any positive sense. They are in Limbo — which can be construed as a perfect place for philosophers, a place without pain, where they can pursue their constant search for knowledge to the very apex, except that the whole thing then collapses, and they have to start all over again, knowing they can never attain full satisfaction of the desire to know.

The problem is: why did Dante save Rifeius, and some others, and why did he not save Virgil whom he loved so much, and with such tenderness (that's the proper word to use for Virgil; the pagans taught Dante something about that feeling, which Christianity increased in him). You can say: he needed a guide, someone who would show in himself how much can be done morally, even without revelation or faith. But I think Dante had something else in mind. Virgil performs a special function which is very important; his value is greater than many of those who Dante saves. Virgil, Dante would have us know, had a torch to illuminate the whole universe, but instead of keeping it in front, he kept it behind himself to light he way for others. What does that mean? It means that Dante wants to make of this great pagan poet, a prophet, even an apostle of faith. And the point is, he could only be that, in the particular role Dante assigns to him, if he remained where he was, saving not himself but others, including Statius and a host of other people.

That raises another question: the danger for orthodoxy in Dante's extolling of pagans. We see it in his choosing Cato to be the guardian of Purgatory. We see it also in something else, to which he returns again and again. He admits what is generally admitted, that in all other nations, the world is such that men politically organized inevitably accomplish some deeds which are good and others which are bad. God is responsible for the good things that are done, and he tolerates the things that are bad. This is true of any State you can think of. But Dante boldly declares that in the case of Rome, there was nothing to tolerate; everything that Rome did was good. In the *Monarchia*, and the *Divine Comedy*, Dante constantly hammers on this monstrosity. Everything that Rome did was directed by God. And, again in the *Convivio*, he comes out with another statement that is monstrous for a Christian: that at no time was the world so well off, nor will it ever again be so well off, as under the pagan emperor Augustus. Under him, human perfection was attained. It is all part of Dante's unrestrained adoration of antiquity.

We see it also in his moral enthusiasm. Naturally, he is always preoccupied with the classification of good and bad, in his poem. A common person might simply say: those who follow Christ are good; those who do not are bad. Dante says: No. Those people are good, who are descended from the Romans; those who are not descended from the Romans are bad. It is a racialism as strong as any of those we have recently encountered. When he comes to talk about Florence, he says there are good and bad. The bad are those who descended from Fiesole, those mountaineers who came down from the hills of Florence; the good are those who descended from Rome. Dante's concept of Rome is not the one which has been utilized by Italians after him. For Petrarch, or Machiavelli, or Mussolini, or Scelba and so many others, for modern Italy, the

concept of Rome is that habitation in a certain place gives one the right to claim descendence from the greatest people who ever lived there. It is hard to see how such folly arises, but there it is; it has been plaguing Italy for centuries. Not so, for Dante: Rome is not the hunting ground of the Italians; it is not for Italians but for the whole world. Just as in the ancient world, people born in Spain, in Africa, in other places, were Romans — being Roman had nothing especially to do with Italy — so for Dante the greatest of Romans in his day, the man whom he wants for Chancellor, is Henry of Luxemburg, Henry VII. He's the true Roman. Dante could not conceive of any other standard of value except the ethnic one of descent from Rome.

2. THE APPEARANCE OF VIRGIL

The *Divine Comedy* is a treatise on ethics; and in the language of the thirteenth century, ethics is a process which enables man to reach happiness, as a man. But the characteristic thing about this happiness is that it comes as a result of another person's love. Dante is able to straighten himself out because someone loved him very dearly. So this ethical tract also turns out to be a love poem, or, the description of an act of love by a woman who died for Dante's sake; and even though her death was in vain, even though she did not then succeed in saving him, she succeeded, eventually, by another kind of teaching in what she failed to accomplish by her death. So the important thing to remember is that the poem gives us the evolution of an ethical doctrine, through the action of one person, and also through the mediation of another, who is a passive agent.

The first appearance of Beatrice, this active agent, under divine control, who regulates the course of things for Dante through an intermediary is at the beginning of the *Inferno*. At the very end of *Purgatorio*, she appears in all her glory, to indicate that all the intermediary phases, all the many acts of purification, point to one end, Dante's final regeneration. In the *Paradiso*, of course, she is Dante's guide. She leads the poet to happiness by love sparked by beauty.

To some, this notion of beatitude may seem strange, this beatitude which for men of Dante's caliber, consists in knowledge which is not really either

13

profoundly or very honestly Christian. It may seem strange, this exaltation through beauty, this love that had to do with disembodied beauty, love of ideas — to express it in Platonic terms — love of principles. The Platonic tradition, the Platonic way of approaching this matter is found in the *Phaedrus*, and the *Symposium*, especially the *Phaedrus*, where Plato helps you to see how naturally you rise to the loving contemplation of ideal beauty, spurred on through moral perfection by a love that at its origin has been aroused by corporeal beauty, beauty in bodily form. So that if Beatrice becomes finally a teacher of wisdom, in the *Paradiso*, that doesn't mean she was always a teacher of wisdom; she was once also a beautiful girl, and that is part of the Platonic development. This Florentine girl was so beautiful that she gradually came to be admired by Dante and by everyone else, and because of that admiration, he and others are morally transformed.

We must not be surprised to hear that this beautiful girl is ready to die, and does die, for Dante, in order to lead him from the love of corporeal beauty to love of disembodied beauty. To indicate the full significance of this development and the close connection between physical beauty and spiritual beauty, there used to be a widely current term which is very fitting, *eros philosophicus*, which might be translated "philosophical erotics," except that in its modern connotation, it might strike some as a shocking term. Or we might go along with the philosophers of the seventeenth century who said simply *amor philosophicus* and let it go at that.

Beatrice regulates the *Inferno* through an *interposita persona*, and that intermediary person is Virgil. Thus we find joined together the two things that

Dante held most dear: poetry and love. Dante tells us at the beginning that, when he reached the age of thirty-five, he realized that theoretically he was way off track; that he did not know what the truth was, and therefore what goodness was, for, in an intellectualistic system the two are the same. In other words, he had fallen into grave error. What that error was he doesn't tell us here. In *Purgatorio* he tells us about it in more detail. It was probably the great Florentine error of the day — Epicureanism, or materialism.

Dante at a certain moment in the *Convivio* has the moral courage — for which courage I certainly don't envy him — to take a passage of the Gospel and interpret it allegorically, to show that three things mentioned there are simply symbolic of three schools of philosophy — a bit shocking to find the Gospel thus treated. Of the three Greek schools that are presented symbolically, Dante says, one is the school of Epicurus, the materialist who denied the immortality of the soul and also the spirituality of the soul. What's interesting is that when Dante comes to write the *Divine Comedy* he puts Epicurus and his sect down in the lowest Hell as the spring and source of the worst evil — or rather because the ideas of Epicurus, whatever his personal conduct may have been, are the theocratic source of the moral infamy of lowest Hell.

He begins with: "in the middle of the journey of our life" (very likely this has an astrological origin). "I came to myself . . . " — the phrase is untenable for *mi ritrovai*, which is the Tuscan phrase, "I found myself." He doesn't want to say how he got there. The *diritta via*, of course, is the way of rectitude. He uses here special terms with a moral significance. From the days of the Pythagoreans down, and still today, we speak of a crooked man, of a straight road; up, above, is good, down, *la bas*, is bad. It's of course the ancient Pythagorean moral geometry. And since it was a dense forest, there was no light — naturally you could not see the straight way. Immediately, the moral is made a function of the intellectual. "How hard a thing to tell . . . with what fear it fills me. . . ." Here you have a series of hammer blows: a single word is heard throughout this first canto: *paura, paura, paura.* What happens to Dante after his hysterical bewilderment, after he has felt fear, is the beginning of wisdom. *Poco è più morte .* . . . Death is used here in the biblical sense, as death of the spirit. Mortal sins do not kill your body, they kill your soul.

 Del ben ch'io vi trovai. The good that he found there, of course, is Virgil; Virgil is the emissary of Beatrice. *Com'io v'entrai.* . . . This period of his life, this sojourn in darkness, where there is no light, is, therefore, a passing through, or rather, a straying, represented as a single night. It might have been one year, three, four, or five years, but it is represented as one long night. When he entered upon this night of heresy and malefaction, he was sleepy, his mental activity drowsed. "When I abandoned the true way. . . . " Any one accustomed to the language of the Gospels, to the language of preachers, knows that *verax via*, in that language, is the word for the Savior: I am the Way, *via, veritas, vita.* So Dante's materialism has to be and was anti-Christian. What else could it be? *Dove terminava quella valle.* . . . This forest, this desert which is a forest with no kind of life in it, comes to an end, and the end of the forest — the reaching of the end of that forest — corresponds to the end of those many years of slumber. He has feached "the foot of a hill," *piè d'un colle,* the hill of knowledge, of wisdom. *M'avea di paura il cor compunto*. Again you have *paura*, but this time joined with the word *compunto* to show this time that it's not the *timor servilis*, but paternal fear, the fear that God inspires. That is brought out by the word *compunto*. At this point, *guardai in alto*. You see Dante all this time roaming aimlessly — remember, this is all allegorical — he is roaming around and all of a sudden he comes to the end, and there is a hill and the summit of the hill is bathed in sunlight. To those who have lived on a plain, this can't mean much; but if you've ever lived in a place surrounded by mountains — it's not common here, but in Germany, in Italy, in Switzerland, you have it — or if you've ever been in such places, you know that no matter how lowly the culture of the people might be, the lowest people will tell you how wonderful it is to see the mountain tops gleaming with the sun's rays when everything else is in shadows and darkness. Dante had some such picture in mind. *Le sue spalle vestite già da raggi del pianeta* already it's morning, the night of error has come to an end. For the Ptolemaic astronomy the sun was a planet, the moon was a planet — *del pianeta che mena dritto*. Again you have here the idea of rectitude, the rectitude which comes from illumination, illumination coming from the sun, which is divine wisdom.

Who was it who started this way of speaking by which God has for a standing symbol, the sun? Who started this symbolism which for thousands of years, people have resorted to, hundreds of thousands of times? Where do we find the first definitive and most beautiful expression or representation of the sun as the symbol for God? Every now and then some smart-alec professor, who remembers the time when every schoolboy knew it, may ask these questions on a test. It's Plato, of course. We find it in the sixth book of the *Republic.* The sun leads all people — you can't see your way unless you have the light of the sun; and in the moral sphere you can't rectify your way unless you have light.

Then comes fear again — *paura. Lago del cor* is apparently a physiological expression, "the cavity of the heart." *Con tanta pietà* — *pietà* for Dante and his contemporaries had two basic meanings, or rather three: one is not so very common — the one that has resulted in the English word *piety* — but the other two are much more common: one is *pity* and the other is *suffering.* You see the connection: one is *suffering,* ηαθος, and the other is *suffering with,* συμηάθεια. *Con lana affannata . . . si volge all'acqua perigliosa e guata. . . .* The greatest thing one can say about Dante — no matter how beautiful, how perfect his images, how profound his thoughts — greater than all the rest, is his capacity to take any situation which would take us fifteen lines to express with vague, blurred images, and give it to us in one line only. You see the picture, the man who has worked hard to reach the shore. *Lo animo mio. Anima,* feminine,is the psychological term; *animo,* masculine, refers almost always to volition: it's not the principle of being in animals but the principle of willing. It is consistently so used in the literature of the time. *Lo'animo mio, ch'ancor fuggiva. . . .* His body had come to a stand-still from sheer fright, but his soul was still running away.

The close adherence to the image is worth not-ing. He turns back to gaze on that deserted, lifeless pass, *che non lasciò giammai persona viva,* the pass which no living person can ever get through. He was drowning spiritually, he had sunk into a terrible error. What it was he doesn't say, but later— as I pointed out earlier — he makes it pretty clear that it was the error of Epicurus. And, as you know, an Epicurian, unless God saves him, is lost. Much that is wrong has been said about the Epicureans in Florence. Many editors of Dante seem to have missed the point here.

This matter of the prevalence of Epicurianism in Florence in the thirteenth century is interesting. Boccaccio, a quasi-contemporary of Dante, was the perfect Epicurian. I suppose he too got scared at the same point, in the middle of his life, like Dante did. Is there anything lacking in the Decameron to make Boccacio an Epicurian?

Then we come to a *piaggia deserta*; "I resumed my way through the desert place." This is followed by a line which I don't know the meaning of and neither does anyone else. Everything that anybody has ever said is only empty conjecture. *Si chè il piè fermo sempre era il più basso*. Of course the trouble with this is he seems to be climbing, and yet the description doesn't quite fit that motion. *Al cominciar dell'erta*, at the beginning of the grade, a steep grade, as the word *erta* indicates, *una lonza leggiera* — a panther? Scholars have written at least 80,000 pages on the *lonza*; but they don't know what it was. Very likely Dante didn't know himself what the *lonza* was; he had in mind the lynx of Virgil. The adjectives he uses are Virgilian. The point is, it is an animal with a certain kind of beauty. The most beautiful of all is the leopard. A very attractive beast, and *presta* — very mobile. *E non mi si partìa dinanzi al volto*. Actually, it was Dante who could not keep his eyes from it. *Impediva il mio cammin* — it kept him from moving forward, not through scaring him, but through its charm; and he found himself again and again on the verge of turning back.

But he overcame this obstacle, which obviously is the obstacle of the flesh, of material pleasures, because of an image of pure beauty which comes before him, and that image of pure beauty is the hour of dawn. The image of the hour of dawn has often been used by ancient writers to indicate purity. How often the poets, after the long night is over, tell us how they are ashamed or pretend they are ashamed of what they have been doing because the dawn appears. The other image is that of spring; it is the vernal equinox. Dante, like so many of his contemporaries, believed that God created the universe at the very moment when the sun was under the constellation of the Ram, which has since shifted from the 21st of March to the 21st of April. Of course, the beauty of Spring is not as consistently used to indicate moral purity, as is the beauty of dawn. Indeed you find Lucretius using it for the very opposite effect. But not so in Christian poetry.

E il sol montava, Dante tells us: the sun was rising among the stars that were with it when divine love, *amor divino*, the Holy Spirit, the creative aspect of the trinity, which Dante always insists should be ascribed to the third person, first put it there. *A ben sperar m'era cagione*, he says. That is, I was encouraged to stick it out, despite the charming leopard, by the fact that it was the beginning of Spring and the beginning of the day. But another obstacle now appears. *Ma non sì che paura non mi desse* — again he is struck with fear — *la vista che m'apparve d'un leone*. The lion terrifies him — the other lured him, fascinated him — *che l'aere ne tamesse*. Here you have *timore*, fear, fright. The very air was affrighted. But he slurs over that obstacle very quickly to get to the real obstacle. *Una lupa . . . carca nella sua magrezza*. We need a good word here because Dante has a very good one indeed — *nothingnesss* — or something like that. It is an oxymoron that perfectly expresses what he wants to say: the idea of sin hollowing you out. This *lupa* is so full of evil that she hardly has any substance left. She is laden with every imaginable kind of evil desire — the evil of which consumes her until she has almost no being. The word *carca* should serve to indicate that we have to deal here not simply with *avarizia* but with the source of *avarizia*, namely, *cupiditas*. *E molte gente fe' già viver grame*. Dante now tries to stress the fact that the obstacle to all proper living, what really blocks the way of those who want to move toward beatitude, is *cupiditas*; and that, of course, is bound up with the political argument that there must be a sovereign to rule the world, who, having all the things he could possible want in his power, is free to stamp out the means and temptations to covetousness for everyone else.

He says of the lynx: *mi porse tanto di gravezza* — before it was *carca*, now you have *gravezza* — this one, he says crushed me with its heavy burden. *La paura ch'uscia di sua vista* was such *ch'io perdei la speranza di sua vista*. Again, *paura*: it weighed so heavily, that I gave up hope. Then Dante compares himself, with some sort of a sneer, to a man who once had wealth and loses it, and is sad over his loss. *Quei che voluntier acquista* — such was I made to feel, *tal mi fece la bestia senza pace*, by the beast that is never satisfied. After all, with the *lonza* nature sees to it that you have to call a halt, eventually, but with *cupiditas* the more you have the more you want to have. But the *lupa* kept at it: *Mi ripingeve là dove il sol tace*. By a beautiful transfer of sensitive images, he speaks of the sun as an object not of the eyes but of the ears: "there where the sun is hushed." Such transfers were used very effectively by the Greek tragedians, particularly Aeschylus.

At this point, something happens to save Dante from the *lupa*; someone comes to his aid *chi per lungo silenzio parea fioco*, someone who hasn't spoken for a while. If you haven't spoken for a while, especially someone my age, the first words that come out when you begin to speak again are apt to come out hoarse. What it probably means here is that Virgil, who had for so many centuries been so highly regarded and read, by the thirteenth century was practically forgotten. Poetry has had its ups and downs, but never in the history of mankind was poetry so badly treated as in the thirteenth century by men who surely deserve our respect. All of them, every one of them, talked about poetry as if it were a thing fit only for inferior minds, for those incapable of reasoning.

Dante goes on: *nel gran deserto* — again the region is described as a desert — someone appears: "*miserer di me — ombra od omo*." The first thing this person does is identify himself by saying: my parents were Lombards. This, of course is a pure anachronism; in Virgil's days the Lombards were off somewhere up in Scandinavia. His parents were both Mantovans. He goes on: I was born *sub* Julio — not *sub* Christo, but *sub* Julio — not born a Christian, though he was born late in the pagan era, the days of the lying and false gods — *dei falsi e bugiardi*. Eventually, Dante changes his opinion of the gods and will give them some other significance.

Virgil goes on: I was a poet and sang of that just son of Anchise — *quel giusto figliuol*. It's hard to indicate the full force of that term *giusto*. For Dante, it came from Troy, when grand Ilium was destroyed. How much moral significance there is here! The great role that Aeneas plays in the history of Rome is determined by the fact that he was *just;* Dante hammers on it all the time. And here also is the lesson of the fall of Troy: was the destruction of Priam necessary?

Virgil asks: *Perchè non sali il dilettoso monte* — and so we know the hill is the hill of beatitude — *ch'è principio e cagion di tutta gioia.* It is what moves us toward joy and the thing where all joy ends, culminates and ends. The idea of beatitude is clearly relayed with the word *gioia*.

---

1. What does the lion symbolize?

Well, it is perfectly obvious, or it was, to every preacher and philosopher in the old days. There never used to be any question about any of these three animals. They are, of course, the famous trinity we find in the first epistle of St. John. What obstructs us in our search for happiness? Three things. One is something which tempts our flesh, our senses, in a very bodily way — primarily sex and gluttony; the other is pride of position, and power, and that's the lion; but the last one sums them all up because when you say covetousness, *cupiditas*, you include all the rest — sensuous pleasure and the exercise of power. It's the desire for more pleasure, more power, more of whatever you seek for yourself. And it's invincible and self-destructive. Everyone who has ever commented on the words of St. John has said this. It was only when literary commentators of Dante were no longer ashamed of their ignorance that confusion set in. In the epistle of

St. John we read: *Omne quod est in mundo aut est
concupiscentia carnis, aut est concupiscentia oculorum, aut
superbia vitae.* But, of course, it isn't enough to read
those words — you have to read what was made of them
by the commentators.

2. Could that *piè fermo* mean the right foot — could
fermo mean "right" in Italian?
      I won't even begin to try to answer that. I can
only remind you of what my old mathematics teacher
used to say. He would set the equation before us and
then bellow: "That's an indeterminate equation, it
cannot be made determinate unless you introduce
another constant." So long as you can't turn up some
new fact, one solution to that line is as good or as bad
as another.

3. THE FIRST EXCHANGE BETWEEN VIRGIL AND DANTE

The first canto of the *Inferno* is very important for the understanding of the whole; and although its meaning is clear enough it is yet misunderstood by many, who have not the slightest idea what the men of Dante's age meant by ethics. What Dante shows us here, as Aristotle does in the closing words of his *Nichomechean Ethics*, is how politics and ethics are welded together.

In his first encounter with Virgil, Dante says (Canto 1, l. 79): "'Thou art that Virgil that source, that fount, that spring, which spreads'" — as a spring dropping into a stream or a river spreads a great stream of poetry. You have to recall that at this time the word *parlare* was fairly close to the etymology in meaning; and all its early meanings are connected with the speech of poetry — not just speech, but inspired speech.

"I answered with lowered head . . ." — Dante feels himself crushed with humility. Virgil had taken the place of Homer; the fascination that Homer had exercised and subsequently came to exercise was now all for Virgil. In addition, he was known as the scientist, the *mago*, the magician. Hundreds of books have been written on the subject; Comparetti's is still the best, containing just about all that is really sound about the impression Virgil made upon the Middle Ages. It also helps to explain Dante's choice of Virgil. Virgil is a poet, but his poetry leads to philosophy. It's the wedding of those two that we find in Dante.

25

"'O honor and light of all the other poets; may I be helped [in your eyes] by the long study and great love'" — that is, I pursued the study of your works, and I pursued it for love, not just for utility or necessity. Of course, whatever we might think when we hear his name, for the Middle Ages Virgil meant the *Aeneid*. "'The great love that made me seek thy volume! You are my master and my authority'." Those two words are very precise in their meaning; Virgil is master in that he has taught Dante, he is the teacher-poet who wrote or sang, so that his pupil might learn; and he is the *autore*, the one from whom he might draw the authority for his arguments. Dante quotes from Virgil as an inspired poet, just as he might quote from David, to the horror of the thirteenth century theologians. Virgil's statements are authoritative and are to be regarded as on a level with the Holy Scriptures.

"'Yours the only one from whom I have derived the style that has brought me so much honor'." That may be difficult or troublesome to understand for those who do not know Dante's theory of style, and who might be tempted to think that style here refers to the *Divine Comedy*, and that behind it is the notion that Dante is writing about a journey through the regions beyond the grave and that Virgil had done the same. I know some authorities have presented it that way, but they are wrong: when Dante meets Virgil, he has not yet written the *Divine Comedy*. Besides, we mustn't forget that when Dante speaks of style, he doesn't mean what we generally mean. There are, he says, three kinds of style — low, medium and noble. The finest example of the noble is Virgil's *Aeneid*. And Dante flatters himself, with some justification, that when he was writing the *canzone* — not only those commented in the *Convivio*,

Style

but the others in the *Vita Nuova* — he was employing the noble style, just as Virgil did in the *Aeneid*. He can boast therefore, and say that in writing his *canzone* he was imitating the noble style of the *Aeneid*.

Such is Dante's reaction to Virgil. But after the initial exchange, we realize that Virgil apparently doesn't know Dante's predicament. He had been sent for, in Hell, to aid Dante, but doesn't know why. Dante tells him his troubles. "'Look at the beast on whose account I had to turn back'" — help me? rescue me? "help me" doesn't sound right — "'acknowledged sage',", *famoso saggio*. Virgil here is not the poet but the recognized — *famoso* is the technical sense of the word — sage, wise man, the great philosopher. That is, as we indicated, why he was popularly represented as a magician. "'For it makes my veins and my pulse tremble'." He has palpitations, through fear of the she-wolf. Break up the imagery here and try to see the man who wants to get back on the right path that he has abandoned, who realizes that the obstacle to his doing so is this one great monster who has swallowed all the other monsters and keeps them, in Augustinian language, all alive in itself. This one great monster is *cupiditas*. When Dante has reached the proper frame of mind, he tells us that it frightened him, that he was horrified by the thought of what he was doing. And then Virgil realizes in an instant what it's all about, and he says: "'you'll have to follow another path'." You can't just buck the hill and go up to the mountain of beatitude, the plain of truth (Plato's imagery) which can be reached by those whom love prods on. "*A te convien tenere altro viaggio.*" The Italian — the sound of it, the rhythm, the cadence — is not simply a joy in itself, but also a help to understanding the proper psychological mood. You

have to take another route, *rispose*, he answered, when
he saw me weeping — if you want to live, if you want to
escape from this savage place, where there is nothing
except vice, vice that bestializes. *Selvaggio*, in Italian, as
in English, as in French, "savage" is connected with
sylva, forest. And the beasts live in the forests. "'For
this beast that has made you shriek, never lets anyone
go by, but harasses him until she kills him'." Again, of
course, this "killing" is the death of the spirit. "Harass-
ing" is the drive for covetousness, as St. Augustine and
other theologians tell us. Most of us don't have time to
do much else but covet. "*E ha natura sì malvagia e ria,*"
this beast, that it can leave no doubt in our minds as to
what it is; "*mai non empie la bramosa voglia,*" it never
satisfies its yearning, its greed.

From earliest antiquity, insatiability is the marked
characteristic of greed: when you have ten you want a
hundred, when you have a hundred you want a thousand. And you know that it is evil from the very fact
that it leads you into an infinite series. Infinity was, for
any good Greek, non-being, non-good. The finite was
the good, they tell us. But, semantically, the word for
perfect in Greek is *teleo* — and that also means end,
finito. Well, they said, if it is so (the great problem
taken up by Dante in the *Convivio*), if it is so, what are
we going to do about knowledge? That must be evil, for
it too is infinite. But Dante denies that it is an infinite
series. The pursuit of knowledge has an end — a perfection; but it must be said of greed that after feeding, it
is hungrier than before.

Many are the animals with which it has, or is
found to be wedded. That is, you don't crave money
simply for money's sake — the Florentines called it
miseria. That meaning has not survived in modern

Italian, it survives in the English word "miser." In Italian that particular craving for money is called *avarizia semplice*. The other sense of *cupiditas* includes all the other vices considered from the point of view of wanting more and more. Is there any other point of view? Yes, of course, but Dante works out this first view in detail — greed in wealth, power, sex; the mansions, the harem — and something worse than these. Worse is when you want to do bad things not in the Sunday school sense, not when you want to do evil things to satisfy a desire, a strong passion, but just for the sake of doing evil, just for the spirit of evil. Dante does not take that up here, but he does in Canto eleven.

"'And many more will there be until the hound will come that will make this beast die in suffering; this one will not feed on land and metal'." The two forms of wealth in the Middle Ages, when they didn't have stocks and bonds, were money and real estate. Money was not paper currency, but metal; and to throw infamy upon it, Dante calls it by the cheapest name: pewter. The force of that is lost now, for pewter today is anything but a cheap metal. The moralists in Dante's time always said: What is the difference between gold and pewter? None!

"*Questi non ciberà terra ne peltro*" — that is, this man will not be actuated by desire to acquire wealth in one form or the other, but will feed on God's nourishment, namely wisdom, love and virtue. These three words are used, here and everywhere else in the Middle Ages, as corresponding to the three persons of the trinity. *Sapientia* is the Son; *Logos*, Christ; *Amore* is the Holy Spirit, the Holy Spirit symbolized by the flame and the dove. The flame has been a symbol for love since the year 5740 B.C., and the dove also as a symbol of love is fairly old. And the Father is power, virtue. Here *virtù* means power. So the one who is to come will be moved not by wealth but by the inspiration of the Holy Trinity. And then comes a line which like the earlier line about the foot, is indeterminate. There have been several tens of thousands of explanations, a new one every day, which shows how useless it is — unless you are one who thinks that an indeterminate equation can be made determinate *ad licitus*, whenever you like.

Who is this man? People who see here the Holy Spirit show that they have not understood the magnificent notion of Dante on the connection between ethics and politics — and show also that they have not read what Dante says in the *Convivio* and in the *De Monarchia*. Why should there be a world monarch with absolute power? So that he won't have to yearn for anything. And not yearning for anything for himself he will be in a position to control the conduct of others, to keep their yearnings at bay. Dante's whole political doctrine is contained here. When the hound comes he will drive *cupiditas* from the world. This emperor must have all things, so that he can maintain peace. Why must we want peace? What's wrong with war? That's a legitimate question. Eagerness for wealth, for power, makes war. Why do we want to avert war? Why do we worry about what is impending? I don't think we have a right to call what is impending today war. We ought to use another name for it. But, in the old sense of the word, we can ask why peace is to be preferred to war. What is Dante's reason? Why is peace necessary?

So man can develop his highest potentialities. What are they? Muscles? No, not even moral potentialities, except in a secondary sense. We need peace so he can develop his intellectual potentialities. Dante speaks of the man who can bring peace, at the close of the *De Monarchia*. In all times there is a unique man who is made by God, or by nature, with a capacity to read the mind of God. He has to be found and elected. And, if the electors lived properly, if they lived well, they could find this man. But they don't lead a proper life; and therefore their choice is often wrong.

Here Dante is still in his Italianate phase: *di quella umile Italia fia salute*, "who will be the salvation of Italy." Dante could never have developed as he did if he had kept at that. After a while, he doesn't worry about what happens to Italy particularly, any more than he worries about what happens to France or Spain. Or else, he is thinking of Italy through Virgil, remembering the role Italian tribes play in the *Aeneid*. He uses *umile* in the Virgilian sense. Remember that beautiful line of Virgil: *humilemque videmus Italiam*. Of course what Virgil probably meant was, "Italy lying low." But Dante adds something else to the adjective *umile*. He will *beg* this emperor, the salvation of humbled Italy, for which the virgin Camilla died, as well as Eurialus, Turnus — those beautiful characters sharply delineated by Virgil in the ninth book, the most beautiful episode in the whole *Aeneid*, for its tenderness; a source of deep moral satisfaction and joy for those who are able to read the great poetry of Virgil.

"'The greyhound who is going after the she-wolf in this forest of evil'," the greyhound who is going to come, will drive her out of every city until he shall have plunged her back into Hell where envy *dipartilla*, from which she was first released by envy. It was Lucifer, in his desire to make man an inferior creature, envious of the role of man, who taught him that awful couplet:

Meam – meam e tuam, – "mine and thine." What's terrible about that? It should be "ours." *Ogni villa,* "every country-house," in Italian, but it could also be a Gallicism, meaning "city." It doesn't make much difference here.

"'So, I for your own interest, think and decree that you follow me; I shall be your guide and I'll get you out, not by that direct route that takes you to the plain of truth on the top of that hill. I shall drag you out of here [*per loco eterno*]'." It and every other place of time, after judgment day will be no more. All that will be left is Hell and Paradise. Purgatory disappears. The rivers, the trees, the earth all go.

Dante will get out of this desert, but instead of following the path he was on, he will be taken by Virgil *per loco eterno,* "'where you will hear the shrieks of despair and you will see the ancient spirits'." He doesn't simply mean that there aren't any moderns in Hell — *antiquo* for Dante has the sense of "evil"; *novus* is the opposite — the regenerate in the Christian sense. "'And you will hear the sorrowful ancient spirits — for they are shrieking for the second death'." We don't know if Dante means that they thought or hoped that there would be a final death, not simply of the body, or of the spirit in the Christian sense, but complete annihilation. That is, *gridare* may have two separate meanings here; in the one case it means crying for, desiring; in the other it means lamenting, deploring the death of the soul. "'And then, after you have seen these, you will see those who are satisfied in fire'." Those in Hell are desperate in fire. The others are satisfied in fire, because they hope at some time to rise to the region of the blessed people to which, if you hope to ascend, there is a soul more worthy to guide you. "'With her I

shall leave you at my departure, for that Emperor'" —
Dante projects his own political system of the world
into the system of the universe. Just as on earth there
is an empire that comprises all peoples, and in this
empire there are kingdoms and republics and city-
states, and duchies and all sorts of sub-divisions, so in
the universe that is ruled over providentially by God.
The whole is an empire, and in that empire there is a
kingdom. That kingdom is heaven — the rest of the
universe is the empire. And God, therefore, is not only
Emperor of the universe but also king of heaven. This
is the common political language familiar to everyone
of Dante's day, particularly used in describing the
actual situation. For the Holy Roman Emperor is the
king of the Romans and Emperor, as Barbarossa said,
of all these lesser potentates indirectly. Directly, I am
King of Rome; Emperor, everywhere else. The Temple
translation has "who reigns up there." No. The Emperor up there reigns as a king.

"'Because I was rebellious to his law'. . . ." There
are three laws: the law of the Jews, the law of the
Christians, and the law of the Moslems. But *His* law is
the law of the Christians. He does not want that anyone
like myself, should ever go there, to the city of God,
Paradise, the celestial heaven. If Dante wants to get
there, he will have to go under the leadership of
someone other than Virgil.

So the emperor "*in tutte parti impera e quivi
regge.*" He has imperial sway over every place but there
he has kingly rule. (I wish Dante would remember
always that going to heaven, if you believe in heaven,
depends not on what you do, but on being chosen by
God.) "And I to him: 'Poet, in the name of the God you
did not know, that I may escape from this evil or worse,

I ask that you lead me there where you said, so that I
will see the gate of St. Peter'" — which is Purgatory —
"'and those whom you say are so sad'," namely, those
in Hell. *Allor si mosse, ed io li tensi retro. . . .* "Then he
moved, and I followed him. . . ." It is a very beautiful
line, very fitting for closing the introductory Canto.

That's the last description of the world in time.
Next, we plunge into eternal night. And this passage
into night is brought out with a famous line of Virgil.
The contrast between the coming of night, with the
rest from toil that usually comes with it, and the
feelings of someone who cannot partake of that rest is
dramatic. Virgil's lines got to be so famous that the
initial words came to be quoted alone: *Nox erat . . . .*
Dante echoes them in the opening of the second canto.
Lo giorno se n'andava, and the dusky air was moving the
animals of earth from their labors; I alone "was ready-
ing for the strife both of the road and the suffering,
namely, this voyage, which will be depicted by the mind
that does not err." He might have been alluding to what
was a commonplace in his day, namely, that mistakes
are possible in the senses and the imagination, but not
possible in the intellectual part of the soul.

"'O lofty genius'," Dante uses the word *ingegno*
to indicate the faculty that enables man to create new
thoughts. To do well, the poet has to have inborn
talent, but that is not enough; he must also be inspired.
"O Memory, that wrote what I saw" — Dante is always
harping on this; here at the beginning of the *Inferno* as
at the beginning of the *Vita Nuova* — he's always
putting before us this interesting construction, that
there are two writings, one inside, the other outside.
At the very beginning of the *Vita Nuova* he says that he
copied from the book of his memory — what you read

is a copy. Dante is the amanuensis who copies what was written inside. You have to interpret these lines in that light. "O Memory that wrote what I saw, here your nobility will appear."

Dante is very firm in saying that there is nobility indeed, but there is no such thing as nobility that comes to man because his father or grandfather had claim to a title. He wrote a magnificent treatise on it; "there is no chivalric nobility, but nobility of one's own character and virtue." Dante's nobility is to be seen in what he does as a poet, not in what his grandfather did. In the *Paradiso*, when he comes to one of his ancestors, he softens this up a little and justly so.

"I began: 'Poet [Virgil] who guides me'.". . . For artistic reasons and in order to bring in Beatrice as the cause of this action, Dante pretends that he is overcome by fear. And Virgil is unable to dispel that fear, except in one way; namely, to reassure him that the force that moves him is love — someone who loves Dante is in back of it all. Beatrice, who died for him, now has done something greater than to die for him; she has descended from heaven into Hell and comes there to provide help for Dante. "'Poet, you who guide me, look and see if my power is sufficient before you give me over to this lofty journey'." Why? Because nobody ever went into the next world, except two people — and here again is the joining of politics and ethics, and again Virgil appears on a par with the Holy Spirit: "'You tell me that Aeneas went, while still alive in the flesh, in his corruptible body'" — of course there's no religious basis for this — God permitted Aeneas to go into the next world because Aeneas was to found the Roman Empire; the second is St. Paul. These two went. But I am neither. Why should I go?

Dante asks. Is there a new faith to be confirmed, or an empire to be founded? The only answer he gets is: No. There's something else behind it, the power of a person that loves you. The question remains unanswered.

4. BEATRICE'S DESCENT INTO HELL;
THE NATURE OF GRACE

Dante is able to show, in a very touching way, how all the action of the *Inferno* depends on Beatrice's devotion, affection for him. The lines in which the encounter between Virgil and Beatrice is set (Canto 2, l. 52) are often quoted. Virgil explains: "'I was among those who are [*sospesi*] suspended'" — they are not damned and they will never be among the blessed. Dante's notion — already old-fashioned in his time, not strictly adhered to then, and long since abandoned by the Catholic Church — was that only those born into the Church, only those who have received the sacraments in the Church, can hope to avoid eternal damnation. That was the doctrine of St. Augustine and, more especially, of Cyprian, and indeed, of the entire Carthaginian diocese of North Africa. From there — after spreading over the rest of Africa — it spread to the rest of the Christian world. Dante adheres to that doctrine. Now, of course, the Catholic Church teaches that adherence to the doctrines of the Church is not necessary for salvation. What is necessary is a moral life, a life lived to conformity with the Gospel teachings, which doesn't, as you can see, exclude very many. Of course, it does exclude the atheists and those who deny that there are principles of rectitude.

"'A woman called me'," *beata e bella*. She was among the blessed and beautiful. These words may seem odd, but in Dante's time, you'll find connoisseurs of painting saying of a depicted face: that head is not *beata*, meaning, there is something missing to bring it to perfection; and what is missing is beatitude, blissfulness, the state of blessedness that appears in the physical features. And here is a very lovely compliment of troubadour origin, rather a commonplace of Provençal poetry: "'So beautiful was she that I had to ask her to give me a command'." She was so beautiful that her beauty compelled obedience. "*Tal che di commandare io la chiesi.*" There are still some traces here of the Provençal style, but much less than in the *Vita Nuova*. Those elements tend to disappear as Dante advances. In his maturity, finally, he rids himself of all that had come to him from Provence.

"*Lucevan gli occhi,*" her eyes were more resplendent, more luminous than the star. Some people have tried to make it "stars," collective; but *the* star, par excellence, is always in all these countries and in all times, one. You see it sometimes in the clear morning; you wonder if it is a star, it is so large, so clear, so resplendent. After sunset, in the west; at dawn, in the east. It is the planet Venus, in the language of poetry, Vesper. In English poetry, in the Elizabethan poets, you always have it before you. It is called Vesper from the Latin, Hesperus from the Greek, when it is east of the sun, and therefore visible just after sunset, the evening star. When it is west of the sun, it is called Phosporos in Greek or Lucifer in Latin, the star of morning; but it is always the same star, Venus. It's *la stella* and we have documentary evidence to that effect.

"'She began'" *soave e piana* — sweet as to the sound, and *piana*, not difficult to understand — "*Con angelica voce in sua favella.*" She no longer had organs of speech as we have, so the only way she could speak was with supernatural organs, *in sua favella*, her speech.

What that means is rather hard to say.

"'*O anima cortese Mantovana*'" — Virgil was born in Mantua, which is in northern Italy. *Cortese*, in Italian has a peculiar meaning, often discussed by Dante; it means good breeding, good manners, such as you would expect from the etymology of the term, such as you find in a court. In other words, it's the manner of royalty, aristocratic courtesy — """the fame of whom still exists in the world, and will last as long as motion lasts"'." Apparently it's not going to be eternal; when motion ceases (time is the measure of motion) his fame will cease. It's rather hard to fathom what's behind that. """My friend and not the friend of fortune""" — most friends are the friends of fortune. Ovid tells us in a very beautiful line: "as long as you are well-off financially, your friends are all at your side; when your fortune changes, you are left alone." """My friend is so impeded on that desert shore""" — Dante seems to stress most, in connection with this place where he went astray, that it's a desert (this is already the fourth or fifth time he mentions it). He's so harried in that desert land, that through fear he has turned to go back. """And I'm afraid he may be already so bewildered, that I may have moved too late to help him, from what I've just heard about him in Heaven. Go to him and with your ornate speech". . . .'"

Dante constantly hammers on the fact that this religious experience has to be escorted, delivered and pushed on by poetry. That is, the accompaniment of poetry goes with all action. "'*Con la tua parola ornata*'," and everything that is necessary for his salvation, that I may be consoled. She speaks here really the language of one who is in love. """I am Beatrice""" — "'*amor mi mosse che mi fa parlare*'." "'It's love that now makes me speak. And when I shall be back before my Lord, I will sing praises to him"'." She became hushed and I began: "'O lady of virtue, the only one through whom the human species can transcend the limits of that sky which has the shortest circle, so dear are your commandments to me that obedience even if instantaneous would be too slow'." Here the question arises: Why is she not afraid to come where the Sun is silent? Because you should only be afraid of things that can really hurt you and so you should never be afraid of physical harm.

This first description of Beatrice — and there are many of them — is clear enough; but, of course, the role which is set forth for her makes obvious the fact that she can't be taken any longer as just a woman. *Donna* should be translated in the etymological sense of "mistress" — she who controls as a master (the masculine equivalent) controls. She is quite a personality. She is mistress of virtue. She is the only one who enables mankind to reach, with his mind, beyond the sky of the moon. How did we get that meaning? Every child in Dante's day knew.

Picture the nine spheres, with the tenth beyond. The earth is the center of it; all around are the nine concentric skies. The first one is the moon, then Mercury, then Venus, and so on. And, naturally, as you go on, these skies are larger and the radii are longer. By sky is meant the whole sphere. The moon, Mars, the sun, and so on — the theologians, the schoolman, and the Ptolemaics before them said — the star you see (in this case the moon, which is relatively small) is imbedded in the sphere or sky. The sky of the moon is not simply the moon. The moon is imbedded in a sphere of the same quintessential matter, invisible because much lighter than the star encased in it, so that in any direction you went up you would find something that might become visible if more dense. In other words, we are here on the earth, enveloped by nine concentric spheres, complete spheres, and each identified by a body, a planet imbedded in it, except that of the fixed stars. The nearest one to us is the moon. And the body in which it is encased is the sky of the moon, which being the nearest has a radius shorter than any of the others (measured from the earth as center). These details are important, if one is to visualize the whole astronomical picture, so essential for comprehending Dante's poem, particularly the *Paradiso*.

What is the meaning of transcending the sky of the moon? Here again, you have an echo from ancient cosmology. Just as the world is divided into two parts, the world of sensibility and the world of intellect — the old Platonic distinction, according to which man is gradually to climb out of the world of sensation, into the world of the spirit — so in matter itself there is a double division. There is the matter of change, of generation and corruption, and that is the matter of the four elements — earth, water, air and fire, arranged in the order already described. The first is earth. A stone, when you let it fall, tries to get as near as possible to the center of the earth, and as near as possible, therefore, to the center of the universe. When you go beyond fire, which is the last of the four, you pass from the world of generation and corruption, to a world where there is no change. Obviously, the things here below, the things of the four elements, are in constant flux, coming into being and passing away; that's what we mean by generation and corruption. On the other hand (this is Aristotle and all that follow him) in the heavens there is no change; the skies are eternally unchanged, and the matter that is eternally unchanged, of which they are made, is the *quintessence*, as Aristotle and the Pythagoreans called it, because it's the fifth, beyond the other four changeable elements. The motion of the other elements is *rectilinear* — a stone moves straight down toward the center of the earth, fire straight up toward the heavens (that's why the boys who went to school had to learn the distinction between *gravia* and *levia*, often they were chapter headings). The first is *gravia*: a stone moves down; the fourth, fire, is light and therefore shoots up. The *quintessence*, on the other hand, moves along a *circular* line. In science, of course, this means nothing; but these phrases — *quintessence*, the world of generation and corruption — exist. The movement of the four elements is imperfect, that of the quintessence is perfect, and therefore the realm of the quintessence is beautiful. And the spirit of man, in its search for the eternal, must pass through that part of the universe which is the world of the circular movement. It's that world through which Dante will pass to acquire the knowledge necessary before reaching beatitude in the sight of God himself.

What Dante tells us here is that this woman, Beatrice, mistress of virtue, because she controls virtue, is the one who enables mankind to go beyond the limitations of perishable matter. In other words, she is the power that makes us act as human beings should act, passing beyond the mere satisfaction of the material immediate demands of our animal nature. How can a woman, or one who was a woman do that? These strange descriptions of Beatrice multiply themselves as we go along.

In what follows we learn that Virgil would not have moved and Dante would not have been rescued, unless Beatrice had come there. She starts the line through Virgil to Dante; but she, in turn, was urged on, through another agent: the Virgin Mary. We see in all this activity the part played by grace, what grace means, even though Dante seems often to brush it aside. Did the Greeks have any notion of it? Do ordinary people today, people not theologically inclined, have any notion of it? Few, surely, and not any who have not been disturbed by certain mysteries of life, both in personal life and in history. What is *grace*? If I have done well in this world and God recompenses me, would that be an act of grace on the part of God? In other words, what is the opposite of grace? It is justice, isn't it? If a thing is due you, if you deserve it, it is not grace but *justice*.

Grace is not merely something given out of generosity, unless you mean the generosity of one and only one. Grace in the theological sense means something given by God, which brings salvation, for which you have done nothing to deserve it. In France, in Italy, there's a phrase, playfully used — *gratis, e per amore di Dio*. What is *gratis* is given gracefully by the love of God. The moment you say that you have done something for it, it's no longer grace. The Christian teachers, some more and some less — the Lutherans more, the Catholics, since the Council of Trent (except the Augustinians) less — have stressed this power of grace. Why does God spare those who do not deserve it, and perhaps damn those who try their best? Naturally the pariah priests try to dodge this, they try to avoid it because even in the hands of very skilled theologians it is difficult. Was it necessary to develop this concept of salvation that is *given* and not *deserved*?

St. Paul makes clear that many are called but few are chosen. Many are called, but only to a few is the inducement given irresistible. What would happen, St. Augustine asks, if salvation, eternal beatitude were given in consequence only of good deeds done; what would be the role of God? It would be reduced, He would no longer be omnipotent. He would be neither omnipotent nor not omnipotent. He would simply be a minister of justice, to use the modern term — a grand steward, rewarding and punishing according to what is due. God has to be something much more than that — what exactly we cannot fathom.

I won't go here into this knotty problem of grace. Dante does take it up, however. In this connection, the thing to remember is that *gratia* is *gratis data* – every child had to know the phrase — grace is given free, free of anything. You don't have to do anything to earn it; it is *gratis data*, and also *grate fascines*: it makes you acceptable to God. In other words, God makes you likeable and then likes you when you have been made likeable. The opposite, as we said, is justice. These terms for a long time were used as the attributes of the king. The last to get rid of them was Italy. To the minds of people no longer trained in this matter, it probably means nothing to speak of justice and grace as the attributes of a king. In other words, when a king pardons, he exercises his right of grace. If a man is pardoned because it is found out that his crime was not so bad as people say, that obviously is not grace. What is necessary in that case is a new trial, so that justice may be done. But if the sovereign, no matter how terrible the crime is, waives the rights of justice and pardons the criminal, that is *gratia*, which is in no way controlled by justice.

Did Dante realize that he was going wrong by himself, and did he get out of his entanglements by himself, or did God intervene? In other words, was it free will or was it grace? Obviously, if it was all by free will, it couldn't be Christian. It is a lowly man, helpless in himself, that needs Christ. Against this situation, in the days of St. Augustine, a great number of people, following Pelagius, came out with a doctrine that practically declared that man is the maker of his own moral salvation. It's called Pelagianism and is destructive of all Christian teaching. Of course it was combated, corrected somewhat, but you can't stress either side without going astray. And so, a certain solution was arrived at that might be called semi-Pelagian. There are two possibilities: one is that man starts to reform, realizing that something has to be done but can't do it by himself. *Gratia* then steps in. The other is the reverse: it's God who inspires you with this sudden change of heart, and it's up to you to keep up with this inspiration. These were commonplace in Dante's time.

Dante apparently takes up the former of these two positions. He seems to have awakened to the fact that he had gone astray by himself; and by himself he tries to make his way out until he is confronted by the last of the three beasts. He would have been helpless at that point, unless grace had come in. The first apparition of grace in the world, leaving out Lucia, is Beatrice, sent by the Virgin Mary. She is the emissary of grace.

So Virgil enters Hell with Dante. And here is the famous inscription, which is the beginning of Canto 3: *Per me si va nella città dolente.* Of course this *per me*, very likely is "through me." "Through me is the entrance to the city of grieving." *Città* in Dante simply denotes

civitas, which means in the Bible, in St. Jerome, in St.
Augustine, in the classical authors, not a city in the
modern sense of the word, but a state; and the two
cities are not so much states but polities. The one is the
political polity of coercion that characterizes all states,
from the first to the last, and that's the city of the devil,
the earthly city that embodies itself in the various
worldly states — now that of the Assyrians, now that of
the Romans, now that of the Holy Roman Empire, now
modern France, England, Italy, Spain, now one state or
some combination of states, next another, all of them
parts of this one diabolical power, the *civitas terrena*.
The other city is that of those who have been saved.
That's the meaning of *civitas* that you find in the
classical authors and in all the authors of early Christianity.

The city of sorrow is the earthly city. This invites
us to look for the allegorical meaning. In the literal
sense, it's the region of the dead, a place occupied by
the souls that will not be saved; but in reality it's this
world of ours, as built up by the people who have lost
contact with God.

"Through me one goes into the city of sorrow.
Through me one goes into eternal pain." Notice the
repetition. The city of grief is of eternal sorrow —
"through me one goes among the lost people" [*perduta
gente*], those who have lost the good of the intellect,
those who are no longer able to see the difference
between right and wrong. *Giustizia mosse il mio alto
fattore.*

Dante asserts here, this time in a very orthodox
way, that Hell is not the work of one eager for revenge,
but the work of one eager for justice. The problem so
often discussed was — Dante must have heard some of

the Dominican fathers arguing the matter publicly in Florence — is it fair that for crimes committed in time, one should be given a punishment, a retribution that is eternal? An elaborate argument was built up. But Dante says very clearly: it was justice that moved my lofty maker. And then to make it even clearer, he specifies: the whole divine trinity, united, made Hell. And the trinity is divine power: the father first, divine power made me; and the loftiest wisdom — as always wisdom is the second person, the word who became incarnate, and then we called Him Christ; and the third person is love — by this time we recognize the Holy Spirit as love.

Next we learn: "Before me there was nothing created that was not eternal." Which means: I was created together with eternal things. Those eternal things Dante will tell us later, in the *Paradiso*, are: first, primal matter, then the spheres of the skies, and then the angelic substances. The soul of man was not created then. All things else are not created but generated. What is the difference between generation and creation? The Catholic Church has called systematically what comes from God directly, *created*, and what is not created, but is made through an intermediary, *generated*. Hell is one of the things created. The inscription ends: "And I shall last into eternity. Leave all hope you who enter."

And so we enter the first circle of Hell, where we find those who live in desire without hope, those who see the truth with their intellect but who cannot hope to attain what they have glimpsed, those who are condemned not because of anything they have done, but regardless of their moral virtues. It is the eternal home of Virgil, Homer, Ovid — of all the great sages poets, heroes of antiquity. (I don't think Dante knew much about the biography of Ovid: if he did, he surely wouldn't have put him there.)

5. THE LUSTFUL

Let me review the various scenes Dante sets before us in the opening canto of *Inferno*. We first see a desolate plain, a desert stretch, terrifying in its desolation; in the background the hill of truth, which, now Dante realizes, is the goal of man, the highest goal, for which all other goals should be put aside. In the effort to reach or rather to climb that hill of truth, he is stopped by three beasts. The next scene is the appearance of Virgil on that plain. After that comes the entrance to Hell, the broken down passage, once locked beyond any possibility of being opened; broken through by Christ, so that many who were locked in there were allowed to pass out. The Apostle's Creed refers to Christ descending into Hell. Who was rescued, why was this gate let down? To let out Adam and all those people who may be called the heroes, religious and military, the prophets and the lawmakers of the Old Testament. For them, that gate was let down; and they passed through that part which had until then permitted no passage to anyone. These are the first scenes. The desolate plain; Dante and Virgil at the gate of Hell.

On the way to the entrance to Hell proper, however, Dante introduces something new, of his own construction. So far he has been on traditional ground, but now he is on his own, though he follows in this, St. Paul. He takes the liberty now to put outside of Hell proper a particular class of sinners — you can't call them transgressors — who are neither for what is right

nor against it. The Italians call them *tepid*; St. Paul calls
them the Laodiceans. They are those who straddle the
fence. The Church doesn't handle them as badly as
Dante does. Here at the beginning of the *Inferno* and at
the end, at the extremes, Dante gives us two pictures
that show his instincts as a man of action, two scenes
that betray his political likes and dislikes based on
principles of political action: the Laodiceans at the
beginning, and the traitors in the lowest circle of Hell.
He shows them as revolting souls.

After this, comes Hell proper, as in the ancient
myths. There's nothing Catholic or Christian about
the topography of Hell, here. What would the Christian theologians have to say about all this? They would
say: it's a mere fiction. The Church teaches that after
death, the damned — those of Hell and those of Purgatory — and those saved, are, until judgment day, disembodied souls. When the body dies the flesh turns to
ashes, to dust; but the soul retains its substance. Pope
Boniface is still Pope Boniface as a soul, although he
has no body.

For those who are materialistically-minded, that
is pretty hard to take; but those familiar with Plato's
line of thought can easily grasp it. In other words, Hell
belongs rather to Greek mythology than to Christianity, because it is clear that a soul that is immaterial
cannot occupy space, obviously, any more than angels
can occupy space. I say this, also, to remind you how
childish many of the eighteenth century critics were,
who tried to discredit Christianity by raising certain
foolish questions as though they had been questions
raised by medieval thinkers. The most famous — I have
a whole list of them — but the most famous, which used
to be repeated in all textbooks, in France where even-

tually they were all done away with, and here, where some still remain, is "How many angels can dance on the point of a needle?" There was no such question raised in the Middle Ages. It came up for the first time in the eighteenth century, the invention of some critic of Christianity, not only ignorant of the historical evidence, but also not aware that zero can never, by any kind of multiplication, become anything more than zero. In order to dance on the head of a needle, in order to take up any space at all, you have to have some matter.

So we should say of the souls in Hell: they cannot occupy space for they have no matter; but Dante treats them as if they do occupy space. He is aware of what he is doing, and he wants us to know he is aware of it. In the course of the poem there is a gradation. In Hell he gives the souls a materiality, almost as on earth. When you rise to Purgatory, these immaterial souls are no longer tangible. A vaporous form surrounds them, so that you can imagine them but you cannot touch them; so much so that Dante, when he tries to embrace one of them, finds there is nothing to embrace. In *Paradiso* the materiality is even further reduced; even the vague contour of Purgatory disappears, and the individual soul is a point of light — changing in intensity according to the value and dignity of the individual soul.

So we have here the Greek Hell, which is all contained around the river Acheron. Acheron means the joyless river — a beautiful image. And here, at the very beginning, all those who are to be damned, congregate. The thought here is not very profound — Dante is not preoccupied with theology — but the poetry is extraordinary. There's nothing in Italian

poetry to compare with the description of the desolation, with the picture of the great mass of people, with
this creation of a naturalistic atmosphere surrounding
these people, the weaklings, and the rest, whose sighs
become a tremor of the universe. The confusion between the psychological elements and the external
conditions of the topography and climate is perfect. It
serves also another purpose, no doubt: as a bridge to
what follows. By the time it is over, you don't know
whether you are actually seeing these things or not, so
deeply does Dante impress the images, the picture on
your consciousness.

The demon Charon now appears with his boat
(depicted in any number of representations), the boat
which takes these souls across to Hell proper. You
have to picture here a plateau on which these strange
scenes take place, and below, a river. You have to drop
down to the level of the river, and cross it to get to Hell
proper. With that you come to the first circle of Hell,
and here Dante pictures for us a situation which was
forced upon him by Catholic doctrine: if you died not
having been baptized, you could not be saved. Even if
you were virtuous in a moral sense, you could not be
saved. Well, if you aren't going to be saved, you're in
Hell; but Dante has created a circle here for those
people who were as good as it is possible to be, yet
weren't Christians. We find noble pagans here including Arabs — not noble Jews, they had already been
saved; Christ had descended into Hell to save them. As
for the Jews of his day — well, when Christianity came,
they had a chance to see the truth. If they rejected it,
they are at fault.

In this circle are those who are damned through
no faults of their own. They include the heroes of the

Aeneid, the heroes described by Virgil in the sixth book of the *Aeneid*; the heroes of early Rome and of the last days of the Republic; the heroes of Greek philosophy — almost a history of philosophy in brief; a great Moslem monarch; a great Arab philosopher. These are the souls of the *sospesi*. Dante pictures these people, who were virtuous in all things except in religion, who have committed no crimes, as not suffering physical misery, only sighing. Why? Because they have seen the truth, the light, and know that it is the ultimate goal that every rational creature wants; they have seen it and therefore they have acquired a desire for it. But they also know they have no chance of ever getting to it: *senza speme vivemo in disio*. "We live in desire without hope."

This is the setting in which we have to make our way now. In the rest of Hell, all is darkness; but here we have a hemisphere of light — not the light of truth, which is reserved for the saved, but a light sufficient to give those souls an idea of what real light is like, the light for which they sigh. The Church softened its view, later, but Dante is more severe than anyone of his contemporaries in this matter. The doctrine of the Church today is that, in order for an individual to be saved, all he has to do, really, is live sincerely in accordance with the Old Testament. You don't have to accept the specific doctrines of the Catholic Church or similar doctrines. That's the current view of the Church on the subject. If Dante were living today, perhaps he would revise his picture.

Next he comes to the place where the real sinners are punished. He proceeds to describe the manner of punishment by dividing Hell into a series of descending circles, one inside the other: the further down you go, the shorter is the radius; and the shorter the radius, the graver the punishment. The shape of this Hell of Dante is a truncated cone, and at the bottom, all is frozen Each circle of Hell is a section of this cone. Naturally, as you approach the apex of this cone, the suffering gets worse and worse.

The fifth canto is the start of real suffering — you can't consider that of the noble spirits of antiquity as a circle of sinners — and has the largest sweep, to indicate how common the sin is and how all-pervasive. If this broadest surface, this largest section of the cone, the furthest away from the apex, represents the most common and the lightest of sins, it must conform to the doctrine of the Church on the gradation of transgressions. Whether you are Catholic, Protestant, Jew, Moslem, free-thinker, you know that the seven mortal sins have been running for a long time. People have been talking about them for centuries and many are still talking about them. They are, in the order of increasing gravity: lust, gluttony, avarice, sloth, wrath, envy and pride. Here we meet with lust — not in the metaphorical sense, but in the literal sense. You are lustful when you put your reason to sleep to satisfy your sensuous desires. That's the sin of the first circle.

Is the Christian the only one who judges that to be morally evil? I remember a fellow who wrote a whole book against Catholic ethics, hoping to overthrow it. Somebody reviewed it and concluded by saying that the author had better explain how his argument does not also do away with pagan ethics. When we come to gluttony and lust, the church does not say you should not eat and get a certain pleasure out of it; that you shouldn't copulate and get satisfaction out of it. So St. Thomas teaches; when you get to St. Augustine, it's a different story. For some, the whole matter resolves itself into one of hygiene, it is all a matter of determining how far you can go without physical ill-effects. Why bring ethics into it, then? How does ethics come into it; and second, how does religion come in? Why is lust a sin — or an error (as Aristotle would call it)? Would Aristotle accept it as sin? Is it, after all, only a question of health? What happens when a man eats too much, drinks too much? He annihilates reason; he tramples the power of reason. Man was made to make use of all these things as a means to exalt his reason. Instead he does the opposite. He makes himself a beast. That's not a matter of hygiene, but a matter of ethics.

So much for Aristotle and for the pagans. What about the Christians? It is a sin, for Christians, because God forbids it. We might go further and ask: why is lust the least grave, and why is pride the worst of sins? Why is lust the lightest? As Dante attempts to point out, the more something accords with our nature, physically, the more that something approaches what is not sinful. Also, if you yield to a natural temptation — no, not if you yield, but if you follow a natural appetite — if you go to excess you are not as guilty as you would be following something contrary to nature. Why are the avaricious placed deeper down? Because it not natural to crave gold. Man was made to reproduce, he was made to live and therefore to nourish himself; but his nature is not such, he was not made that he should make love to a heap of gold, or to a plot of land. Here avarice is simple avarice and not *cupiditas*. The difference between the man who counts his gold and counts the number of fruit trees on his land, the difference between that and *cupiditas*, is that, although the desire to acquire wealth is the common element in both, in one case the sinner stops there, with wealth as an end in itself, while in the other, wealth merely serves to feed all the other vicious appetites.

We have gone through this hemisphere of light, with its noble castle and, symbolically represented, the seven virtues, and the seven sciences. The seven virtues are the four moral or cardinal virtues, and the three intellectual virtues. Are there any others, any more besides these? Surely. There are also the three theological virtues, but they have no place here; the seven sciences are the *quadrivium* and the *trivium*. These classifications held for a long time but have been abandoned.

We are now in the fifth canto. Dante has descended from the first circle down into the second, *chè men loco cinghia*, that encloses less space, that has a smaller circumference than the one above, *e tanto più dolor, che pugne a guaio*. The smaller the circle, the more the pain, so that it stings you until it makes you cry out. The word *guaio* means yelling from torture.

Here we find Minos, the noble character of antiquity, Minos the law-giver, relegated to a lowly function. Dante had a strange view of the island of Crete. It was, of course, the land of the minotaurs, and of all sorts of unnatural creatures. Sailors shunned the sight of the place, for the mere sight of some of the things that went on there was enough to damn a person. This strange notion about Crete became popular — the myths about the minotaurs, the stories of the lustful Pasiphae, who, at one time, had herself put into the shell of a cow to satisfy her unnatural desires. Poor Minos, who was a rather respectable man, in Dante's Hell is here performing the lowly role of judge. By rolling up his tail he indicates to what circle the sinners are damned.

He objects to Dante's coming; so far everybody has objected to Dante's coming. You are a living man, why do you come here? You are now a good man, why do you want to fool around with sin? There is a moral problem here. Is there any justification for going into the vicinity of sin for your own good? Or should you avoid such a test? The view — from St. Ambrose on — is that you can't avoid it; it's the way to go. You must test yourself. Do not be afraid to face sin. If you can't resist, it means you need more grace. Face them all — all except one; from one you are supposed to run away. And this seems to be in accord with the teachings of the Gospel. If you are susceptible to irascibility, see if you can face the situation without succumbing to it. If you are susceptible to gluttony, again, see what you can do when you are in the midst of people who gorge themselves and vomit. So also with pride; so also with the rest. But, as I have said, from one you are supposed to run. And that is lust. Why? Well, apparently because the lure is greater and also because it is harder to extract yourself from it once you have sunk into it. But Dante goes into the midst of it to indicate the revolting aspect of lust, something in love that we fail to see when we are tempted. Face all the possibilities of sin — if you are really virtuous — to test yourself, except for lust.

There's a famous poem represented as a play — it's one of the earliest plays of the Middle Ages, of the tenth century — that treats this very theme of facing the allurements of sexual love, contrary to the teachings of the Church. It's about Thais and Paphnutius the monk. Thais was a courtesan. The story was that the poor monk thought he could take the vice out of her and save her beauty for Heaven. Well, he did save her, but damned himself in the effort.

In canto five, Dante draws the picture, builds up the scene simply by elaborating a metaphor, a metaphor fitting both in antiquity and for us today. He draws a picture of sexual love as a storm. This circle of the lustful is described as a plain convulsed by a terrific storm: "I came to a place devoid of all light." Dante doesn't say devoid, he says *mute* of all light. He does again what we have already seen: transfers the characteristics of one sense to another. The place bellows like the sea in a tempest when it is beaten, lashed by contrasting winds, *bufera infernal*. The hellish storm which is inside the lustful is here presented as also outside: the hellish storm that never stops, that always goes on, that drives — *mena* — the spirits with its whirling, smiting them, tormenting them without rest. All this, of course, you have to carry over into an allegorical significance; it is the soul that forgets everything, because it is in love.

When they reach the great ruin, there the cries — *quivi le strida, il compianto e il lamento. . . . Compianto* is a hard word to translate. It is not simply crying but the crying as you fall into the arms of someone else. There are three or four touches here that tend to extenuate their fault. First we hear them *bestemmian quivi la virtù divina,* "as they curse the divine power" — something not easily extenuated. Dante understands, he says, that to such torments are damned the carnal sinners who subject reason to their desires. To show how numerous they are, Dante throws before you a familiar image — famous even to people in New York: they are as numerous as starlings, congregating in great numbers for flight. "And as the starlings are

borne by their wings, in the winter [*nel freddo tempo*], in
a huge extended swarm, so this storm" — *fiato* is rather
derogatory, "so this wind bears the evil spirits, this way
and that way, down and up it drives them; no hope ever
consoles them," *nulla speranza gli conforta mai*, "not
only not of rest, but even of less pain." On top of this
comes the melancholy sound of the crane. In addition
to the starlings, startling with the sound of their huge
numbers, we now have the cranes, with their sorrowful
song. *E come i gru van cantando lor lai*, "and as the
cranes go forth singing their woes, making a long
streak of themselves in the air, so did I see, trailing
cries," *ombre portate dalla detta briga*. "And I asked:
'who are these people whom the black breath [*l'aura
nero*] chastises?'" The storm is now the black breath.

[handwritten: Starlings / ↓ / CRANES]

6. THE POWER OF LOVE: PAOLO AND FRANCESCA

In describing the punishments, the tortures of Hell, Dante gives us popular representations, popular images — not only here but also in Purgatory. We have already seen this, in connection with his representation of love as a storm. Reason, which regulates all things, which is supposed to overpower everything, is overcome by something that seems more than anything else to be capable of overpowering reason; namely, love. In the fifth canto of the *Inferno*, Dante represented the power of love as a storm. Lovers carried away, as in a storm, by their love, while alive, here are punished, for all eternity, by a storm that never rests, for what in life was but a moment's pleasure. Same with gluttony. In the circle of the gluttons, the main character is Ciacco. Ciacco is a pig, for gluttony is a piggish quality. In ancient times, in the Christian era, down to our day, the man who gorges himself is compared to a pig: so here in the *Inferno*. Ciacco was a pig on earth: he is a pig in Hell. That's his punishment.

The same thing happens in Purgatory, only there the punishments that the souls suffer for their sins serve to purify them. They purify in one of two ways; rectification or nausea. The proud, who on earth strutted, their heads thrown back, their chests out, trying to make everybody bow down before them, here are so cowed, so bent over that their chins touch their feet. By their punishment they are rectified, the starch is taken out of their spines. That's one form of purification. The other is the disgusting realization of what they were doing or longing to do. The avaricious are driven in life by love of wealth, of money, of land; well, in Purgatory they get the land they loved, and they have to eat filth, manure, so that they get disgusted and are purified. Those are the two lines that you will see Dante regularly following.

Here in Hell the representation of the penalty is very much based on popular images, but there is something very remarkable in this circle. Usually, in one way or another, the effect produced by the spectacle of punishment is one of disgust. But here that is not the case. Dante can't be disgusted here. He is so grieved, in fact, that he faints. Perhaps he is trying to show how defenseless one is apt to be in the presence of love in keeping with the Church's teaching — which always urges us to face up to every temptation, except one. We should turn away from the temptation of carnal love because we are most defenseless there. Or perhaps he wants to draw a picture, a final homage in remembrance of what in his early days must have been his attachment to love. This canto, like so many others, serves to impress on us the fact that Dante is a great poet, not just an expounder of philosophic ideas. It's one of the ten scenes in Dante most highly elaborated artistically.

We have found that the punishment in this very large circle is persecution by a great wind. People in Dante's day — when most people were exposed to the open air more than we are today — to anyone used to the outdoors, the madness that can be caused by the constant attack of winds was well known. And Dante is here relying on the reader's knowledge and experience of the effects of unrelenting winds. Here in the outer circle of Hell is a windstorm that never rests, except in

homage to Dante, when he wants us to hear the story
of the two lovers who met death for love. As you would
expect, this circle is crowded more than any of the
others, because so very many people have lost their
reason to love. And to give you some idea of how many
they are, Dante gives us, as we said, an image of
starlings in flight. I don't have to point out how
appropriate that is. All you have to do is to look
around and see how numerous starlings are: this was
the image used in earliest antiquity, when writers wanted
to indicate a great throng, or crowd.

To give us some notion of the pathos of these
souls, still in the sphere of birds, Dante calls upon the
crane. Anyone who has ever lived where there are
migrations of birds must be familiar with the melancholy spectacle of the crane in flight, because of their
sad cry. Dante no doubt saw them coming out of
Germany down to Africa, passing over Italy. *E come li
stornei ne portan l'ali* — he gives with the phrase, with
the construction of the sentence, an idea almost of the
passivity of the loved one — *ne portan l'ali, nel freddo
tempo*, that is, when the cold comes on, *a schiera larga
e piena* [*schiera* — almost an army] — *così quel fiato li
spiriti mali*, "so does that breath.". . . Dante does not
always use flattering terms for this wind that carries the
lovers. *Di quà, di là, di giù, di sù il mena. Menare* had an
entirely different sense than what it has now. You can't
say *leading* — it's a *driving* wind — driving almost to
destruction. Here, there, down, up, it drives them. No
hope ever comforts them, not only of rest but even of
reduction of pain. Of course, every time you introduce
one of these abstract terms like "reduction" you break
up the texture of the poetry which Dante has so beautifully woven together. *Non che di posa, ma di minor*

pena.

Here, as he so frequently does elsewhere, Dante operates by contrasts; he hammers on the contrast of motion and rest until he makes you feel that what these souls who had in life been carried away by storms of love really want, after all, is the opposite of this motion: peace and rest. And a hymn to rest finally does come from the lips of Francesca. This terror of her emotion explains why peace and rest and quiet are so exalted. *E come i gru van cantando lor lai,* and as the cranes go chanting their lays (not lay, but woeful lay), making a long streak of themselves in the air, so did I see coming, trailing," *traendo guai,* "shadows carried by that powerful storm." Dante asks: *"Maestro, chi son quelle genti,"* "'Master, who are those people whom the black air lashes?'" *Briga* is a confusing, overpowering swarm of things; "black air" should be "black wind." Dante likes to use these transfers of qualities. It is the wind that is black here, in this region of darkness.

The necessity of making darkness visible forces him to create these phrases. *Auro* could never be air, as some translators would have it: *auro* is always breeze, wind — here: the black blast. "'The first of those of whom you would like to have knowledge,' he then replied, 'is an empress of many peoples'." She was so broken by the sin of lust that she made the desirable, what she wanted, legal by her law. As an empress, she passed laws declaring that to be lawful which she found pleasurable. Dante intends this phrase of his, *libito fe' licito,* to shock us — but in reality we tend to do more and more of that all the time; the crime of Semiramis no longer shocks us. It's one of the great progressive programs of modern times, that we should legalize everything that we find pleasurable, provided it does

not interfere with the pleasure of our neighbors. The
Latin and the Italian couplet, *libido-licito*, which is
wollen and *sollen* in German, has no equivalent in
English.

She made the *libido licito* to remove the blame
into which she had fallen with her people. She made it
appear that what she ought to do was what she wanted
to do. You couldn't say she was lawless, because the law
was to follow your appetites. "*Ell'è Semiramis. . . .*"
"'She is Semiramis, of whom it is read that she succeeded Ninus, and was his spouse; she held sway over
the land which Soldan now controls'," namely Egypt.
The other is she who killed herself — "*che s'ancise
amorosa*" — and broke her pledge to the ashes of
Sichaeus. This is Dido, who had promised eternal faith
and fidelity to her husband and instead fell in love with
Aeneas. You see Helen, "'*Elena vedi per cui tanto reo
tempo si volse*'," on whose account so many years of
suffering followed, for she was the cause of the Trojan
war. The phrase is very effective: on whose account —
per cui tanto reo tempo si volse — so many years of
suffering followed. "*E vedi il grande Achille,*" brave
Achilles, who had resisted love all along, as the great
Homeric stories tell us, until finally he fell in love and
while loving was killed, caught in a trap. "*E vedi il
grande Achille, che con amore al fine combatteo; vedi Paris,
Tristano*" — Tristan who loved Isolde — "and more than
a thousand shadows he showed me pointing them out
with his finger, shadows which love had taken from
our life." The break in this passage is especially effective. *Poscia ch'io ebbi il mio dottore udito nomar le donne
antiche e i cavalieri* — "After I heard my master name
those ancient women and nobles," ancient not in its
hellish significance, but in a sort of troubadorish

sense, "pity overcame us."

Here Dante is very unorthodox. Pity should not overcome us in Hell. The just punishment inflicted by God should not arouse pity. *E fui quasi smarrito*, I was almost lost. Lost morally perhaps. Religiously, because he felt pity. "I began: 'Poet, I would gladly speak to those two.' ..." This sudden transition dramatically clouds or obfuscates all the rest. Paolo and Francesca are thus isolated. "'Gladly would I speak to those two who go together',", "*che insieme vanno*." The others have been torn apart, one from the other; these two are treated exceptionally "'and seem light on the wind'." They offer no resistance, they are carried away, lightly, indicating that the love that had carried them away in life still continues here.

At the very beginning, we are told that love continues to be the eternal bond of union for those two who offer no resistance, in spite of the fact that it is their infernal torment. Dante has created a kind of beatitude in this canto — not the highest kind, from a moral point of view, or from any point of view, but a little corner of light which seems to dispel all the horror which should be connected with this infernal scene. "And he to me: 'You will yourself [speak to them] when they are drawn closer to us'." Dante, the lover, himself should do the beseeching: "'ask them, call to these souls who loved and died for love, and ask them in the name of that love which drives them, and they will come'." "*E tu allor li prega per quell'amor che i mena; e quei verranno*." A request in the name of love, for love and by love, will bring them to you. *Sì tosto come il vento a noi li piega* — This blast, this wind, this storm that blows now here now there, will push them his way, and then he will be able to speak to them. *Mossi*

la voce — "'O souls in anguish, come and speak to us if
no one'" — meaning God, or devils acting for God — "'if
there is no one to prevent it'." Of course, *affannato*
must be taken again in the troubadour sense: it's not
the infernal *affanno*, but the *affanno* that accompanies
every surge of love, the panting of love, the anguish of
love.

He had been asked to call them in the name of
love and he does so by referring to the *affanno* of love.
Quali colombe dal disio chiamate. . . . Dante appropri-
ately falls back on an image which is one of the two
eternal symbols of love: the dove and fire. A cupid
always has a dart or a torch in his hand. On sepulchral
monuments — which are perhaps the highest expression of Greek art — on the sepulchral monuments of
young girls and boys you are apt to see the bas-relief of
a cupid with the torch turned down to indicate that the
flame is coming to an end. *Quali colombe dal disio
chiamate, con l'ali alzate e ferme al dolce nido, vengon per
l'aer dal voler portate* — carried by their longing, like
doves that come to their nests, not by moving their
wings but by gliding, carried not by any propulsion but
by their longing, *cotali uscir de la schiera ov'è Dido, a noi
venendo per l'aer maligno, sì forte fu l'affettuoso grido* — so
strong was the affectionate cry. Dante had been asked
to call them in the name of love; he had called out, "*O
anime affannate!*" And he wants to remind us, now,
here, that his cry had been of love — an *affettuose grido*.
It is that cry that makes them come to him gliding
through the air, carried by love.

"*O animal grazioso e benigno.* . . ." In that word
"*animal*" is a very sweet touch; they realize that whereas
everything around them is a soul, here is one that is
not only a soul but an *anima* in a body. To translate it

as *animal* is ridiculous in this context. If you say living creature, then there is no contrast between Dante and the others. You need something to bring out the contrast. Dante is distinguished from everyone else present; the others are *anime*, but Dante alone is *animal*. And he is gracious and kind. "*O animal grazioso e benigno*" — that's the vocative, an invocation — "*che visitando vai per l'aer perso* [dusky air]," "'we who painted the world with blood.' . . ." Because of their love, much blood was shed. "'If the king of the universe were kind to us, we would pray to him for your peace, seeing that you have pity for our [*mal perverso*]'." Perverse is not a good word for *perverso*; "distortion," perhaps, "inhuman." Notice the word *pace*. In the eyes of these people, happiness has been equated with rest, tranquility, cessation of the storm. The happiness they would ask God to give Dante is *pace*, peace. Why? Because he has pity on them. "*Di quel che udire e che parlar vi piace noi udiremo e parleremo a vui, mentre che il vento, come fa, ci tace.*" "'Of all that you want to hear and say we will hear and speak to you — while the wind is quiet for us'." And then comes what is perhaps the most famous passage of the *Divine Comedy*. "'The land where I was born'" [Rimini], said one of them, Francesca — *terra* is city in Italian, in the Italian of the Middle Ages — "'the city where I was born [Rimini], sits on the shore where the Po descends'" — the Po is the great river of northern Italy — "'to find peace'," again, peace, this constant obsession with peace, "*per aver pace co' seguaci sui,*" *seguaci*, the retinus, being all the affluences on the left and on the right side of the Po.

And here comes the lesson on love. Why did Paolo fall in love with Francesca? That's the first *terzina*. In the second *terzina*: why did she fall in love with him?

And the third *terzina*: what happened as a result of that love?

In the *Vita Nuova*, Dante expressly says that to fall in love one must have a *cor gentile*. One must have a heart capable of loving: that's the definition of nobility. Love that quickly seizes the noble heart seized him. Of course, what always captures the love of man is beauty — we hammered on that long enough. He had been seized by love because of the beautiful body of Francesca, "*della bella persona che mi fù tolta*" — "'because of the beautiful body of which I was robbed'," robbed because she was killed by her husband, "'and the manner in which it was taken still hurts me'." That is, she was killed so suddenly that she had no time to atone for her sin and therefore had no time to avoid eternal damnation, "*e il modo ancor m'offende.*" These *terzine* are chiseled to perfection: "*Amor, ch' a nullo amato amar perdona,*" "'Love that never refuses requital of love to those who love'." He loved her because she was beautiful; she loved him because of the necessity of requital. That's an old theme; real love forces requital, and that old theme is here put forth very forcibly. "'Love, that never permits one that is loved from not loving back'," "*mi prese del costui piacer si forte,*" seized me so powerfully, because I realized how much he liked me, so strongly, "*che, come vedi, ancor non m'abbandona,*" "'that he still, as you see, lingers about me, does not leave me. Love led us to one death'."

There's a certain amount of exaltation here; we were killed, yes, but we were killed together — one death. And what happens to the one who killed them? He's down in the lowest place, Caina, named after the first fratricide, "*Caina attende chi vita ci spense.*" "These words reached us from them. From the time I heard those injured souls, I bowed my head, and kept it low so long, that at length the poet said to me: 'what are your thoughts?' Answering, I began" — here, in two lines Dante compresses the contrast between the sweetness of love and the eternal sorrow for a love that was carried out in a way contrary to divine law. "*O lasso, quanti dolci pensier, quanto disio menò costoro al doloroso passo!*" Dante wants to know what happened in reality — how strong a desire led them to that sorry path. "Then I turned to them and spoke: 'Francesca, your torments make me weep sadly and piteously, but tell me'" — this story was unknown until Dante made it popular — "*ma dimmi:*" "'at the time of the sweet sighs'" — that's a phrase that Dante has made famous, *al tempo de' dolci sospiri,* the time when those who are soon to be bound in love one to the other are still uncertain, still sigh in doubt; but there is hope in their sighs, therefore they are sweet. All these are eternal phrases, elaborated by poets in all languages. "*Al tempo de' dolci sospiri, a che e come concedette amore che conosceste i dubbiosi desiri?*" The *dolci sospiri* is now explained by the expression *dubbiosi desiri.* "And she to me:" "*Nessun maggior dolore, che ricordarsi del tempo felice nella miseria;*" "'there is no greater sorrow than to recall happy days in the midst of misery';" "*e ciò sa il tuo dottor*" — "'as your master knows'."

Of course, Dante has so many masters — who is this one? Boethius? Some have even suggested Aristotle. (Aristotle does have a line like that.) "'But if you have such a great desire to know the first root of our love'," if you have such a great desire to become familiar with the source of our love, "'I will be as one who speaks and cries'." Here is what happened. "'We were reading one day for our pastime the story of Lancelot, how love

seized him'" — that, of course, is still a famous story —
"'we were alone and without suspicion; more than
once did that reading bring our eyes together'." You
know what that means. The Italian is very lovely. *"Per
più fiate li occhi ci sospinse quella lettura."* That story
gradually lifted the eyes of one and the eyes of the
other until they met, *"e scolorocci il viso,"* "'and we grew
pale'," the color drained from their faces. That, of
course, is a commonplace; all lovers grow pale at such
moments. "'But only one point was it that overcame
us'," that is, they would have resisted the temptation
except for one thing. *"Quando leggemmo il disiato riso
esser baciato da cotanto amante,"* when we "'read of the
longed-for lips'," but instead of saying lips, Dante says
lips smiling for love, *disiato riso,* "'longed-for smile',"
when we read about the exchange of kisses, "'this one,
who shall never be separated from me, all trembling
kissed my mouth'." Notice again, the exaltation: they
are in Hell, but surely they make the most of it. "'This
one, who shall never be separated from me, all trembling kissed my mouth'." *"Galeotto fu il libro e chi lo
scrisse."* Galeotto, of course, is a name from Provence
that has lived through the centuries, for the man who
brings lovers together.

Galeotto is the one who brought together
Guinivere and Lancelot. But here, it is not a man who
brings them together, who functioned as the go-be-
tween, but a book, and he who wrote it: *"quel giorno più
non vi leggemmo avante."* A sort of homage, if you will,
to poetry. While one spirit was saying all this, the other
says nothing. He is built out of silence, this lover of
Francesca; but although silent, he is eloquent. "The
other wept so, that through pity, I swooned as if dying,
and fell as a dead body falls." Here in Hell, instead of

being mindful of the justice of God, Dante faints almost to the point of dying, for these two who died for love. I can't do justice to the perfection, the metrical perfection of the canto, the correspondence from one part to another — it's built up almost like a symphony.

We come next to the circle of gluttony. And, we must again ask: what's wrong with gluttony? What's wrong with Ciacco and the rest? Why put them in Hell? Why not put them in a hospital? One answer is: It's contrary to reason. Man wasn't made to find joy in gorging himself, but in reasoning. He has to live, and therefore he has to eat; but he must eat in order to live, and live in order to reason, and not the reverse. The ancients understood that. But a new factor enters into it for Dante and for Christians. Not only does philosophy condemn this — make of it a monster — but God has forbidden it. Therefore, it's not only δμάρτημα as Aristotle called it, but also a sin.

7. THE FLORENTINE EPICUREANS: FARINATA DEGLI UBERTI AND CAVALCANTI

After the circle of the lustful, smaller in circumference, deeper in position, where the sinners are tormented more cruelly or painfully, comes the circle of the gluttons, symbolically represented by that ugly beast that has all the earmarks of over-indulgence. Here we find those who have eaten too much and drunk too much. All the muscles are consumed except those of the abdomen; and you go on from there to a still smaller circle, that of the avaricious and the prodigal. Dante now is following the usual classification, the orthodox classification. When he reaches the circle of the spendthrifts and the misers, he falls back on the usual device to describe those vices as extremes in accordance with the Aristotelian teachings.

In the satisfaction of our natural desires we can go off in one direction or the other. Our reason is there to help us see to it that we don't, but we often do go astray. In eating, we can eat too little and we can eat too much. So with all our impulses; in addition to the desire to eat and drink, we have sexual desires, and we have to have a certain desire to accumulate wealth. For surely, as we have the desire to eat, in order to live, and the desire to copulate to continue the species, so we have the desire to accumulate, to store, wealth, money, material goods, for community life. No political group can maintain itself without some accumulation of economic wealth. However, one is not to go beyond what reason dictates. One is not to go beyond what Horace calls *aurea mediocrite*, the golden mean.

It is to this vice only that Dante limits the Aristotelian doctrine. In treating other vices he is limited, for, in some cases, what were extremes and therefore vices from the pagan point of view, for the Church, for Christian teachings, have become virtues. Here he avoids altogether the Christian view. However, when he comes to *Paradiso*, he has more courage; he defends extreme poverty. With regard to wealth he says, there is no mean. Any desire for wealth is too much. It would be better that there were no wealth. It is not a very practical view socially, but it is one that was imposed on Dante by his realization, by the conception he has of *cupidigia*, of covetousness, as the source of all sin, and therefore to be absolutely overcome. In *Paradiso*, to bring this emphatically before the reader's mind, he gives as his sublime example St. Francis, who considered it a sin to keep even the little bit of bread that might be left over after a meal. Don't keep it, give it to the poor. Keep nothing. One of the extremes of Aristotle, punished as a vice in Hell, comes to be praised as one of the highest of Christian virtues.

From this point on in Hell, Dante seems to be troubled by his scheme. Instead of following the orthodox classification of evil as he seemed to have intended, he changes his mind, he jumbles the remaining sins together in the fifth circle, in that swamp, contrasting the impression of the swamp with the fortified city that is in that swamp. There he finds the wrathful, the envious, the proud and the slothful, all jumbled together, hardly distinguishable. We find, first of all, a magnificent description of military architecture and the accurate account of how a fortified city was organized to defend itself and to ready itself for attack — all of which, of course, is to be symbolically interpreted.

You have this huge swamp; in the distance are towers and walls — the towers and walls that surround the city. Then two lights are seen flashing, as a signal for the boat crossing the swamp to approach. (Some of these swamps or moats that served as part of a city's defenses still exist. If you go to Lucca you can see the residue of the old canals around the walls.) We see the boatman who is taking Virgil and Dante by devious ways across the moat toward the fortified city. The moat is there, and the towers; so that no defilement, no surprise attack can be made. The towers are protected by terrible demons, and it is announced that one is more terrible than the others: the Gorgo. The meaning of Gorgo is not clear. It is a figure that strikes man to dumbness, turns him into stone. Dante makes clear that we have to consider it allegorically. Is it the sight of a heresy that is so fatal, spiritually, that it will destroy all faith, every sense of ethical and moral values, in the heart of the one who looks at it? Hard to say. But Dante wants us to understand that he is in great danger.

Virgil himself is helpless: the faithful guide himself doesn't know what to do. Here, for the first time, the necessity arises for miraculous intervention from Heaven. The important line here is the strange verse in which Dante indicates that we are to look for other meanings. He invites us to break through the veil, to pass beyond the allegorical statement to the true sense. *O voi che avete gl'intelletti sani, mirate la dottrina, che s'asconde sotto il velame degli versi strani.* Break the veil and the doctrine will come through. Virgil and Dante are forced to a stop. But finally, by the help of an angel that intervenes, they are allowed to go through;

they enter the city. From the external aspect of it, they expect to find a city full of soldiers; instead they see a fiery burning cemetery.

To get the reader to visualize the scene, to conjure before the reader's mind the picture of this fiery cemetery, Dante introduces his representation by calling to mind two very famous scenes, known to the people of his day: one is the cemetery at Arles, and the other is Pola. The fact that Dante goes from the Adriatic to the Rhone Valley for his examples, shows how accustomed these people were to going from one place to another. At Arles coffins were thrown into the Rhone and floated down to be deposited where there is a bend in the river. Most of it has been torn down, four fifths of it to make way for the tracks of a railroad yard, but there are still parts of it left. It's worthwhile seeing, to get an idea of what Dante had in mind in describing this cemetery which is so carefully defended by devils, thick walls, high towers, and deep moats. The other, Pola, is all gone. There's nothing to be seen there.

Ora sen va per un secreto calle, tra il muro della terra e li martiri, lo mio maestro, ed io dopo le spalle. They have finally come into the city and go through a semi-hidden passage that is next to the walls. If anyone has ever seen the walled cities in Italy, he knows that there are usually roads, narrow winding passages, near the walls. Today they are employed for ignoble professions, mostly, undertakers, slaughter houses, etc. *Terra* means a fortified city. A strange meaning for *terra* but that's what it is. "Now, by a hidden passage, between the wall of that city and the torments my master goes, and I right behind him. 'O power supreme, you who lead me around these evil turns, speak to me and

satisfy my desires'." Can the people that lie in these
sepulchers be seen, can one see the inhabitants, the
townspeople that occupy these homes of the dead?
"*Gia son levati tutt' i coperchi . . .*" "'The lids are lifted
and therefore there shouldn't be any difficulty'," "*e
nessun guardia face.*" "'And there's no one to keep
watch over them'." Dante is still talking military language; it is the talk of one who has been in a military
milieu all his life. "And he to me:" "*Tutti saran serrati,
quando di Josafat qui torneranno coi corpi che lassù hanno
lasciati.*" "'These lids are open now, but on judgment
day they will be closed down on them, after the bodies
which they have left behind will be joined to the souls
that you now see'." A touch of bitter irony here: the
Epicureans had said the soul dies with the body and is
buried with it. To represent the terrible suffering of
these souls, Dante places them in the coffin where they
thought they would have rest. "*Suo cimitero da questa
parte hanno con Epicuro tutt' i suoi seguaci, che l'anima col
corpo morta fanno.*" It is the cemetery of the Epicureans:
of Epicurus, that is, and all his followers, the sect that
holds that the soul dies with the body. As to the
question you asked me, says Virgil, you will be satisfied; you will be able to see the people here, as you
asked me; and also the answer will be given to a wish
that you have not asked explicitly; namely, if you can
see some of your friends that you knew in Florence.
The Epicureans were powerful in Florence; Boccaccio
tells us that one of Dante's best friends was an Epicurean, the poet Guido Cavalcanti, whose father we will
meet here.

One might ask: why is this heresy, this Epicurean pagan doctrine flourishing in the Middle Ages, in
such a religious age? Dante says that he refrained from

saying what he wished, because he feared Virgil would scold him for talking too much.

Suddenly, from the silence of the tombs, comes a voice, the voice of Farinata degli Uberti, a man of great courage, great magnanimity; a man who was ready to sacrifice everything for his party, who believes there is no value higher than love of party. He embodies the first stage of the process which Dante has adopted. You start with love of party, and from love of party you pass to love of country, and from there to love of humanity, and finally to love of God. It's hard to see how all this follows necessarily, but they thought so — Cicero and the rest: they thought there was a continuous ladder, from the bottom to the top. What Dante describes of these damned souls is not the sin that put them in Hell — that's spoken of in passing — but what extenuates the sin. It is done very effectively.

The very first word indicates the character of this man; he would not have been interested in the passing of anyone or anything, except that he had heard someone speaking his own language, the dialect of his town. "'O, Tuscan!'" he cries out; and with that word Dante proves how with one name, a geographical designation, great poetry can be made. "*O Tosco*" — "'you who go through the city'" — "*la città del foco*," the city of fire; these blazing tombstones, "'and go through it alive'" — still living — "*così parlando onesto*," "'speaking so nobly, stay a while. Your speech shows you to be a native of that noble fatherland of mine'". . . and there, all of a sudden, he realizes that like all loves, love of fatherland carried to excess is dangerous and damaging: "'which perhaps'" — what a great deal of pathos there is in that "perhaps" — and in the midst of this expression of love for Florence, his native city, he is reminded that perhaps he loved it too much, "*alla qual forse fui troppo molesto,*" injured, bothered it too much. "Suddenly this sound came from one of those sepulchers. I drew close in fear to my guide. And he to me —" Here Dante comes out with the greatest homage that he is capable of; he makes even Virgil enthusiastic in his regard for this great Florentine partisan. "*Volgiti: che fai?*" "'Turn there; not to me!'" "*Vedi là Farinata*" — "'that is Farinata, standing up erect; you can see him from the belt up'." Not below, because the side of the sepulcher prevents that. *Io avea già il mio viso nel suo fitto.* As soon as he hears the name "Farinata" Dante fixes his look on him.

And here begins the description of the haughtiness of this man compared or in contrast with the cringing humility of his fellow-Epicurean. *Ed ei s'ergea col petto e colla fronte*, "he stood up with his chest and his brow high" *come avesse lo inferno in gran dispitto*, "as if he had nothing but supreme contempt for Hell." He doesn't know and he doesn't care whether he is in Hell or Paradise; the only thing he knows or cares about is his party. "And the courageous hands of my leader, ready for the task, pushed me through the field of sepulchers, toward him, saying: 'let your words be brief [*conte*]'." *Conte* is a very difficult word because it has at least three meanings, and any one of those three meanings can fit here: "brief," "few," or "relevant." *Com'io al piè della sua tomba fui, guardommi un poco, e poi quasi sdegnoso mi domandò: "chi fur li maggior tui?"*

After stressing Farinata's love of country, Dante now depicts pride of family. Farinata comes from perhaps one of the greatest families of Florence — Longobard nobility — going back to the early seventh century. Like many Ghibellines of ancient nobility,

Farinata had a lot of contempt for the merchants, for the mercantile civilization of the later Florentines. "When I was at the foot of his tomb, he looked at me a little and then almost disdainfully asked: 'who were your ancestors?'" Dante, who is himself usually very proud, this time is humble. "I, who was desirous to obey, did not conceal from him who they were, but told him all — so that" *ei levè le ciglia un poco in soso*, "he raised his brows."

In the eyes of Farinata, those ancestors of Dante's were an obscure people; he had to lift his head, close his eyes, in order to meditate as to who they were. "Then he said:" *Fieramante furo avversi a me e a' miei primi e a mia parte, sì che per due fiate li dispersi.*" A proud statement: "'Fiercely were these people hostile to me and to my elders and to my party, so that twice I had to scatter them'." This, however, is too much for Dante, who answers: "'If they were driven out they returned from all sides both times; but your people haven't learned that art'." After the terrible disaster of Montaperti, the great defeat at the hands of the Ghibellines, when peace was settled between the factions, a few families were selected to be forever banished from Florence, never to come back, and the Uberti were one of these. So Dante says: "'Mine have learned the art of coming back but yours have not'." And with this disdainful answer the scene shifts.

"There now arose out of the ground next to this one" — *scoperchiata vista* — this open space from which Farinata had emerged — a shadow, that was not seen while Dante and Farinata were speaking. Instead of standing erect like Farinata, this other figure is cowed, hidden up to the chin: *credo che s'era in ginocchio levata*: "I think it had lifted itself up on its knees." Cavalcanti

is supporting himself on his knees, and the only part
that projects in his cowering humility is the part above
his chin. "He looked around as if to see if someone else
were with me." He is looking for, hoping to see his son
Guido, Dante's friend, with him. Guido Cavalcanti is
the first man that Dante mentions in the *Vita Nuova*;
theirs was an exemplary friendship. When Cavalcanti's
expectations prove empty, when he saw that his son
was not there, he says weeping: *piangendo disse.* . . .
This man weeps for his son, the other doesn't care
what happens to the rest of the world. Cavalcanti says:
"'If you go through this dark prison because of the
loftiness of your mind, where is my son, why is he not
with you?'" Guido Cavalcanti at this time was as famous a poet as Dante himself. "And I to him: 'I do not
come here of my own talent. The one who is waiting
there, leads me through this place: a man for whom
Guido had not perhaps sufficient respect'." What exactly Dante means by that we have no clear notion. We
know nothing at all of any disregard of Guido for
Virgil; but very likely it's not lack of regard for Virgil
the person, but for what Virgil symbolized. Guido
probably did not believe in Virgil's standard of morality, that certain kinds of moral evils were a necessary
step toward the good. Dante now explains why he
could answer so readily when this man questioned
him. "His manner of speech and the punishment had
already revealed his name to me; therefore I answered
him at once." But then, the pressure of paternal affection breaks through and forces the kneeling figure to
do what he did not do before.

"'What did you say? You said he had?'" "*Egli
ebbe?*" The word used by Dante in relation to Virgil and
Cavalcanti was in the past, which could be understood

perhaps to mean that he had once been disdainful of Virgil and had changed. But Cavalcanti interprets it to mean that his son is no longer alive. "'Does not the sweet light of life strike his eyes?'" In this blind alley — this *cieco carcere* — this blind prison, which is really the blindness of sin, the significance of the sweet light — *lo dolce lume* — of life is a powerful contrast. It's not just a poetic paraphrase he is using. "When he became aware" — *quando s'accorse d'alcuna dimora ch'io faceva dinanzi alla risposta. . . .* "When he became aware of a certain hesitancy that I was going through before answering him," — *supin ricadde*, "he fell supine and appeared no more." *Supine* is the opposite of prone. Prostrate.

As a counterpoint, the great magnanimous Farinata reappears on the scene, *quell'altro magnanimo* — the word magnanimous here does not mean munificent; it is simply an adjective that describes a man who, to attain an end, is ready to sacrifice his life and his wealth, whereas munificent means he's ready to sacrifice his wealth only. Farinata had not changed his aspect nor moved his neck nor bent a rib. Resuming where he had left off, he continued: "'If my family has not learned the lesson of returning, that fact torments me more than this bed'." Don't miss the irony of calling those burning stones of the sepulchers a bed, "*ciò mi tormenta più che questo letto.*" "'But not fifty times will be renewed the face of the lady that reigns here'" — that takes us down to when Dante finally lost hope of having his own condemnation and exile rescinded, so that he might go back to Florence — "'when you too will find out that it's impossible to return. And so may you.' . . ." There is something here, stylistically, that is pretty hard to translate; it's a sort of response, stylistically, between what Farinata says here and what Dante says some lines later. "*E se tu mai nel dolce mondo regge*" — which does not mean "if ever" but "so *may* you" — we shall find a similar phrase used by Dante to apply to Farinata.

"'Tell me, why are those people of Florence so cruelly impious against my people'," "*perchè quel popolo è sì empio incontro a miei in ciascuna sua legge*," "'in every one of its laws?'" When pardon was given to almost all the other families, the condemnation against the Uberti was reiterated. "And I answered him: 'the butchery and bloody slaughter that made the Arbia flow red with blood'," that is, the battle of Montaperti that was won partly by the bravery of this man here, "*tale orazion fa far nel nostro tempio*," "'makes us utter such prayers in our temple'." Farinata had said the people of Florence were impious; Dante takes up the metaphor and uses it here by speaking of "our temples." So great was the slaughter heaped up by the Uberti that the Florentines thought it best not to let them come back. *Poi ch'ebbe sospirando il capo scosso;* "After he had sighingly shaken his head:" "'In that battle I was not alone,' he said, 'and I would not, without cause have stirred with the others. But I was alone there where it was proposed and agreed by all to destroy the walls of Florence'." It was he alone who openly defended the city. At the Congress of Empoli, the Ghibellines decided to destroy the walls of Florence which meant the city would be reduced to a defenseless village. And here is Dante's response mentioned earlier: "*Deh, se riposi mai vostra semenza*" —not if ever, but the expression of a hope that his seed may have rest. "*E par che voi veggiate se ben odo, dinanzi quel che il tempo seco adduce, e nel presente tenete altro modo.*" "There is a problem here that has completely bewildered my understanding; solve this problem for me, and if you do, may your offspring find rest. You seem to know the reality of the future, you seem to know what the future will bring, yet don't seem to know what the present holds'." He knew what would happen in 1304, and yet Cavalcanti did not know that his son was still living.

"'We have power of seeing like one who has' [*mala luce*]'," no, not imperfect vision, *mala luce* is the precise term for the defect which we call far-sightedness, one who sees things "*che ne son lontano. . . .*" "'We can discern things so long as they are in the distance'." "*Cotanto ancor ne splende il sommo duce.*" "'To that extent almighty God is still generous with us, still allows that we see something'." When things are becoming present, or are actually so, everything becomes blurred, and, unless someone comes to inform us, we know nothing of what has happened in your human state. "*Però comprender puoi che tutta morta fia nostra conoscenza da quel punto che del futuro fia chiusa la porta.*" "'Since we can only know the things of the future, you can well understand that all our knowledge will cease from that moment on when the door of the future shall close. Then, of course . . . the future will cease too, and that will be on judgment day'."

The difficulty that Dante plays on here is the fact that Guido Cavalcanti was still alive then, in the Spring of 1300, and that his father could not see when his son was going to die, because his vision had become blurred; the event being near at hand. In fact, Guido died that very summer. "*Però comprender puoi che tutta morta fia nostra conoscenza da quel punto,*" the line is very effective, "*che del futuro fia chiusa la porta*", "'when the gate of the future will be let down, will be locked,

forever'." *Allor, come di mia colpa compunto,*"then, as if
in compassion for my sin," in not having explained
properly the situation to Cavalcanti, "I said: 'Now you
will inform that fallen one'" — "*quel caduto*" — Dante
here shows a touch of contempt for him, "'that his son
is still among the living; that if I was slow in speaking
in answering him, let him know that it was because I was
thinking of this error, this problem which you have
resolved for me'." And so the scene ends, and Dante
goes on to describe the other souls that are here, in this
circle of the Epicureans.

What the reader should carry away from this
canto is the sharp contrast between these two very
different souls suffering the same punishment: one, a
humble, weak man, who cares only for his family, his
wife and his children, and is indifferent to other things;
the other, Farinata, the proud man, who cares only for
his party, whose love is all involved in the first phase of
love of country. As a whole, this canto stands out for
the magnificence of its structure. The scene is indeed
extraordinary from many points of view: the military
apparatus; the constant play between the death of the
soul and the death of the body, and so on.

The eleventh canto, which follows, is surely not
one of the greatest esthetically; it has none of the
dramatic beauty that is to be found in canto ten, but it
is important primarily as one of classification.

8. EVIL AS DEPRIVATION OF BEING; THE QUALITATIVE CHANGE OF SIN IN LOWER HELL

After the circles of lust, gluttony and avarice, there is a change in scenery, which points to a radical departure from the earlier sins. We encounter now a different, more serious kind of sin — real depravity. Until now, all these people — Francesca, Ciacco, and those others — all they wanted was pleasure, the satisfaction of their natural desires. Where was the sin? Or, put another way: where does man's real good lie? What is wrong with trying to find beatitude, as in the case of Francesca, in the arms of a handsome lover? Just a few days ago I heard a sermon by a very naïve pastor on the evils of overeating. He explained that the Christian religion forbids it, because it's bad for the health. He confused morality with hygiene. What is the blunder here? What's wrong with overeating? What's wrong with the good that some people find in overindulging in food? When is an act, a moral act evil? What is evil in general, and what is moral evil in particular? That's what we have to deal with now.

Plato, Aristotle, St. Thomas, Dante, looked upon evil as the deprivation of good. They say: evil has no essence. You know how that has been ridiculed by anti-Christians. Look at these foolish Christians; they see suffering everywhere, evil everywhere. How can they dare to deny that evil exists? The answer is: they don't deny evil — and I'm speaking of the pagan philosophers as well as the Christians — they deny that evil has *essence*, that there is something essential which you can call evil.

Evil is a void. Make a hole in a wooden floor and you have a real hole. But if you proceed to tear up and throw away all the remaining boards surrounding the hole, you won't have a large hole, you'll have a void — nothing. Evil is a deprivation of good, and when you say deprivation of good you mean also deprivation of all *being*, which in turn means an equation of good and *being*. Anything, insofar as it *is* — I'm following the language of the schoolmen and their pagan masters — is good. Earlier, I gave the example of blindness; blindness is a deprivation, but do we say that a blind man is evil? No, because, although deprived of a certain kind of good — the good of *seeing* — although deprived of that, he still has *being*. He can walk, he can speak, he can think. And insofar as he can do these things he has much that we can call good. If everything were bad, that is, if he were deprived of all good, no *being* would be left, obviously. Therefore, there is no such thing, according to the Church and the ancient philosophers, as a completely evil thing; or, the way the Church presented it against the Manicheans: there can be no possibility of establishing a religion with two supreme beings, one supremely good, the other supremely evil, because, when you try to pass from limited evil to infinite evil, what happens to *being*? Can there be an infinite principle of evil? Not in this context. Infinite evil is zero being.

In the language of mathematics, the God of the Manicheans, the God that is supposed to be the principle of evil, is zero, non-existent. Dante was aware of this commonplace — for it was certainly one of the commonplaces of his century. And to place this commonplace visibly before you, Dante has shaped Hell like a cone, a truncated cone: that is, it has a base but not an apex. And all these circles through which we have been passing, at least the upper eight, above the last which cuts off the apex of that cone, are planes, conic sections, drawn parallel to that last one which cuts off the apex. That is the shape with which Dante intended to show how evil obviously increases; the lower down you go, the worse the evil, and space decreases. The three worst sinners, the three terrible traitors are with the most awful enemies of God, the anti-trinity. For we have an anti-trinity down there that inspires people with an ecstasy of horror just as the real trinity inspires people with an ecstasy of love. Why does Dante not put that anti-trinity at the point that would be the apex of the cone? Because he has to give that trinity some being. If he tried to represent it as absolute, infinite evil, he would have nothing to represent; there would be zero *being*.

So, for Dante, moral evil is a deprivation of *being*; but it was natural with him, as it was natural with so many hundreds of other people, to recall that the being of man is essentially *rational being*. Moral evil is therefore a deprivation of *rational being*. And, since this has to do with the practical more than the theoretical reason, the *will*, therefore, has something to do with it. This deprivation of being, the sinful act which reduces the plenitude of *being* becomes an act that also reduces the plenitude of love. You can measure evil by showing to what extent the act of the sinner, of the evil-doer, has made him proceed along the way toward the destruction of love. There is the first act that destroys the natural bond of love, and then, as Dante tells us in the eleventh canto, the act that destroys that bond and another that is superimposed. A sin, therefore, is an act which is destructive of love; of course it must be a voluntary act, otherwise it cannot be a sin.

The schoolmen considered the question of how, no matter how evil something is, it is still essentially

good. St. Augustine devotes some of his most brilliant
pages to it, and never tires of repeating the precepts
that once upon a time every schoolboy used to have to
learn: *omnia ideo est quia unum est*, everything is, insofar as it is one; and then the poor lads had to immediately learn another: *omnia ideo est qui bonum est*; everything *is*, insofar as it has goodness. And then the
teacher would triumphantly show the relationship of
three things: *being, goodness* and *unity*. They don't
figure in the logical configuration by which our mind
operates rationally; they are beyond the categories,
they flow everywhere, they act everywhere but never
can be predicated of any category of things; they never
can be put in any particular box. These three things are
called *transcendentals*. People have loved that word. An
artist, wanting to bamboozle his audience, may speak
of his work as *transcendental*, or he might go on to say
metaphysical — hard to tell which is the more imbecilic.

We are still using transcendentals when we
speak of a thing as such, or *res*, or the more usual word,
aliquis. These rays of a sun which appear first in a sky,
then break through to shower themselves on science
and philosophy, until they come to rest on the table of
Porphyry — one substance, and nine accidents — thus
pass down to individual things. But that has nothing to
do with our subject here, except to clarify what the
relation of *bonum* is to *unum*, and above all, what the
relation is to *being*. (An interesting study would be to
trace how humanity has reacted to this idea of *bonum*
and *being* and *unum* in language, in thought, in art.) It
is impossible to think that *being* can ever be multiple.
You can't think unless you reduce multiplicity to
unity. And this applies in all things. That is the lesson
that Plato taught, and that all serious philosophy
teaches.

So: you go down this spiral of Dante's, from the

beautiful storm-wind of love (which many people would like to be caught in) from Paolo and Francesca, through a series of ups and downs, to the opposite extreme of that storm, reaching finally a place where vice has brought life almost to a complete standstill, a place frozen over with ice. Here you have, first, people who can no longer move around, then people who can't even change the position of their limbs; then people who can no longer speak, where all you can hear are low, beastly grunts. At the bottom, you get to a place where not even sound is possible, where all activity ceases. This is the place of the greatest sinners; those who betrayed political and religious sovereignty.

The people who are almost completely stripped of *being*, who have only enough passive *being* to make them suffer for their sins are Brutus, Cassius and Judas. Dante give us allegorically the picture of diminishing, waning *being* and waning love. Having explicitly stated what his notion of evil and sin is, he brings it before your eyes by showing you this progression to a point where you can't stir your limbs, you can't even make a sound. He shows you the world almost completely deprived of being. If he had gone a step further, Brutus, Cassius, and Judas would have disappeared.

An evil act, therefore, is not something that is simply detrimental to your health. We have got to get away from the confounding of hygiene and moral acts; or, perhaps, we should say, an evil act is detrimental to the health, but to the moral health of *reason*. We must stress that, when we say *act* in such discourse, we mean *human* act; and an act may be said to be human only when it is voluntary. If I happen to do something by accident, if my muscles twitch, or anything else like that, it is not a human act. A human act, a voluntary act, is evil when by itself, voluntarily, it works to deprive itself of something which is inherently owed to

it. This is a pagan doctrine; God does not come into it.
The precepts of revealed religion don't apply at this
point. What is owed to man? Or we should ask, rather:
what is owed to any act, any deed, any performance?
How do we know what is owed? How did the ancients
attempt to determine what is the due of anything?

What a thing is determines what is owed to it. In
other words, this kind of morality is based on ontol-
ogy. An act must be done because the individual belongs to a certain species, because it is so made. If man
were a beast — of course the hypothesis doesn't make
sense — but if man were a beast, he would have another
nature, and therefore you would say that the act that
he must perform must be such as not to deprive him of
anything that is his due as a beast. But man is not a
beast. And the something which is his due as a man is
reason. In other words, only man, no other animal, has
been created to constitute a species which distinguishes
itself and rises above all the others because it possesses
reason. Therefore, as all the pagans and the pseudo-
Dionysians and the rest taught: when you speak of the
good in connection with man, you mean a good that
has to do with *reason*. Man's goodness consists *essentially*, not by some kind of participation but *per se*, of
some kind of *rationality*. Man is good in that he is
rational. Which does not mean, however, that he must
reduce himself to an act of pure reason; he is also an
animal, and there are other goods for him in addition
to rationality. There is the good of the stomach, of the
sexual organs, of all the various parts of the body and
of the animal passions. And that being so, the virtue of
reason in this is to control and regulate.

The definition that has been in place now for
2,000 years is that an act is evil when it results in a
voluntary diminution of the fullness, of the plenitude,
of what man is. A dog is evil, or rather, the evil of a dog

consists in the diminution of the plenitude of his sensory capacities. Of course, dogs don't do it voluntarily — but, if they did, evil for them would consist in the diminution of the faculty of sense. And so with all other examples that might be given. Does that mean that reason can be injured in its theoretic as well as in its practical side? When we speak of evil as a diminution of reason, we speak usually of reason insofar as it operates to regulate our appetites. But we can also speak of evil with regard to reason in the theoretic sense. It is no sin to refuse or neglect to study astronomy, except if you belong to a class where you would be failing in moral responsibility by so doing. But there is a point in the sphere of pure reason, however, to which it is an individual's moral duty to go, and therefore a sin to refuse to attain; namely, when a man refuses to avail himself of the use of reason when he is able to do so, to a point sufficient to institute rational control of the animal appetites.

In other words, theoretical reason, because it has a bearing on practical reason, can be a sphere of sin. Sin or evil in this sphere can go to a point where you can no longer tell the difference between good and evil. Of course, some people are unfortunately born that way and we excuse them. But there are those who were not born that way but became that way, made themselves that way, who were once capable of distinguishing good and evil but can no longer do so. Do they commit a sin? Does the definition apply to them? Can you blame such a person? Was Francesca in that stage? Obviously not. In the second stage, you can no longer quote the two famous lines: *video meliorem,* I see the better thing, *probeque,* and I approve, but (like Francesca) follow the worse one. Since Ovid's day, poets have used these lines hundreds of times.

The people in the upper third of Hell are those

who have sinned that way, knowing better. But if you keep on doing the wrong things until they become habitual, the force of habit will result in the dulling of reason, an incapacity to understand that what you're doing does not accord with reason. It's what the psychologists have in mind when they call alcholism a disease. The poor drunkard is not to blame. He can't control himself. Build a monument to him or to his species, inconvenience everybody else for their benefit, destroy anything you want, but don't touch these people or say a harsh word, because they're not responsible. Is it true that the drunkard, the alcoholic, is not responsible? Well, maybe not now; but he was once. He has become what he is now because of his earlier acts. There was once a time when he said: I know this is bad, I know that it will destroy my stomach and my eyes and so on, but I'll do it anyway. But does it stop there? No, by dint of doing such things you destroy the capacity to distinguish good from evil. You have committed sin or evil in the theoretic sphere, as well as in the practical sphere.

You can get all this out of the pagans. What Christianity has added to the dictates of reason is a positive divine law. God has given two people, the Hebrews and the Christians, a law that distinguishes the pagans (so noble in philosophy but so ignoble in religion), that separates the religion of Olympus and the religion of the Jews, out of which comes the Christian religion. Is there anything more disgusting, more atrocious than the theogany of Olympus, the generation of the deities? When people compare the Greco-Roman religion, the Greco-Roman deities with the Christian, Hebraic religion, to show the superiority of the one over the other, all you have to do is recall the ten commandments — that's as far back as you need go — the deliverance of the Decalogue. If you want to

know about the other, about Olympus, read Hesiod
and Homer.

What has Christianity done? Christianity has
added, with regard to morality, a revealed positive law.
What we have called *natural* is what is written in the
human heart. But for the Christians there is something
else, for the Jews there is something else. They have a
table before their eyes, if they're real Hebrews, if they
are real Christians, and that table contains orders,
commandments, absolute commandments. These commandments contain the will of God. If you disobey
them, you have no doubt transgressed against reason,
you have committed the act described by Aristotle, but
you have also violated the explicit verbal positive command of God. So when we talk of sin in the Christian
world, everything we have said so far applies; but you
must finally resolve the whole thing into this: we call
sinful that act, that thought, that utterance (for it too
is a sin, is it not? — you don't have to actually hit a man
on the head to commit a sin) which has been positively
prohibited by God.

You kill reason when you abuse it or cause it to
deteriorate. First you act counter to it, then you dullen
it, and finally it is killed; though, after being killed it
may seem to gain new life, it may begin to operate in an
inverted way, as when you are urged by perverted
reason to commit evil for its own sake.

Dante has come through six circles. There are
three more to go. This sixth circle is apparently a circle
for sinners in the theoretic sphere, where people are
condemned for having committed a theoretic sin.
Although their religion taught them otherwise, they
insisted on a certain theoretic view. Farinata and
Cavaleanti and the great Frederick and many others
are found here, among the "heretics," the Epicureans
who deny the existence of God and the immateriality

and the immortality of the soul. The Epicureans taught that maybe the gods are there, but they don't care about this stinking world of ours; they're up there having a lot of fun with their backs turned on us. It's the Boccaccesque attitude. It is a theoretical sin; there is nothing here of the stench we get as soon as we go beyond this point, where we have to stop because of the terrible smell. By limiting the stench to a point beyond this wall, Dante pays homage to these sinners, whom he distinguishes from the gross ones. To blind yourself to the truth about the soul, is an error, but it's a theoretic error. The sin of this circle is terrible but not as revolting as the others are, in the lower circles.

In this sixth circle, we are inside a walled city with all the moats and towers and canals of a city, in addition to a swamp and a ferry-boat. We see the defense of the towers, the walls manned by devils, everything that pertains to the art of military defense of a fortified city. Angels intervene at last, and we then come to the city of the heretics, of the Epicureans, which turns out to be nothing but a burning cemetery. Dante turns to the right upon entering and skirts along the wall. He doesn't go to the center, to the part where the cathedral is. In every city there is a central square, with the city hall, the manufacturing district, and of course the cathedral. Dante turns and goes along the wall, away from the center of the city, and reaches the end of the plateau upon which this walled city lies. There he comes to a halt because of the awful stench. The plateau is rimmed around by a sort of ravine. Picture the Palisades twisted into a sort of circle, and you might get an idea of what Dante is describing: a circle of big boulders that are almost perpendicular. Just below, is the circle of the violent. After that comes the circle of the fraudulent, who kill natural love. The last circle is for those who kill both natural love and acquired love, over and above the natural. That completes the nine circles.

At the edge of the passage between the sixth and seventh circles, on the edge of this ravine, Dante tells us, there is a heretic pope — he doesn't want to put him clearly in the sixth circle, where he belongs (because in a way this pope stinks). Then comes the usual guardian. At every passage you have someone who stops Dante, stands in his way, kicks him, or tries to grab him. Here the guardian is the Minotaur. He represents the infamy of the place, the sins against nature which are found in the lower part of Hell — unnatural sins. The nature of man is rational; the moment you go against your reason, therefore, you go against nature. To that extent you can say that all sins, including that of Francesca, are against nature. But there are gradations; and as you go along, at a certain moment, the quantitative change is so great that the result can no longer be described in terms of quantity; the result is a change in quality. This is the great lesson of Aristotle. You can push something so far quantitatively, but at a certain moment the change becomes qualitative. We see it before us now, in our day: you can push the progress in arms so far — you can push war so far that it becomes something very different. What we call war today should no longer be called war; it is something qualitatively very different from what we meant by war before.

9. THE REVISED STRUCTURE OF HELL

In the eleventh canto, Dante marks an important change. *Inferno* wasn't originally planned this way; we witness here a rectification of the course followed in the earlier cantos. He didn't start out this way, but he was learning as he went along, through the many, many years he took to write this poem. In the process he straightened himself out, he repudiated a great deal of what he had previously thought. And now he thinks he can give a plan to the *Inferno* that will best conform to his design for the poem as a whole. Later, another rectification will have to be taken into consideration in the middle of Purgatory, and still another at the end of Purgatory.

Dante and Virgil had to stop at the edge of the ravine because of the terrible stench. To utilize the pause in some way, Dante asks Virgil to explain the structure of the part of Hell that has yet to be covered and to review that part of Hell they have already been through.

"'My son,' Virgil tells him, 'within these stones'" — the boulders that make up the ravine — "'are three little circles'," concentric circles, all conic sections of diminishing size. He calls them here *cerchietti*, small circles in contrast with the large ones. "*Di grado in grado, come quei che lassi*," "'they taper down progressively like those we have just left. All of them are filled with accursed spirits'." Notice how full of a kind of school-boyish rhetoric Dante's poetry still is, compared with the sublime effects of the *Paradiso*, where there is not a smattering of rhetoric. "'I will tell you about them now, so we won't have to stop later'" to explain; you will understand how they are pressed in, "*intendi come e perchè son costretti,*" how they are restricted in this cone, and the reason for it.

And then comes a famous and much debated *terzina*, "'Of all *malizia.*'..." Obviously *malizia* doesn't mean malice in the modern sense of the word, nor for that matter, in the modern Italian sense or French sense. *Malizia* — whether you take it in the technical sense, as the translators of Aristotle used it, in the sense of *kakia*, which is moral perversity, indulging in evil for itself, or in the sense of something not good mistaken for a good, or a good mistaken — has nothing to do with malice in the ordinary sense. Malice ordinarily signifies a certain meanness, a low fraudulence. Here it must be understood in a more magnificent sense; it involves a grand defiance of the deity. I know it's bad, and I want it that way; the devil take it. It is this *malizia* which is hated in heaven.

For all kinds of *malizia* — for all activity and so for this — there is an end. This idea, we saw, is the universal finalism of scholastic and Aristotelian philosophy. In this particular sphere, there is an end aimed at by this *malizia*, which has determined the action and brought it about. These evil ones are aiming at *injuria*; they are aiming at doing injury. *Injuria* is not injury in the physical sense, nor in the juridical sense of the term as in modern Italian and Latin, in which sense it is the opposite of justice. You may think of *injuria*, as we said, as the jurists think of it — the precise opposite of justice. You've heard the phrase: *summum jus summa injuria.* When you try to become too just you become most unjust. On the other hand, any half-baked Italian student will think of *injuria* as insult, which is the ordinary meaning of this word in Italian. Well, *injuria* here means none of these things. It is the act or the intention of a human being to do harm not for self-defense, not for passion, but simply for the sake of doing harm. In other words, it's connected with the Aristotelian *kakon*, which is the Greek word corresponding to *malizia*. These people, who are hated in heaven because they act contrary to all justice, want to hurt something or somebody. That is their end. And every such end is reached either through force, violence, or fraud.

Here Dante introduces, like a bolt out of a clear sky, a very important classification; not very significant philosophically, perhaps, but very significant in the history of ethics and politics. It figures large in Machiavelli. Every human being, he says, is a malefactor, everybody south of the Alps and east of the Rhine; and malefactions take two forms: one, that of the fox; and the other, that of the lion, i.e. violence and fraud. It is very old; Cicero formulates it, Dante has it. By itself it doesn't fit very well here, but Dante has to find some way to patch up his disrupted scheme, and this, with all its imperfections, serves his purpose. In other words, *malizia*, which is to do harm for its own sake, is reached either by violence or by fraud. But since he says that fraud is an evil act peculiar to man — *proprio* — the word proper in English unfortunately can't be used any more in the sense we need here; we do have the word property in that sense, but when we use the adjective, what do we mean? The property of the magnet is to attract iron, the property of a thing is that character which every individual of a species has, and which is not found in any individual of any other

species. We have maintained property in this sense
because it can be used in science without being misunderstood. But can you use the adjective that way? Can
you say that fraud is proper to man? Hardly! Too much
meaning of another sort has filtered through, in connection with that, to allow us to use the word that way.
"Peculiar to man," might do.

"*Ma perchè frode è dell'uom proprio male*," that is,
it's a *proprium* of man because, according to Dante, in
spite of Machiavelli and of the ancients, the fox is not
fraudulent. Why not? Because to defraud you need
intelligence, intellect; it may not be a high use of
rationality, but you need it, and no lower animal has
this. And since it's peculiar to man, this complete
revulsion of rationality, it is most displeasing to God.
"*E però stan di sutto gli frodolenti.*" "'For that reason the
fraudulent are below on a lower level, and suffer more,
correspondingly'," "*e più dolor li assale.*"

"*De violenti il primo cerchio è tutto,*" "'the first
circle is entirely made up of those who were violent'."
Then he goes on to say — but this is something that he
will repudiate very solemnly later on — "'you can be
violent against yourself, against your neighbor and
against God'." Therefore in the circle of the violent
there must be three sub-circles, again tapering down in
the order of the gravity of the sin. "*A Dio, a se, al
prossimo si puone far forza.*" You can do violence to
God, to your neighbor and to yourself. And you can
do violence to the substances themselves, to man as a
substance, or to the things that belong to man. The
same for your neighbor, the same for yourself, and the
same for God. "*Dico in loro, e in lor cose. . . .*" As far as
the neighbor, the man himself, the neighbor himself,
you can harm by killing him, or wounding him, or you

can harm him by doing harm to the things that belong to him. Death by violence and grave wounds can be dealt to him personally; as to his things, you can deal him *ruine*, ruins, *incendi,* conflagrations; i.e. you can destroy his house, burn it; and *tollette dannose. Tolle* is the word from which you get the English word "toll." Here they will find "'murderers and those who inflict wounds unjustly'."

Dante wants you to understand that sometimes you can deal wounds with justification. He is no absolute pacifist; *omicidi,* homicide, does not mean just to kill a man, but to kill him unjustly. We don't say a man commits homicide who kills in self-defense; he is not a murderer. A homicide is one who kills for *injuria* — "*guastatori e predon,*" devastators, wreckers, plunderers, brigands, all are tormented in this first circle in different categories. "*Tutti tormenta lo giron primo per diverse schiere.*"

Dante, with pedantry which is hard to explain but very orthodox indeed, continually reminds us that as to rewards and punishments there are never two alike. There are, true enough, many mansions in my father's house, but there are many mansions in the house of the enemy, in the father's enemy's house also. Next comes violence against self. "*Puote omo avere in sè man violenta e ne' suoi beni.*" "'Man can lay violent hands against himself and also against his goods'." It is mete, therefore, in the second of these sub-circles, that the sinners should suffer without the possibility of useful repentance — that is, whoever "*qualunque priva sè del vostro mondo,*" "'whoever has deprived himself of your world'" — Virgil no longer belongs to the world to which Dante belongs — suffers uselessly. not only by depriving himself, but also by destroying violently his belongings, *"biscazza e fonde la sua facultade,"* "'destroys his faculty'" — that is, his property, either by lavish spending or by gambling, "'and weeps there where he ought to be rejoicing'."

One might ask: how did the prodigal escape this lower Hell? They are punished so much more lightly than those up above. The others got fun out of spending their money; these are not looking for fun. These do violence to themselves and their goods, they kill themselves and they kill their possessions simply to do something atrocious. The line that explains this very beautifully is *"e piange là dove esser dee giocondo,"* "'and weeps where he ought to be happy'." One may also do violence against the Deity. How? By attacking Him and by attacking His things; against God Himself or against nature. Following the line of thought of Aristotle: we have to regard nature either as God or as the long hand of God, the executor or executrix of God's design. One may do violence against the Deity in a rage — that is, if in fit of rage you curse God, or deny Him. That's not the crime here considered; the crime here is denying and cursing God in your heart — not simply in a rage but when you mean business, as Capaneus and others did. That's the crime against Deity in itself; then, the crime against His things: *"e spregiando in natura sua bontade,"* depreciating, despising in nature the goodness of God. Nature manifests the goodness of God and, by the way you treat nature, you show the way you regard God. Therefore, the smallest of the circles *suggella* — rather powerful, that word; Dante lets us see across these circles of Hell what he really means, namely, what happens when the souls on earth let themselves be seized by these sinful habits — *"e però lo minor giron suggella del segno suo e Sodoma e Caorsa, e chi*

spregiando Dio col cor, favella" "'stamps with its signet',"
impresses its signet, stamps with infamy those who
offend God, namely the Sodomites, the homosexuals,
and the usurers. Instead of calling them by their name,
he calls them by the name of the cities where they
operated. France had the monopoly on usury at Cahor,
as far as Dante was concerned. Of course, the French
could reply, and with much justification, that almost
all usurers for centuries, almost everywhere, were called
Lombards, were Italians. The stamp of infamy is put on
those for whom those place-names are the symbols;
and not only on them but also upon those who despise
God, with their hearts, not merely with their lips.

Next comes fraud: "*la frode, ond'ogni coscienza è
morsa*," "'fraud by which every conscience is bitten'."
Fraud is brought out in man in two ways; against one
who trusts him — "*ch'in lui fida; e in quel che fidanza non
imborsa*," "'and against him who does not pocket trust'."
This second way, that is, fraud against those who are
on their guard, seems to cut from behind because that
is what fraud is: if it cuts from in front it would be
violence, not fraud. That second kind of fraud only
cuts the tie of love which nature makes. By nature, all
men should love one another, whether they are friends
or relatives or not; that is the great doctrine of Christianity: men, as such, are intended by nature to love
one another. The second kind of fraud seems to kill or
wound only that kind of love. Then come hypocrisy
and flattery.

Strange, that all through classical antiquity, way
back in Athens, then in Italy, people made such a fuss
about flattery; probably because, with tyranny, it was
the greatest public menace. The flatterer is feared by
all; with his words he turns the head of even the tyrant

and makes him do what he wants. So you find here hypocrisy, flattery, sorcerers, those who practice witchcraft — *fattura* is a kind of witchcraft — counterfeiting, theft, simony, not the kind of people you find in the circle of simple fraud. Simony is corruption in church matters: when a bishop, a metropolitan, appoints a bishop of a subordinate town for a consideration he is guilty of simony. Here too are ruffians, grafters — *baratto* is corruption not in the administration of the church but in the administration of the civil government — and similar filth. *Lordura* is the worst possible word for filth.

In the ninth circle, there's another fraud, more destructive of love and more severely punished. The simple version is punished in the eighth circle, where: *"quell'amor s'obblia che fa natura,"* "'that love is forgotten that nature makes','" and also the love of husband for wife, of father for son, of friends, *"di che la fede spezial si cria,"* out of which not the generic confidence of the other, but the specific confidence of those who are united in personal friendship is created. Here, in the smallest circle, the ninth circle, *"nel cerchio minore ov'è il punto dell'universo,"* "'where the center of the universe is'" — *punto*, of course, means the center, technically — we find *Dis*.

Dante looks upon *Dis* — whether he was aware of the older pagan notions on the matter or not is uncertain — primarily as a city: the city of the devil. In that last circle, *"qualunque trade in eterno è consunto,"* "consumed," is hardly the word. "Undone"? *"Ed io —"* "to this I answered, 'Master, very clear to me is your line of reasoning, and very well have you marked out, or distinguished this *baratto*, and the people in it, but tell me' — "

He is coming to an important point; he wants to put the patch in. He has apparently finally learned the thing which every Aristotelian student should know from the very first, and by means of which he now hopes to put order into the structure of the *Inferno*. "'Tell me, those in the thick swamp'," the one they crossed, where the wrathful and the sullen are steeped in mud, "'those whom the wind drives'," the lustful; those whom the rain beats on, "'the gluttons'," and those who clash against one another with sharp tongues, "'namely, the prodigal and the misers'," why are they not crushed inside the fiery contours of this city? Why are they not punished inside this city with the rest, if the wrath of God has descended upon them?'" Why is there a different way of treating those we saw before and those whom we now find? "And he to me, 'why does your intellect'" — *ingegno* of course has always the same meaning in Dante: that of the intellect directed to the discovery of something new, the capacity for mental discovery; and *delirare* (Dante must have known the etymology of the word) according to the lexicons of the time means to move aside from the furrow — *lira* means furrow and therefore to *delirare* is to move aside from the straight line that the plow makes — "'why does your mind move from the straight track? Or do you have something else in mind when you ask that? Do you not remember those words with which your ethics treat.' . . ." Why *your* ethics?

People have said so many things about this. It has puzzled many, yet it is very simple. Does one have any need of ethics in the next world? Or, put it this way: ethics, with Aristotle, is bound up with the capacity to sin. Can anyone in the other world sin? Aristotle asks scornfully: can you imagine the gods being subject to ethical rules? Can you imagine a god having to practice moderation, having to regulate his sexual desires, or other passionate appetites? Ethics presupposes passions such as possess our vulnerable nature. After death that vulnerable nature no longer operates — not in the damned, and surely not in the saved. Do you not remember the words of your ethics that treat of these dispositions? Disposition is a technical term. By dint of repeating certain acts, what happens? If a child, starting at the age of three or four or five, is made to respect his elders, at a certain age he does it instinctively, and with pleasure. That's what people who thought seriously about these matters used to think. (But, of course, modern educational theorists have thought otherwise, and you can tell with how much justification from the wonderful results.) By repeating certain acts one forms habits. If they're good, we call them virtues; if they're bad, we call them vices. If someone were to ask what are habits, what predicate should be used? In defining anything, you have to predicate, until you reach the last possible predication, and of that there can be no predication; but until then you have got to supply an answer — a predication.

So, what is a habit? It's a disposition; and with the disposition you pass into a large world. There are three dispositions *"che il ciel non vuole"* "'that heaven doesn't want'" — incontinence, *malizia*, and a third, which is not very clear in Aristotle, less clear in St. Thomas, and very confused in Dante: *"matta bestialitade,"* mad bestiality. It seems to some to be a malice so great that you think of the one that performs it as some kind of mad beast. Others have explained it as simply a lack of reason, similar to that which we find in the violent; but it's hard to say. These are the three dispositions: *incontinenza, malizia,* and *la matta bestialitade.*

Do you remember that from your ethics? Virgil asks; and how, since the first one, incontinence, offends God less, it is therefore punished less severely? *"Se tu riguardi ben questa sentenza,"* if you consider, if you give the proper attention, to what I'm now saying and if you recall to mind who those people are *"che su di fuor sostengon penitenza,"* "'who are punished up above, you will see why they are separated from these [*felli*]'." *Felli* is a hard word. Felons, might do. It means evil, but without any connotation of any particular kind of evil. You will see why *"men crucciata la divina vendetta li martelli,"* "'why divine justice hammers them with less wrath'." All along, Dante stresses the rage of the divinity; this is the third or fourth time. Of course, it's a figure of speech. God cannot possibly express rage; rage is a passion, and there are no passions in God. In God there is only justice; though to our eyes, what he does appears to have passionate significance.

"'O sun, you who give sight back to my disturbed vision, you satisfy me so, when you remove the clots you satisfy me to such an extent that doubting is almost as pleasant as knowing'." Dante treats for a first time the famous Aristotelian doctrine of doubt, which he will take up more fully in *Paradiso.* Doubt, according to Aristotle, is the *sine qua non,* the root of all knowledge. Those can never know anything for whom doubt does not exist. Dante wants to know why Virgil said earlier that the usurers first of all offend nature and secondly why, offending nature, they offend God. How does usury offend nature? The answer, of course, is what you should have expected. Nature shows us, internally, and externally, that to get our livelihood we must work; everything that possesses life and produces life does so by some kind of work. The cow will produce a kind of animal like itself; the plants also reproduce their kind. All this reproduction takes place within the sphere of nature. The miser, on the other hand, sits down and lets gold coins reproduce themselves. That is against nature. Gold coins don't reproduce themselves the way the cow does. In saying this he is, no doubt, using the well known Aristotelian criterion. The word for the usurer's advantage is not *interest*. In Italian we have the word "frutto." The Greeks use the word *tokos* which means child. In Latin the word is from the vegetable kingdom, in Greek from the animal kingdom. Coins cannot, by nature, reproduce; they cannot bear fruit, therefore usury is contrary to nature. If you can't accept Aristotle's explanation, go to the Bible. We find in the book of Genesis that you are supposed to get the bread you need to eat not by sitting down and counting coins, but by the sweat of your brow.

10. THE PAUSE ON THE EDGE OF LOWER HELL; THE IMPORTANCE OF ASTRONOMY

This eleventh canto is basic for the entire *Inferno* and indicative of the change of mind in Dante's ethical thinking. He deduces ethics from love. It's an ancient notion, older than Christianity. It is the effort to show that the four natural virtues, the cardinal virtues, are phases of love. All the others are related to them and regulated by them. They are *justitia*, *temperantia*, fortitude, and *prudentia*. Of course in the Catholic Church, in Plato, in Aristotle we have to be careful about *prudentia*, particularly when we come down to Aristotle, because *prudentia* is not the same as *phronesis*; Aristotle distinguishes the two, and that distinction is carried on by St. Augustine. There is wisdom, an intellectual virtue, pertaining to theoretic reason; *prudentia* pertains to practical reason.

When these people spoke of such matters, they distinguished not only a higher reason and lower reason, but also a practical and theoretic reason. When your ratiocination has for its object pure ideas in themselves, and in relation to one another, we are dealing with higher reason; it is intellect operating as theoretic reason. But when your reason is busily occupied with things here below, with the objects of sense, then it is lower reason. The distinction is carried down by St. Augustine. The distinction between practical reason and theoretic reason, and between reason and intellect, the distinction advanced by Aristotle and by the schoolmen much more than by Aristotle is that we use our mind in two ways: one to grasp the thing in its immediacy — intuitively — and the other, to grasp something discoursively, proceeding from one thing to a related thing. We call the latter discoursive reasoning, a reasoning that runs along. For instance: I grasp the notion that I am a man; if I know what "man" is, I can proceed to say that I must be able to think and that I must be mortal. In all languages we call that a discourse, ratiocination; thinking, grasping something intellectually, not in its immediacy but in its relation to something else. The English philosophers of an earlier time knew the distinction between the Greek words *noetic* and *dionetic*: *noetic* is what is grasped intuitively, in a non-running manner; *dianoetic* describes the activity of reason as it proceeds from one thing to another.

Sapientia has nothing to do with *prudentia*. *Prudentia* operates only in the practical sphere of life. Practical of course means moral; practical philosophy means moral philosophy. In French books, Italian books, you still find *prassi, la prassi*, used philosophically to mean moral, without further explanation. How does Dante relate these four virtues to love?

They are very old, as we said. There's the Stoic articulation of them and an Epicurean one, and others. You see, the human mind is not satisfied with just the four as such; it wants them articulated. And to articulate means to find a common root. The Epicureans did it, and every one else. St. Augustine is the articulation followed by Christians, *caritas* as the root. In the schoolmen and in St. Augustine, charity doesn't mean alms-giving, although alms-giving is a phase of *caritas*, because if you love your fellowman and you find him in need, you will give him some material benefaction. Charity is an unfortunate restriction of a

very noble word. The Gospels and St. Paul especially
put a great deal of stress on *caritas*.

Love is the root of the four cardinal virtues. If
in the exercise of your love you encounter danger, you
are expected, if you are a moral man, to be brave. So,
fortitude is the virtue of love you are expected to
exercise when the object of love is being menaced. But
what exactly is to be loved, in the Christian sense? God,
per se, for Himself, and your neighbor, not for himself
but for the sake of God. And what happens to you?
Well, when you love God, and indirectly when you love
your neighbor, you exalt yourself to the highest possible level, spiritually; but the man who lusts for material prosperity, who loves himself materially, destroys
love, repudiates love. Love yourself, yes, but in such a
way that you can reconcile such love with love of
neighbor and love of neighbor as a phase of your love
of God.

What is temperance in this context? The capacity, the habit, of moderating your appetites, your
egotistic appetites, for the higher appetites. Love of
neighbor is to be subordinated to love of God. Of
course you can say: eat, drink and be merry for tomorrow we die. If tomorrow you die, or if you don't die,
you are supposed to love God and your neighbor; and
if you don't, you have gone counter to the purpose of
human love.

What is *prudentia*? It's the activity of the mind
directed — we said, it's practical — to knowing and attaining the object of your love. In this, you have to use
your rational faculty, not just your volition. Your
mental activities directed to the satisfaction of your
highest appetite or desire — which is love of God — is
called *prudentia*. And *justitia* is the virtue whereby you

love each thing according to its due; God first, then your neighbor. And love of neighbor begins at home. The proverb is ugly, hard-sounding, but properly understood, it's very appropriate. The reduction of ethics to love is important because it takes a particular form in Dante.

The eleventh canto starts off with a description of an overwhelming stench. And that stench was intended to indicate the distinction between the lot of the heretical, the Epicurean philosophers and what lies below. After all, the philosophers may be sunk in error but they don't stink. The stench from below is so powerful that they have to stop and wait to get used to it.

Keep one eye on the literal, and the other on the recondite meaning — the meaning that applies to this life here on earth. When you examine unsavory moral and ethical matters, you can't just hurry by; you can't just take a sniff, say phooey, and run on. You've got to be able to stand the stench and see what you can do about it. To get themselves accustomed to what is coming, Dante and Virgil wait and occupy their time with a long discourse, an ethical analysis. Then Virgil says: it's time to go; but he says it in round-about language. He says the Fish are leaving the horizon and the Wain; the chariot is in Taurus, that is, in the northwest.

Not very long ago someone raised the question: aren't these astronomical observations of Dante usually quite meaningless? Of course not; they have a great deal of meaning in Dante; and he expects you to get something out of what he says about the celestial phenomena. Let me give you a very quick survey of the situation. As he goes through the realm of the damned,

Dante is moving toward the center of the earth, which
is also the center of the universe. In his system, the
earth is a sphere; it stands at the center, and it stands
suspended in space. How, they admit they don't know,
but they offer all sorts of explanations, some of them
very funny. It stands at the center because the pull of
its appetites is the same in all directions. It is like the
donkey who died of hunger surrounded by hay, because all the bales of hay were equidistant and equally
stimulating to the appetite; and therefore the donkey,
equally drawn on all sides, starved to death from
indecision.

Incidentally, Dante asserts again and again and
builds up his whole system on the fact that the earth is
a sphere. You still find in textbooks one of the many
blunders out of that famous book which contains
1,000 egregious blunders, which blunders you still
have to learn in order to graduate from some high
schools and even to graduate from certain colleges
and universities. The error to which I refer is the
popular one that Columbus, when nobody else thought
so, established that the earth was round. The fact is
that everybody in the Middle Ages, knew that the world
was round — and only humorists of the time ever said
anything to the contrary. Men established that the
earth was round in the days of Aristotle. The three or
four chief proofs, some very cogent, some less cogent,
were already familiar in the fourth century B.C.

Here's Dante, then, moving down to the center
— not in a straight drop — but on an incline, to the left
mostly and sometimes to the right. He goes sideways to
break the fall. The sphere of the earth, the center of
which Dante reaches at the end of the *Inferno*, is the
center of the universe of time, the center of moving

things. And, of course, the physics of the day rested in the fundamental distinction between matter that moves in a straight line and matter that moves in a circular line. Of the first kind of matter are the four elements, some moving rectilinearly, downward, like earth; others moving rectilinearly upward, like fire; the rest have rectilinear motions in between these. This matter that moves in a straight line, is made up of the four elements, those pestilential four elements, which have plagued science for centuries. This matter of *levia* and *gravia*, of perishable things, extends to the sky of the moon, the first or lowest of the celestial bodies as astronomers had established.

The moon is a body of matter that moves not in a straight line but in a circular line. It is not made of any of the four but of a fifth element. And that fifth element or substance or essence of which all the stars are made, is called *quintessence*: which means fifth element. The Pythagoreans called it by the term which is the Greek equivalent of quintessence, but Aristotle called it *ether*, a word that has lived on through the centuries. Ether, astronomically, is not that stuff you get when your teeth are pulled out. It's not as anesthetic: it is the *quintessence*. It is matter not subject to decay, or genesis. In other words, it's not matter that goes in a straight line; it moves in a circular line.

This region of the fifth essence is where the Fish are to be found. It's divided into skies. The oldest natural philosophers did not speak of skies; they said, there is the moon, the orb as we see it, and there are the other bodies. These old philosophers ordered the celestial bodies with the moon first, then the planet Mercury, then Venus, then the Sun and Mars, then Jupiter and finally Saturn. The order is correct: the outermost is Saturn, the next one is Jupiter, and the next is Mars — but below that, they are sometimes right and sometimes wrong. Mercury and Venus were made to move around the earth instead of around the sun, as they do, so that sometimes they appear nearer than the sun and sometimes further. The order given is true when those planets are on this side of the sun. It is only a partial error; they had sized up the situation pretty well.

Until Ptolemy they had been satisfied to say: there is the moon and there is Venus and so on. But when Ptolemy came along, who was primarily an educator, there rose the necessity of giving it a more tactile representation. Instead of thinking of the body of the moon in the sky, they put the moon in a big sphere, like a pearl encased in a ring or, better yet, in a bowl. They did that for every one of the planets. The difference between the matter that you see in the skies and the matter that you don't see, is that the former is compressed and the latter is not. The schoolboys of the time were supposed to know that, no matter in what direction you shoot off from the earth into the sky, you will encounter this ring or hollowed sphere with the body that's encased in it — encased is the very word they used; it is a word that comes from the language of jewelers.

So you have these various skies that go on to Saturn, these seven planets; but beyond them you still see a lot of other bodies, and the astronomers assumed from long observation that they all moved together. They called them *fixed stars* and observed that they were all more or less equally distant from the earth and encased, again, in a single heaven, a sky which, coming after that of Saturn, is therefore called the eighth sphere. There, the quintessential matter comes to an end. In the days of Plato and Aristotle the natural scientists were satisfied with this astronomical scheme of eight spheres; but when they discovered the procession of the equinox, when they observed that the eighth sky also had a motion from west to east, they introduced the ninth sphere. And thus we have the nine celestial spheres, that Dante utilizes, building up his entire *Paradiso* on this scheme of nine concentric rings, which are the heavenly spheres.

You can see how this structure is used for practical purposes. What are the various measures of time astronomically? One of them is obviously the day; another is the week, (significant astrologically, not astronomically). The next astronomical unit of measure is the month and the next is the year. How do we get these measurements? How long does it take the moon to go around the earth? Not its daily motion across the sky from east to west in approximately twenty-four hours; the moon and all the other erratic bodies have a counter-motion, the motion that takes them from west to east. When you see the new moon, it's in the west. It's new because it's practically stamped against the setting sun; and the day after, at the same time, you see it higher in the west, and the day after a little more, and a little more, always in a more easterly position, always waxing, until at last you see the moon rising in the east, no longer the new moon, but the full moon. It continues in the same direction until it has gone all around. These different phases take twenty-eight days. That gives us the month, which has been juggled around in order to fit into the other astronomical units, especially the year, the time it takes for the sun to go around the earth from west to east.

The sun goes around the earth from east to west in one day — apparently — but to go around in the opposite direction, from west to east, it takes that length of time we call the year, 365 days. How can we tell? With the moon it's easy. Even if you don't get out and look for it, you can't help noticing its change of position in the sky, going from west to east. You can see that the moon is nightly among different stars. But how did they observe the counter-motion of the sun? By noticing the constellations opposite to it, after setting. That motion gives us the year. And the astronomical motion that measures the day is the time it takes a given star, a fixed star, to go from the meridian around and back to the meridian. They, of course, could not say that. The day for us is the result of the rotation of the earth on its axis, but from the point of view of the Ptolemaics and Dante: since the earth stands still, it's the passage of the eighth sphere in its entirety, across the meridian.

If, on any given night, you look up to see what stars are directly overhead, and then look again, twenty-four hours later, you will see the same stars overhead. And they will be overhead every twenty-four hours *in eterno* — for, the ancients said, unlike the planets, the fixed stars have only one motion, that of east to west, which all the ancients called the motion of the *primum mobile*. If a schoolboy in antiquity and through the Middle Ages were asked: what is the day? he would answer: it is the unit of measurement based on the revolution of the *primum mobile*. The *primum mobile* has a motion which is not precisely the same as that of the heaven of the fixed stars, but the latter's motion was a sufficiently accurate measure of the day, just as the rotation of the earth is sufficiently accurate in our system. We have done away with the revolution of the eighth sphere by substituting the rotation of the earth on its axis. And instead of saying the sun moves around the earth, we say the earth moves around the sun.

In addition to the daily movement from east to west, these planets have a counter-motion from west to east, which takes one month for the moon, thirty-odd years for Saturn. The fixed stars don't have any west to east motion, only east to west. All this helps in reading the *Paradiso*. Still, one might ask: why the ninth sphere? Because, when, by a brilliant observation, the so-called procession of the equinox was discovered, when it was discovered that the eighth sphere — needed to account for the twenty-four hour motion — had two motions, the daily motion from east to west and a very small counter-motion (a change they figured at one degree in a hundred years), they had to posit another sphere with a single motion to account for the twenty-four hour measure. They had to invent the ninth sphere, without a visible body, having a single motion from east to west that takes every celestial body around — the moon, the planets and the stars — all of which, including the eighth sphere, have a counter-motion of their own.

That gives us another measure of time beyond that of the thirty-odd years of Saturn: something much bigger, the Platonic year of 36,000 years. That number comes from the calculation of one degree of counter-motion in one hundred years. To complete the measure of 360 degrees therefore, will take 36,000 years. This calculation was very important with the ancients for their theory of the reconstitution of phenomena, the notion that we, everything, will all be here again, even as we are now, you, touching your little finger, I, talking, everything that has been will be again, when the whole world is to be reconstituted to run its course again after the so-called Platonic year. For the Christians, however, even in the Acts of the Apostles, that measure of time will not be completed. The idea was fulminated against by Christian preachers, naturally, but it persisted. It has no scientific value, except that it shows how well they observed what we call the procession of the equinox, which they interpreted as a revolution of the eighth sphere from west to east. Their calculation of a motion of one degree in a hundred years wasn't absolutely accurate, but very close to it.

---

1. I don't see how they get the notion of fixed stars; the stars change their position, do they not?

Relative to the planets, yes; but not relative to themselves. In relation to one another their positions are fixed, there's no question about that. It was against the background of the fixed stars that the countermotion of some of the heavenly bodies was observed. In other words, how did all of this begin? In the beginning, no doubt, all that was observed was the general motion of all heavenly bodies from east to west in twenty-four hours. Then some shepherd on a mountain top observed that the moon didn't move with the rest; and then someone discovered that Mars — a certain reddish brilliant star — also didn't have a simple motion from east to west, but another from west to east. And so, gradually the erratic bodies were isolated and distinguished against the sphere of the fixed stars. Even as late as Galileo, they thought that all the fixed stars were in a single sphere more or less equally distant from the center. Galileo wavers at times, in his writings on the subject; but he doesn't have the courage to plunge through the eighth sphere, like Newton did afterward. It took a long time to make the plunge into infinite space.

Next, we have to see what the reference to the Fish, at the close of the eleventh canto, means. In that connection we will also have to try to form some picture of what the ecliptic is: that great avenue of the heavens along which the moon and the sun and the other erratics move. In other words, we'll have to ask ourselves: what do we mean when we say that the sun is in Aries?

11. ASTRONOMY AND THE ZODIAC; THE MINOTAUR AND THE APPROACH TO MALEBOLGE

We have considered briefly what might be called a representation of the heavens, not to explain Ptolomaic astronomy but to provide in detail, a cosmological picture that might be useful not only for understanding the structure of the *Paradiso* but also to make some sense out of Dante's astronomical figures. The mind, in its naiveté, at first saw all the stars going around until, to take up the image given us by Greek poetry, a shepherd on a mountain top, with nothing to do all night but look at all those stars (which is not a bad way to spend a night if you have nothing better to do and can't sleep) discovered that they were not going around all together, in a single motion, but some had a motion in the opposite direction, discernible from night to night. And gradually, in the course of centuries, one after another of these stars were distinguished.

Further observation showed that the erratics, the planets — for that's what the word erratic means — were seven in number and don't conform in their motions to the movement of the fixed stars. One of them approximated in its motion the unit of measure we call the month. Then they discovered the erratic motion of the sun, which completes its circle in 365 days, giving us the measure which we call the year. Another star that attracted attention was that very ruddy star which many have found, and some still find, awe-inspiring to look at — the ancients said the sight of it was awe-inspiring — I'm referring to Mars. And so on to the slowest moving of the planets, for that reason called Saturn. All of them are circling around the earth.

But of the stars, one might say: you don't see them overhead every day, or at the same time of night. Certain stars up there now won't be there six months from now. Does that mean the stars have altered their course? No. It means that the sun has moved around among the stars we formerly saw and out-dazzles them. The stars keep their even course. The seven planets, instead, the seven erratics, move around within a definable portion of the sky. They have, in other words, all seven, an avenue, a broad avenue along which they move and they stay within that band. You never find the moon straight overhead in these parts, for instance. You know the old phrase: the man who was foolish enough to think he could see the reflection of the moon in a well. The phrase must have originated among people living north of the tropic of Cancer, south of the tropic of Capricorn. For the moon and the sun, and the rest of the erratics, never go northward or southward beyond the limits of those two tropics. They all move to one side or the other, within a broad belt, not very wide, not parallel to the equator, but inclined to it twenty-three and a fraction degrees, so that it is partly north of the equator and partly south of it.

Anyone who has studied something of that useless science which is astronomy, if only the rudiments of it, will know about this inclination of what is called the ecliptic, this belt which is called popularly the Zodiac. Ecliptic is the accurate term, but it was called the Zodiac, popularly, because the various patterns or groups of stars in moving in it were imagined pictorially and represented as animals. Therefore, the whole belt is called the belt of the animals, or Zodiac. Ten animals make up the belt, ten animals which I would guess were the most famous group of animals in the world from the most ancient times down to as late as 1920. There wasn't anybody who didn't know what the animals were, or who couldn't represent them, draw them easily. Everywhere, even in the United States, in every community, beginning with New York, the representation of the Zodiac must have numbered in the hundreds and thousands. There isn't an important building that doesn't have at least one representation of the Zodiac in it. Here, at Columbia, there are at least nine or ten. There's one, at least, in Butler Library, and one in Low Library, and there are a dozen others scattered all over the campus. Of course, if you don't know them you won't recognize them even if you see them — these animal representations of the mental pictures inspired by the constellations of the ecliptic, which have come down to us through so many centuries.

You see, of course, what all this means when projected upon the earth. The sun is pretty hot in the summer, here, when it's in its most northerly position. And when it's noon or two or three PM it doesn't hit your window and spares you that misery of heat because it's on the roof. Then, in the winter, when you don't mind the sun, you see it at noon relatively low on the southern horizon, so low that unless you have a window pretty high up in this city, it won't come through at all. And, of course, this is a result not of a motion up and down, but of the fact that the sun in its yearly motion moves along a circle, part of which is north of the equator and part of which is south.

The Zodiac, these constellations, which make up the belt which is the track of the erratics, is what we have to have in mind when we try to understand what Dante or anybody else means in saying that the sun is in Aries, or that the moon is in the Fish. It doesn't mean these different planets have been pushed off into the eighth sphere but simply that if you were to draw a line from the center of the earth, from the center of the universe, through the center of the moon, that line would strike, after it had traversed all the intervening skies, the central point of the constellation of fixed stars called the Fish. In the European churches, in the cathedrals, they sometimes represent these signs on the pavement near a window, located so that it lets through the light in a way that indicates the position of the sun in the Zodiac — something like a sundial. There used to be various mnemonic devices to help you remember the sequence of the signs. The names of these constellations were put down in rhyming or rhythmical lines; in order, they are Aries, Taurus, Gemini, Cancer, Leo, Virgo, Libra, Scorpio, Sagittarius, Capricorn, Aquarius, and Pisces. Fish is the last, coming just before Aries.

So what we have, to summarize, is this sphere of ours, the earth, surrounded by these globes, each with its star, up to the seventh; then another globe that envelopes them, which has not one star but an almost infinite number of stars; and then, beyond that, another globe that has no stars at all. For a long time the sky of the fixed stars was considered the last globe, until it was discovered that it too had an erratic motion of its own, which is very, very small and therefore, according to the Greeks, would take 36,000 years to complete — which period, however, according to the Christians, is never to be completed because the world will end before then. The motion we calculated to be approximately one degree in a hundred until — according to the ancients — there would take place the reconstitution of all phenomena, the reconstitution of all being.

The Christians, as we noted, rejected the whole theory of reconstitution. Most Christians had started off thinking that the end of the world was imminent, just around the corner, until St. Augustine warned them that the corner might not be so near as they thought — that it might be pretty far off, in fact. In the tenth, eleventh and twelfth centuries, it was declared heretical to speak of an imminent end of the world. You've heard how people amused themselves repeating the old tale that the world was expected to end after the year 999? There were many years that people expected to be the last, but 999 was not one of them. The Church got sick of it, and declared it heretical to speak of an imminent end. But Dante doesn't take notice and keeps talking of the end of the world.

Their pause comes to an end with Virgil saying: we've got used to the stench, let's move on; "*'seguimi oramai che il gir mi piace'.*" *Mi piace* doesn't mean "it pleases me"; it's a legalistic term of command, deriving from the same Latin word that gives you the *placet* of royal sovereignty. In other words, it's not a question of pleasure but an order, authoritative language. "'We have to go now, because it is nearly dawn, and we must not tarry'." Dante has somewhere a very beautiful line that admonishes "those who love to lie on soft downy beds all day" that they will never become famous. Here Virgil says, "'Follow me, it's time to go; it's dawn'." But

instead of saying it's dawn, he uses language based on
the picture of the heavens as I have described them.

It is spring, the time of the vernal equinox;
which means that the sun is in one of the only two
constellations of the Zodiac whose position, with regard to the earth, is such as to give you equal days and
equal nights; one is the Ram, Aries, and the other is
Libra, which is the position of the sun at the autumnal
equinox. If the sun were rising, if it had been already
dawn, the constellation which would be on the horizon
would be Aries; but it's not dawn yet, it is two hours
before dawn — so the constellation that is on the
horizon is the Fish, Pisces, the one that precedes Aries.
In the metrical enumeration it precedes Aries, which is
the first.

So we know that dawn is approaching; you
would also know that by the position of the Wain, the
great bear, *Ursa Major*, that great constellation which
the ancients described in a very beautiful image. They
spoke of this group of stars as never quenching its
thirst in water; that there is around the polar star this
group of stars that goes across the sky and comes
down toward the horizon, but not far enough to touch
it before circling up again. Of course, if you go down
south far enough, you will see these stars touch the
ocean and if you go further down toward the South
Pole, they will disappear altogether. If you happen to
be out of doors some clear night for any reason, and
have nothing better to do, you might notice this group
of stars circling about the polar star. You would see
them at ten, in the east; later overhead; then in the
early hours before dawn you would see the group far
off, as far west as it can go, right over the Caurus,
Dante says, which is the wind of the northwest. After

that, of course, it continues in its circle down and around and up again, without touching the horizon.

The Fish are on the horizon, Virgil says, the Wain is over Caurus, and we have a long distance to go. They have to pass through the next horrible circle, the circle of the violent. Here we no longer have the heretical philosophers whose sin is an intellectual error, or those passionate souls who did horrible things but wish they hadn't. The people we meet now are benighted souls — the more benighted as we go along — people whose acts of violence, acts destructive of rationality, have brought them to a point where they hardly know what's good and what's bad any more. These violent are represented as guarded in their various positions of punishment by the Minotaur, a form of beast, of a violence that would appear to have consisted in the slaughter of his fellow-beings. Half-man and half-bull, the Minotaur is also considered by Dante the result of a crime against nature. Of course, all sin is a crime against nature; either against the nature of the genus or against the nature of the species. The crime against nature as to the species is the crime against reason. Every time you trample on reason you commit a crime against nature, analogous to sodomy in the sphere of reason: we can speak of sodomy, therefore, in the figurative sense or in the literal sense. The other is a crime against the nature of the genus — more loathsome, less dangerous.

Of both, particularly of the latter, this Minotaur is an example: first in his composition and then because of the image it carries of his procreation. He is the product of Pasiphae of Crete, who fell in love with a bull and managed by an unnatural process to generate this monstrous creature that guards the passage through the circle of the violent. Crete for the Middle Ages was a land of horror; all horrors came from Crete — bad legislators and a lot more. One should note here Dante's humanism: whereas most Christians traditionally treated the ancient pagan gods as devils and locked them all in Hell — from which few, if any, managed to escape — Dante puts in Hell only Pluto, Perserpine, the monstrous Cerberus, and the Minotaur. In other words, you find in Hell only those deities that the pagans put there themselves — which goes to indicate the rather unchristian respect Dante had for the deities of the pagans. What of the other pagan deities? According to Dante, they really never existed. They were only men, human beings who had lived under the influx of certain stars, by virtue of which they acted in an extraordinary manner, so that they came to be called gods. But they weren't gods; they were only human beings. Venus is not a woman, but a star. A certain woman got that name because she acted under the influence of Venus in an extraordinary manner. So ancient Olympus is broken down into the stars on the one hand, and, on the other, the human beings who lived on earth under the influence of these stars.

This canto has been admired for its artistic beauty. We realize, once again, that Dante is much more of a poet than a philosopher. Even in *Paradiso*, where he is a philosopher, he is always exclusively a poet, with the result that he gives us there an entirely different kind of poetry that reminds us of nothing that we ordinarily call poetry and which is not to be found described in any *ars poetica*. He says at the very beginning of the canto: the point which we had reached in order to pass on was *alpestro* — which doesn't mean alpine, but precipitous, like the Alps. It was very steep:

that was one difficulty. The other was that there was
something there that had to be overcome, and that was
the Minotaur, *ch'ogni vista ne sarebbe schiva*. Getting
past him was so tremendously difficult that every sight
would be struck by the terror of having to get past him.
Then, in order to give the reader some idea of what this
steep descent is like, he makes some comparisons
which indicate that he must have expected his readers
to have traveled a great deal: the images he draws have
no very great importance, but they are picturesque. At
any rate, one gets the impression that in his day people
generally must have traveled a great deal; not like those
of the seventeenth and eighteenth centuries, who stayed
at home. The Italians of Dante's time loved to travel;
and images of far-off places would excite a ready interest. Of course we know from the histories of the times
that people were always on the go. So much so, someone has said, that the number of Florentines who in a
single month went from Pisa to France in Dante's day
was greater than the total number who went to France
in the entire eighteenth century, which is quite possible.

　　　Here Dante puts before our eyes the Adige,
where, on its bank, this side of Trent, the Italian stock
begins, where Dante says, there was a ravine similar to
that which he has now encountered, watched over by
the Minotaur. Like that ravine, *ruina* he calls it, on this
side of Trent, a ravine created either by an earthquake
or by a land fill — that's pretty sound isn't it — often by
a combination of both, *che da cima del monte, onde si
mosse, al piano è sì la roccia discoscesa* — which simply
means that the torrent rushing strikes the mountain
and erodes it. This process of erosion in the course of
centuries excavates a cavern, and finally the pressure

above is such that this grotto which has been eroded collapses. And he proceeds to tell you that from the *cima del monte*, where this ravine starts, the land is so precipitous that no path or passage could be found. Of course the reply that comes immediately is: there must have been a path because Dante has found it; if there had been no path he could not have arrived there.

Like the precipitous ravine near Trent, such was the descent here. And on the point, *sulla punta della rotta lacca*, "on the point where the infamy of Crete was outstretched. . . ." Note now effective that *infamia di Creti* is. You have often heard, no doubt, that abstractions are to be avoided in poetic composition. Already in the *ars poetica* of the twelfth and thirteenth centuries the contrary was asserted. Very beautiful poetic effects can be given by a skillful use of abstractions and Dante here gives us a very fine example — the infamy of Crete, *che fu concetta nella falsa vacca* — *concetta*, conceived in a counterfeit cow. Dante says this to justify the traditional condemnation of Crete as a place of unnatural *eros*. This Minotaur was conceived in a cow that wasn't a real cow but a wooden cow. *E quando vide noi*, when the Minotaur saw us — here is a good image of rage, impotent rage, for rage is always impotent — *se stesso morse*, it couldn't bite anybody else so it bites itself, *si come quei cui l'ira dentro fiacca*, like one inwardly consumed by rage. "And my sage, Virgil," *lo savio mio*, "cried against him," as he has done all along, when these pagan deities have tried to obstruct Dante's passage. In other words, the spirits of evil are very eager to see that no one gets away from their grasp. My sage cried against him — partly as a threat and partly as a sneer: "*Forse tu credi che quì sia il duca d'Atene*," "'You may think you have the Duke of Athens here'." Reference to the Duke of Athens is sort of amusing, particularly if you remember that the Duke of Athens, Theseus, was a very important person in Dante's day. What's humorous about it? Well, "Duke" is such a medieval term. To hear the noble Theseus, *"che su nel mondo la morte ti porse,"* "'who handed out death to you in the world above'," referred to by this peculiarly medieval term is somewhat disconcerting. *"Partiti, bestia."* Notice how finally Dante has become, and will continue to be in the cantos that follow, almost brutally contemptuous toward the damned, sneering cruelly at sinners, until finally we will find him treating them with downright abuse.

"Partiti bestia, che questi non vien ammaestrato dalla tua sorella" — "'move aside for this man doesn't come here guided, schooled, by your sister'." What had the sister done? Seduced by the charm of this Athenian, she gave him that famous *filo condottier*, the thread that enabled him to come out of a maze, that guides you out of a difficulty. She gave, she provided the thread that enabled Theseus to come out of the labyrinth where this monster had been confined. By means of the thread he was able to come out into the sun again; with the help of Ariadne, sister of this monster, Theseus retraced his steps and got rid of him, because the blood that the Minotaur had to be given to drink had to be milked out of beautiful Athenian youths. "'He comes here not schooled by your sister'," *"ma vassi per veder le vostre pene."* That's a very important line — he comes in order to see how your people suffer, not because he's cruel and wants to enjoy the sight of suffering but to learn what happens, both there in Hell and on earth, to those who abandon the way of reason, the right way which we are commanded

by God to follow.

What follows is a very effective literary device that seems awkward at first; this semi-bull this monster in his impotent rage is compared to the antics of a bull in a slaughter house, about to be slaughtered — *si slaccia in quella c'ha ricevuto già il colpo mortale, che gir non sa, ma quà e là saltella.* Once he's been struck a mortal blow with a mallet, *gir non sa,* he can't move about "'but jumps up and down'." It is an accurate picture; horrible,very photographic, and with something more that no photograph can give. Such were the actions of the Minotaur, as I watched, says Dante. The picture is very effective; Dante wants us to see that these are not the violent motions of a fierce bull but the motions of impotence; like those of a beast in the proximity of death, as he grows weak.

At this point, Virgil tells Dante to take advantage of the moment, while the beast is helpless in his fury, to move by him, quickly. *"Corri al varco; mentre ch'è in furia è buon che tu ti cale."* "'While he rages, it's a good time to run past and go below'." Dante must have had something more in mind here, for he imparts to the verse that familiar cadence which he so often uses when he wants you to know there is something to be understood beyond the letter. *Così prendemmo via giù per lo scarco,* "So we began our downward way over the precipice." *Scarco* here is a good word. All along, Dante has kept before our eyes the image of this precipice as that of a ravine, a mass of stones more or less loosely stuck together, and so inclined that a very slight impact will set them moving. He must have seen some of these ravines — the use of the word *scarco* suggests it — a *scarco* is an artificial unloading of rocks. Dante would have seen an artificial accumulation of rocks unloaded down a mountainside in quarries, where a large cube, or parallelepiped is cut from a place up high, cut roughly and then divided and sub-divided and then further sub-divided until it is cut to the desired size and shape, and the useless parts rolled down the mountain side. That is the *scarco*. They are still there to be seen in many places. Some go back to the most ancient times and some are recent. Almost everything has become precious now; nothing is thrown away: Even the *scarchi* have come to an end. But for 4,000 years or so, in Greece, in Italy, and also in Africa, they were present. *Così prendemmo via giù per lo scarco di quelle pietre, che spesso moviensi sotto i miei piedi per lo nuovo carco* "down into the abyss". The stones are loose, and therefore they move *sotto i miei piedi per lo nuovo carco*, "under the weight of a heavy body." Dante is still a heavy body. *Nuovo carco* means a strange load — strange to these people who have no weight. The Italian is magnificent, its beauty lost in the translation. The entire scene, the sight of this vast ravine plunging downward and this strange heavy body that moves the stones, is a very beautiful image.

The next stop is *Malebolge*, where we meet Ulysses.

12. THE TOPOGRAPHY OF THE INFERNO; THE NUMBER NINE; TYRANNY; THE OLD MAN OF CRETE

The topography of the *Inferno* is built on nine sections — the same as in *Purgatorio* and *Paradiso*. What induced Dante to use the number nine? You can hardly escape it in any cultural milieu that has been under the influence of the Pythagoreans. It's one of three or four key numbers. There is also the perfect number six, and then, of course, the universal number three which seems to have greater justification than any other number to be set apart, for it seems to be essentially involved in our human way of thinking.

Nine, from earliest times, had a special importance; you can see what Dante does with it in his earliest book, the *Vita Nuova*. The number three is, of course, directly involved in the trinity, and nine is the square of three. Possibly when he came to think over the plan of the whole poem, Dante may have been influenced by the fact that the *Paradiso* could not avoid being divided into nine classes, because the scheme of the *Paradiso* is based on the nine spheres of heaven, which are not Dante's making. The first eight we get from astronomy and the ninth from philosophy.

In the details of observation, the construction of the eight spheres is pretty accurate on the whole; it accords with what we see when we look at it. But the ninth comes in as a result of a philosophical preconception that posited a single motion to the *primum mobile*. The eighth sphere at first was regarded as the *primum mobile.* But closer observation revealed that the eighth sphere also had a counter motion, however slight, and therefore another external sphere had to be posited as the one that accounts for the passage over the meridian of all the celestial bodies, once in the space of twenty-four hours. That is the motion of the ninth sphere, which is replaced in modern astronomy by the rotation of the earth on its axis. There you have the nine spheres described objectively; Dante responding subjectively may have decided to conform the rest of his design to it by giving nine circles to Hell and nine sections to Purgatory.

Why nine in Purgatory, where the scheme differs from that of the *Inferno* and the *Paradiso*? The scheme of Purgatory is a construction based on the seven mortal sins, a construction which he quickly abandoned in Hell but decided to reserve for Purgatory. But how do you get nine out of seven? With an introduction and a conclusion. You have a pre-Purgatory and a post-Purgatory.

First you have that part of the mountain where people who held back, who delayed until the last moment to make their peace with God, wait before they can begin purgation. And then you have the series of seven ledges where the seven sins are washed away; and then you have one more, the last, on top of the mountain, in what you might call the locale of earthly beatitude, Eden — the mountain that, had it not been for original sin, would have preserved the perfect life of man on earth. Now, instead, it's available only for those souls that have gone through a process of moral purification and divine justification where, according to Dante's picture, certain cleaning functions take place which really have nothing to do with Christianity. Two fountains flow there: one, Lethe, washes away all the memories of bad deeds (a very pagan notion obviously). The other is the fountain that restores the memory of all good deeds, a notion that doesn't figure very much in pagan mythology, in nothing comparable to the significance of Lethe; yet there are traces of it here and there. At any rate, both these fountains are introduced by Dante as part of the process that has to do with the reconstitution of human nature after the purgation is over — from which it emerges enriched with good memories and washed clear of bad memories. That's the ninth division of Purgatory.

I thought I would explain this for those who might at some point have to say they took a course on Dante and who might be expected to give some picture of the general structure of the poem. I wouldn't want anyone to find himself as unprepared as the poor soul in the story about Henry II, of whom it is reported (among other things having little truth in them) that he once acted as an examiner: a man who had studied hard and wanted very much to pass his examination was told he should be prepared to answer three basic questions and would have little trouble, The questions were: first, what is your name; then, what are you looking for; and the third: have you studied? When the time came, the man got all confused. When asked his name, he answered "Holy Orders"; when he was asked what he was looking for, he gave his own name; and when the examiner asked: Are you trying to make a fool of me? He answered, Yes. Should anyone ever have to face such a situation, he may find this little outline useful.

To go through this series of nine parallel planes of the truncated cone of the *Inferno* would be pretty dull reading if one could not find in it some integrating thread to carry his interest along. There are such threads; one is obvious, clearly pictured for us; the others are spiritual and escape our immediate attention only too easily. But the obvious one is something that develops as we go along, and Dante particularly calls our attention to it. It's an artistic unity that proceeds from a topographical unity. These nine circles of Hell are united by a stream that flows along with ever-increasing misery with ever-changing names. It starts off as Acheron, the terrible Acheron, the river that so dismayed Dante upon his entry into Hell. Then it becomes Phlegeton, the river of boiling blood. It continues down, not precipitously, but in an ample curve, not difficult to follow, descending gradually toward the center of the earth, to end in Cocytus, where the terrific heat of Phlegeton is changed to ice. And here the various depths of this boiling stream of Phlegeton (seething with the blood of the violent) are a hydrometer of the gravity of punishment of souls. What that means is that the very worst sinners are immersed more deeply than the lesser sinners. If you have ever seen a hydrometer set in a great river where there is danger of flooding, you will have noticed that the hydrometer is used to indicate the regime of inundation. Well, here you have a regime of inundation for sinners — some are completely submerged, some are submerged only up to the eyes; some up to — I was going to say up to the mouth, but it is, more properly, the snout. And then, finally, there are those whose whole body is above the river's level, at a point where the river becomes shallow, a kind of swamp, where Dante and Virgil are able to cross. So you have the unity of artistry brought out by the unity of this hydrographic image. It helps in trying to orient one-self in Dante's world if one can call together a multi-tude of pictures by one word. Hydrography is such a word. The hydrographic system of America is built on the Mississippi River basin. It's a system of rivers. In Dante's hydrographic system, we are now at the point of extreme heat in this flowing river; later we will reach the point of extreme cold, where people are again immersed, not in boiling blood, however, but in ice.

The water of this river comes from two sources; but these two sources unite only at the end. One is the filthy water that flows down from Purgatory carrying with it all the sins washed away from the souls purged there. It flows down into the earth, making an opening as it sinks through, and it's through that opening that Dante will eventually make his way up out of the *Inferno* almost in a directly vertical line. When this water reaches the center of the earth, it meets and joins another stream of water, the water that has flowed down the long-winding channels of the infernal stream just described. Both of them are made up of filths: the filths of sins washed down. Incidentally, Dante follows up the description of the violent, these people who have reveled in the flow of other people's blood and wealth, in the usual tradition of tracing their violence to the source of all evil of this sort: tyranny. *Ei son tiranni che dier nel sangue e nell'aver di piglio* (Canto 12, l. 104).

What is the point of interest in this matter of tyranny in our western world? Obviously it's connected with freedom, which is a notion so dear to most of us in the West that we assume it must be so for everyone else. The fact is that great majorities of the peoples of the world in the past have lived, have gone along and

still do, without any real notion of freedom, and
certainly with not a vital attachment to the idea. But
there is a little corner of the world that has made a
great thing of liberty. And, of course, it goes pretty far
back, long before Plato and Aristotle, this matter of
tyranny and liberty. Among the Athenians there was
heated discussion on the evils of tyranny. Plato, in his
Republic, deals with it. And in Rome, Cicero writes
some warm pages on how tyrannicide can be justified.
Even cautious Christian thinkers have discussed it:
you are told never to take a life, except if you are a
sovereign or an agent of sovereignty, acting for the
public good, and therefore obeying the commandment of God; otherwise, the commandment is "Thou
Shalt not Kill." But, some Christians said, there is an
exception: you can kill a tyrant. Even St. Thomas, the
mild St. Thomas, in his youth let himself be drawn to
the idea of justified tyrannicide. Later on, when he had
thought more deeply about it, he rejects it. But there's
a whole school of churchmen in the sixteenth century
and seventeenth century that favor it. Dante belongs to
that tradition.

It's one of the chief themes in western civilization, this worship of liberty; indeed the chief theme,
perhaps. The Athenians had their unknown God and
we also have our unknown goddess, which we call
liberty. In this canto, Dante plays on the theme very,
very hard, although he is not too careful in distinguishing the political crime from the personal transgression. The circle is divided into three sections. In
one we find those who have done violence against their
neighbors; in the next the violent against self; and, in
the third, the violent against God and, of course,
against nature. What did the people of Dante's time

mean by nature, when they spoke this language, when they said, for example, that a miracle is something done without reference to nature? It's a very important matter in Dante's scheme, as it was for Aristotle and St. Thomas.

The harmony of the universe means that the animate and inanimate things — the falling stone, the rising fire, the winds, tides, birds, men — all obey the voice of God; in their multiplicity of motions there is unity of purpose. How do the stones and tides comply? We need not ask how animals comply, because they have some kind of obviously purposive motion; surely man has. But the inanimate things have not. Who guides the tides, who guides the stones, the animals and plants? God, no doubt, but not directly; God through his intermediary. God through his long hand or, if you will, through his art. And this intermediary, this long hand of God, is described by Aristotle as Nature or Physics, very often interchangeably: God or Nature.

In man, too, nature operates in activities that go on not as a result of chance or human design but as a result of that same motion, that pushes, that operates in all things, that drives the heavy bodies down, fire up, and so on. What is it for instance that man doesn't do by deliberation? Well, according to Aristotle and St. Thomas, and according to Dante, there are very many such things that man does not do as a result of deliberation, and one is his political activity.

Man is, not by deliberation but by very nature, a political animal. He doesn't say: fellows, let's try to get together, make a nice little group, put various people at the top — which is typically the eighteenth century colonial system. Things don't happen that way. Just as a man is driven to eat in order to live, to copulate in order to reproduce so as to carry on the species, he is also driven to get together to form a political order. This is not entrusted to his deliberative faculty, but implanted in him by a divine force, and that force is Nature.

Would you get such a notion from the usual English usage of the word Nature? What some people mean by nature today is hard to figure out. Often the word is used to describe the inanimate world, excluding man and even lower animals. Nature is the beautiful forest, the mountain. Some include animals in the setting. You can expand the popular conception of nature to embrace all that is included in that of Aristotle; but the important thing that Dante and others included in the idea of Nature, what we don't include, is the notion of law. In Dante's universe the idea that would predominate in the mind of everyone, in connection with Nature, is the notion of law. With Dante, you would say: in this universe which is providentially ordained, there is a section given to man; and there man, operating in accordance with the will of God, builds up his own universe as part of the whole, which is built up as a result of the operation of several forces. One is the power of human volition, free will, free use of reason; another is the power which we all call chance; and the third is what we've been talking about — nature. Where is evil in all this, in this providential system of God, which is a result of nature, chance and free will? How does evil come in?

It comes in *negatively*, as a privation — which means that evil has a great deal of goodness in it. Insofar as it is, it is good. Therefore its presence in the providential scheme of things is good. The idea of the

presence of evil, justly punished, fits in with the goodness of the universe. To get to this meaning of the
word, don't look it up in the dictionary; consult
Aristotle and consider this explanation.

Nature, of course, goes all the way down the
line. There's the law of nature in man, operating in him
insofar as he is a heavy body. There is the law of nature
in him as a vegetative being. Man is also an animal,
naturally, and oriented accordingly. And finally, man
is a rational being essentially, so that natural law in
him, his natural consistency, natural orientation is not
that of a heavy body, or of a vegetative being, or of a
lower animal, but of a being endowed with reason. At
all these various levels, transgressions are possible,
and you may call such a transgression unnatural, sins
against nature. If you try to do what Icarus did, fly, you
are committing a crime against nature, on the level of
inanimate nature. And when we try to find out too
much about anything or everything — I'm giving you
now the opposite extreme — that's a crime at the
highest level.

Those who seek infinite knowledge, commit a
crime against nature at the highest level, because God
meant the human pursuit of knowledge to be not
infinite but finite. So you can have a crime against
nature at the level of the *primal genus* and as high up as
the ultimate species. But what is a crime against nature
in the usual parlance? When you speak of an unnatural
crime, what do you man? Perversion, yes. That's all it
is. The violation of the laws of the *primal genus* or of
the ultimate species, is no longer called crimes against
nature. We refer it only to the animal *genus*; it has to do
only with sexual and other carnal animal appetites.

What is the picture in this circle of the violent?

First comes the stream of blood; then, after the stream of blood, you have a forest of deadly, dry crackling wood: the suicides that have become crackling trees. This is really a very beautiful homage to Virgil; when a writer uses the work of another writer openly and extensively, obviously it is meant as homage. In this case, Dante is paying homage to Virgil, to a book of his that here is raised almost to the height of all possible praise. It's a picture which even the translation can't spoil, an effective and impressive spectacle of the forest of deadly wood, with the harpies that torture and feed on the souls of these wretched suicides.

After this second scene, you have a Sahara with fire beating down upon it, as a symbol of the crime against nature in the sin of the Sodomites, those we call homosexuals. The tendency in our time is to find a good name to wash away the distinctions and frame a so-called ethics which includes everything, good, bad, and indifferent — the old stoic distinctions forever abolished. Here, as a symbol of this crime against nature, you have fire — but fire falling, instead of rising, as it does naturally.

Dante says, concerning free-will, that it is so free that nobody can daunt it; you can press it down but it shoots up again like fire. Here fire symbolizes the crime against nature, by falling. And then, when the whole thing is done, after this Sahara, at the end of the plain of burning sands, Dante remembers those who have sinned against divine art. He wants you to understand that they are so insignificant that they are put in a corner; Dante is in the next circle before he remembers them, the usurers, who have sinned against nature. It's simply the embodiment, the configuration of the usual sense of the word which, in Italian, in French, in German, in Greek, in Latin, is used to signify the interest of usurers. The word for interest is fruit, *child*; the Greek has *child* the Italian has *fruit*. Here Dante says: these are not children; gold does not reproduce itself. That field does not reproduce itself; if you want to get anything from that gold or from that field, there is only one way: through hard work. Or as in the Biblical admonition: by the sweat of thy brow.

Dante has this old habit of passing compliments internationally from one side of the frontier to another. What do the Italians, and the whole world because of the Italians, call syphilis? They call it the Celtic infection; the French call it *mal di Napoli*. Today you have a lot of things that some writers blame the Italians for, and the Italians blame the Americans for. Dante here takes what is one of the finest regions of France, both in its climate and in its people, and stamps it in the memory of his many generations of readers as a hot bed of usurers; when, in fact, it was nothing of the sort, when compared with what the Italians of his day were doing all over the world — the great money-lenders of Italy. Of course, one might point out that, without them there wouldn't have been trades and therefore their contribution is meritorious.

How did they prove that usury is a crime against nature? By a reduction to absurdity. If it were true that money can reproduce itself, in a few generations what would happen? If there were any soundness in the doctrine of the usurers, a few pennies would soon have more value, would produce more wealth than there is in the whole planetary system. What happens if you multiply two by itself again and again? Were they familiar with these progressions? Yes, Nothing seems to happen up to 28 or 29, then very strange changes

take place. It is interesting to observe that although for
a while historians used to point it out as one of the
stupidities of the Middle Ages, recently they seem to
have become better disposed to it. Now some of them
say: there must be some way to break down the argument against usury as presented by the medieval thinkers.

The next circle is that of the fraudulent, the
seventh circle. We are on the edge of a big rock; below
there is an abyss, or, if you like, a canyon. Dante has to
go down on a sort of airplane; the description as you
read it is so accurate an account of the sensations you
experience descending through the air as you approach the level of the earth that you might think
Dante had actually experienced it for himself.

He subdivides this section down below,
Malebolge, into ten parts. In English, *bolge* (it's Gallic,
Celtic in origin) is a word for what you would call a
pouch. *Malebolge* is made up of pockets, pouches.
That meaning of the word has survived, in English,
with the word budget.

In this passage we learn the origin of the infernal streams or rather that infernal stream that flows
down until it finally hits the spot where that other
stream arrives. Again, this stream begins in that land
that once was so good and beautiful and now is all evil,
the island in the middle of the Mediterranean of which
Plato and Aristotle said much, once so noble, now
become so corrupt that all crimes against nature were
said to originate there. It is located, according to
Dante, halfway between Gibraltar and Jerusalem. We've
mentioned it already: the Island of Crete. Dante puts
there that great man found in of the book of Daniel, a
figure made of various metals: his head is made of

gold, a portion of the body is silver, some is brass, and
so on until you come down to something that is not
even metal any more. One boot is made of iron, but the
other is made of clay, meaning that it will not stand up
and soon the whole thing will collapse. This picture
described in the Old Testament represents allegorically one of the two doctrines regarding the course of
civilization in the ancient world. There is the Hesiodan
doctrine, the doctrine of primitivism that says the best
is at the beginning; and the Pythagorean, Lucretian,
Democritean doctrine which states that the beginnings
are crude and there is continuous progress. We'll call
it Democritean, although the man who explains the
doctrine most clearly is Lucretius. He represents man,
at the start, like a very lowly beast that gradually
improves himself, evolves and develops.

Which of these two does Christianity adopt?
Primitivism, obviously. Adam was perfect wasn't be?
But you can also adopt the second view, if you start
with Cain, immediately after the fall. Almost all the
original endowments of Adam are lost after the fall —
even natural law is almost silenced in the heart of man.
Then progress begins, there is a rectification in the
natural sphere, with the Pagans; the Hebrews are given
particular commandments whereby man may live better; and finally you arrive at the coming of the Christian era.

This old man of Crete produces, from the distil-
lation of pain, tears that seep through crevices in the
corroded metals of the statue — tears that falling make
a hole in the ground, which is the source of the stream
that descends from level to level as Acheron, Styx,
Phlegethon, down to the bottom where there is no
more descent, and where it joins the water of that other

stream, descending from the mountain of Purgatory into frozen Cocytus.

13. THE DEFINITION OF LOVE; THE APPREHENSIVE AND APPETITIVE FACULTIES

In Canto eleven, we saw what fraud is, relative to treason and relative to violence. This eighth circle is divided into ten subdivisions. Dante tries to give us the impression that they're philosophically articulated, but the arrangement is really haphazard. He has merely gone through his own experience picking up particular manifestations of fraud. At this point, he wants to determine the basic principle in relation to the establishment of what is good and what is evil. Or, to put it another way, he now indicates more clearly that the axiom on which his whole system is built is *love*: Love directed to God through the proper channels is good; love directed away from God is bad. And the greater the deviation from God the greater becomes the guilt.

The question is, briefly, how can you justify this love-ethics in relation to Aristotle and St. Thomas, and the main current of intellectualistic Christian teaching? Something is good, morally (leaving out the religious consideration that God wills a thing), not because you say so, or I say so, but, Dionysius tells us, because it is in accordance with reason. In other words, since all beings have, by necessity, to operate with full regard for their nature, and since man's nature is his rationality, if he wants to be natural, if he wants to comply with the demands of nature, he has to use his reason; he must use his reason in its own sphere and in the other pursuits that he has in common with the lower animals. This is basic. An action is good when it conforms with reason; there's no way out of it. An action is bad — use any word you want here; I am using the generic one — or evil exists in this Christian Platonizing universe, not as an essence, but as a void, a privation, a diminution of what is natural.

The nature we have described, in its plenitude (without discussing what establishes and maintains it) uses reason to understand, to comprehend what accords with it, as a heavy body, as a procreative being, in all that pertains to the substance and accidents of man. For Aristotle and for St. Thomas the plenitude of nature consists of an activity that takes into account all of these, for man is not merely rational but also animal and has all that goes with being an animal. He is a rational animal. When this plenitude is hollowed out, diminished on any level, you immediately give a blow to your nature and to your creator. That's when sin or immorality come in. How do you reduce the plenitude of nature? By going against rationality up to the point where your reason no longer functions.

Where does love come in? Here is Aristotle, here is Dionysius, here is St. Thomas, here is St. Bonaventura, all repeating this statement — although of course the last two bring St. Augustine into it, whose thought pertains distinctly to a religious universe and not to a philosophic one. The question is, how do you harmonize this, how do you reconcile love-ethics with this? The way Dante does: instead of operating with reason you operate with love. It's no longer the plenitude of reason that is being diminished by this process, but the plenitude of love — to a point which is not zero but almost zero. We find it, in Dante, down in the plain of the traitors.

Someone might ask: isn't Dante's conception

that reason leads to love? Well, *brodez*, as Roxanne used to say — that's the idea, but work it out, define it a little more philosophically. Reason leads to love, not theoretic reason according to Aristotle and St. Thomas, but practical reason. *Praxis* has to do with activity that is directed toward an end; and for Aristotle and the Aristotelians that meant what is good. Every schoolchild had at some moment to learn the famous axiom, *bonus et finis convertuntur* — the end and the good are identical terms, they're convertible terms. If it is an end, it is a good. If it is a good, it is an end.

Obviously this has to be true. All human activity is directed to an end; and for practical reason the end becomes an object of desire, and every object of desire is a good. When a practical philosopher considers the whole scheme he will speak of an appetite of the end; a poet will maintain the same idea but talk not about the appetite of the end, but about love. Love is an appetite. From the most ancient times, all activities of every animal are comprised under a classification that is two-fold. Everything that you do has to be put in one of two boxes. One is the apprehensive faculty — but not what is meant by apprehensive today. When I learn theorems, I apprehend; I am not fearful, I am learning. The other faculty is the appetitive one. It is obviously a faculty shared by all animals, although the ancients and the scholastics applied it also to inanimate things by assuming that inanimate things had a kind of appetite, an inclination toward an end, that comes to them through nature. The stone doesn't fall, fire doesn't rise simply of itself; these things all move the way they do, are what they are, because they are all pervaded by this force which is called nature.

So, all animate and inanimate things have in

themselves, or borrowed from something else, these two forms of activity: the appetitive and the apprehensive. St. Thomas — with all his sobriety and all his care to avoid the metaphors of those despicable people called poets — speaks of love in inanimate things. What is love in the ultimate analysis? How does one define this appetite we call love, in the light of this distinction between the appetitive and the apprehensive faculties? Or we can put it in the form of a question current in Dante's day: What is love, and what arouses love? We're speaking of love on a higher plane, but of course we can begin by asking what aroused the love that Dante had for Beatrice, and then generalize from that.

What aroused it? Beauty. And how does one distinguish the beautiful from the good? For this we fall back on Plato. The beautiful applies to one of these two categories — the apprehensive — and the good applies to the appetitive. The question is: when you contemplate beauty and you are satisfied with that contemplation, can you call that love? Dante says: no. Love is not satisfied with contemplation; and this applies not only to the kind of love that is inspired by beauty, love in the sexual sense, but to all love. But love in this particular sphere, the sphere of the beautiful, begins with a phase of experience that pertains to the apprehensive.

When a man contemplates a beautiful woman, what does he contemplate in reality? These people say when a man looks at a beautiful thing, what gets into his soul is certainly not the thing itself. It is what the schoolmen used to call the *intention*, the perception of reality, not as reality but as a non-material projection. Some might call it images, but that's not quite accurate; or in German you could call it *Vorstellung*. It's something immaterial that comes in, not the substance of the thing. This applies to all things that you perceive; you grasp them not as substances but as forms or species *intentionalis*.

This applies to all love. As soon as your perception gives you an intention of beauty, something that you call adorable — not necessarily having to do with sex or the friendship of men and women, but with many other spheres — as soon as you have in you this intention of beauty, instead of being satisfied in calmly contemplating it, you want to find the thing from which the intention proceeds. This is, of course, the doctrine of Averroes and all his contemporaries. You find it in all the ancient writers, except that they don't have the same words for these two faculties, the apprehensive and the appetitive.

Once in your consciousness, as projections of external reality, however, they do not satisfy, as in theoretical reason. When you grasp the notion of a cylinder you don't go out and say: I want to put my hand through it. That might be helpful at the beginning, but once you have the mathematical habit of mind. you want to operate with the intention. When love is generated, you don't rest, thus satisfied, with the intention; you're impelled to move to the appropriation of that thing from which the intention proceeded. In this scheme of ethics, when the point is reached where love is introduced to replace reason, there is no contradiction between the concept of evil as a diminution of the plenitude of love, and the other which describes it as a reduction of the plenitude of reason. Love pertains to rationality but it's that rationality which we call practical. It is reason that aspires toward an end and is therefore a form of love.

I started off with the beauty of Beatrice, merely to get to the problem from Dante's position, but what has been said certainly applies to friendship. When you think longingly of a friend, you want to see him, to talk with him, let him see how happy you are in his company, and so on. Beauty comes into it, of course. Dante gives us a very precise and unmistakable description of man, born with a potency for love — that's another way of saying very briefly what I just mentioned: *l'animo ch'è creato ad amar presto*, the soul which is made with a capacity to love, *ad ogni cosa è mobile che piace*, moves toward anything that pleases it. The practical reason, the *praxis*, the appetitive faculty is mobile. Man is born to love. but that love is potential until a certain age; then potential love become act. *Tosto, che dal piacere in atto, è desto*: this slumbering love, awakened by that mysterious something that we have repeatedly mentioned, that has always been a mystery, though people don't worry much about it any more, that slumbering love is awakened by *piacere*: the condition by which you say, I like so and so, I like something. Not pleasure, but likeness, the capacity to like.

Then Dante proceeds to explain how it operates; he describes the process of the development of this *piacere* in the intention. *Vostra apprensiva*, your apprehensive faculty *da esser verace*, your apprehensive faculty draws, extracts your *Vorstellung*, this representation, from a real external thing, *esser verace*, and begins to move it around. You begin to dream about it. It starts with apprehension of the intention, and when this intention is in you, the mind begins to operate until finally — and this is the point — the force of this beautiful thing that has awakened the *piacere*, drives the one that experiences *piacere* to seek *la cosa in se*, the thing itself, from which the intention proceeded.

Dante explains all this in Canto 18, 1. 19 of *Purgatorio*: *l'animo ch'è creato ad amar presto* — *l'animo* of course, throughout the *Divine Comedy*, in the masculine sense, means the soul; but in a definite sense, one of the two capacities, the volitional one, the appetitive not the apprehensive — the soul which is created by God is ready to love. *Ad ogni cosa è mobile che piace*: is ready to move in the direction of any thing *che piace*, anything which it likes. The ancients had shown that they had seen the mystery of that *piacere* by being much more philosophical than those people who say that love is stirred up by the beauty or goodness in an object. They said that appetite which we call love is not determined by what is intrinsic in the object but by itself. You like something not because it is beautiful or strong or because of any other quality in it worth liking, not because there's a promise of great joy in it, you like it because you like it — that's all. But this, of course is not scholastic.

Tosto che dal piacere in atto è desto. As soon as it's awakened into act — by reflection, act evokes the word potency, which Dante speaks of only metaphorically here — as soon as the potency of love is awakened by *piacere, vostra apprensiva* (here comes the other of the two; first, the appetitive, the *animo*, now the perceptive faculty), *vostra apprensiva da esser verace*, your apprehensiveness, your knowing, your receptive faculty draws, *tragge intenzione*, draws an intention (the only thing to do is keep this word because it has a very particular meaning), *tragge intenzione, e dentro a voi la spiega*, and keeps revolving it inside of you. We all have been struck at some time by something, somebody you liked; we know what this means. You can't keep your mind off it, *sì che l'animo ad essa volger face*, until it draws the attention of the will. The appetitive is polarized by this intention, *e se, rivolto in ver di lei si piega.* It turns toward it.

So far you have a sort of free fancy; now it has been directed toward this one object, it bends toward it. In the use of *si piega*, bends toward this thing, from the verb *piegare*, you have an image of love that you find in every language, including English. What is *penchant* in French? *J'ai un penchant pour* — whatever it is. You have it in English I'm sure. *Quel piegare è amor*, that inclination is love, *quell' è natura che per piacer di novo in voi si lega* — love transfigures you; as a result of this love you get a new nature, a nature that is newly constituted in you, as a result of *piacere*:

In other words the attraction of somebody transforms you; the fact that somebody forces you to say, I like it, changes your nature. And nature, according to Aristotle, is the beginning of action. *principium motus.* Now you begin to move, not only move your feet but move yourself. *Poi come il foco movesi in altura . . . là dove più in sua materia dura, così l'animo preso entra in disire, ch'è moto spirituale, e mai non posa fin che la cosa amata il fa gioire.* Having a new nature, you are a new being with a new form and a new matter. Nature is the principle of motion, and the principle of motion moves you like fire moves upward, because of the form which nature has given it — *che nata* means nature gave it its form, makes it climb where it lasts longer in its matter. Here below fire is a fickle thing, a short-lived thing; but when it reaches its sphere, it's a thing that lasts perennially.

So the enamored soul, *l'animo preso*, the soul taken by love moves, with its new nature. *L'animo preso* is the technical term from ancient times down through the centuries — even the peasant girl newly fallen in love says it: *son presa*. You have it in Ovid and in many other poets. Desire is motion toward something that you do not have but which you want to have. It indicates a lack, a want, accompanied by anguish and frustration, until the end is reached. So the soul that is taken enters upon desire. Desire is a motion, but not a physical one; it is a spiritual motion, *moto spirituale. E mai non posa*: and never stops. This desire keeps on going, and the poor benighted person that cannot understand this transformation remains in anguish; this motion continues, until the *cosa amata* — not the intention but the thing that draws it, the beloved — gives you joy. The result of desire, if it is satisfied, gives you joy.

This is Dante's fullest account, or explanation of love. It doesn't mean simply sexual love, you can apply this to other kinds of love. The two forms of love in this natural sense are *Eros* and *Philia*. *Philia* is friendship. The ancients distinguish love from friendship (read the *Dialogues* of Plato). This applies to both *amor* and *amititia*. In the case of *amor* it's pretty obvious; but what about friendship? In friendship you have the kind of joy that Plato and Aristotle described as far superior to anything else. For them, the joy of love was not 1/1,000,000th of what the joy of friendship was. The one belongs to nature, and the other is really divine. And when you look at the pictures the poets give you, poets like Virgil, there's no comparison between the two: the most moving love scenes are those connected not with *eros* but with friendship. It's the same in Horace and many others.

There's nothing in the *Divine Comedy* that better

enables you to see how keen Dante is in his observations than his description of the descent to the level of the fraudulent: his flight downward in the dark, where he can see nothing and yet is able to discern whether he is turning to the right or left, and his description of what motion in space is like generally. He describes very accurately what happens to the soul, the dread you feel when you no longer have anything solid to stand on or to hold. Of course, that's all gone now, with the common experience of the airplane. Still, there is a strangeness in the moment when the last support is taken away. As a young man, I saw many people who did not fear to climb steep mountains, but as soon as they left the mountainside in the suspended chair and felt the air rush about them, they got panicky.

---

1. In St. Thomas, what is the psychology of esthetics, in the work of art?

St. Thomas is very clear: the aesthetic apprehension and appreciation is exclusively in the theoretic sphere; he follows Plato in placing art at a very low level of apprehension. It's a knowing form and has to do with a kind of knowledge which has to do obviously with a sensory perception. It's a line of argument which serves to explain love but not to explain aesthetics. In St. Thomas of course — and he takes it from the ancients — we have a hierarchy of the senses. First of all we have a group of ignoble senses and a group of noble senses. The noble ones are the eyes and the ears. The others are ignoble. You first find this all in the *Phaedrus*. This hierarchy has, of course, a direct bearing on the present discussion. Dante wants to make of it a fundamental idea in the *Vita Nuova*. Why can't you be satisfied merely with the intention; why do you want to find the *cosa*, the thing itself? The question is urgent for him, because when he did come upon the *cosa*, what happened? He got all confused; it caused him much pain and sorrow. Why could he not be satisfied with the intention?

It's strange that they should maintain that, when at the same time, they made so much of music. Dante puts more stress on the beauty of music than anything else. The last of the vanities is, at the beginning of Purgatory, music. And he says of music that it integrates the soul, unifies all the faculties and makes them one. All you have to do is read Franz Schubert, to see how, without knowing a thing about philosophy, he got at this very idea. At any rate this hierarchy of the senses has gotten into language, has become a grammatical point. When do you say *buono* and when do you say *bello* in Italian? Of course, the southerners have a way of inverting these; that's the characteristic of southern climates, everywhere. When, ordinarily, an Italian speaks of seeing and hearing he says *bello*. When he speaks of the other senses he says *buono*. A *meridionale*, a southern Italian, is apt to reverse these in a way which is the source of immemorial jokes on the part of the other Italians.

14. *LOWER HELL*: MALEBOLGE

We are now in *Malebolge*. Dante takes us there by
means of all the aids that a subterranean river can give
us — the roaring noise, the crash, the thundering
downfall. This is one of the many masterpieces that
ancient and modern literature have left us of subterranean rivers. We have a river running through caverns
measureless to man and into a sunless sea. The river
falls down to the level of this circle, which is the eighth
circle — a sort of inclined plane — given over to those
who have betrayed the cause of natural love through
fraud. It is shaped as a hollow cylinder; the walls all
around are a sheer drop perpendicular to the plane,
which is divided into ten zones, belts, so to speak, or
tracts, separated one from the other by ridges.

There is a military fancy working here again, as
we saw before, in connection with the approaches to
the City of Dis. We have here ten moats hollowed out
of the surface of this eighth circle. The banks of the
moats are such that one side is raised higher than the
other, which is so because the plane of the whole circle
slopes down to the edge of the ninth circle. Besides
this, and again it is a point of military construction,
over each of these ten moats is a bridge, a natural
bridge of rock, and each bridgehead becomes the
point of departure for the next moat and so on. So you
have bridges and castles as in a dungeon, *dunjón*, I
should say, of a fortified castle. Instead of drawbridges,
there are bridges of stone and at each end of each
bridge is a rudimentary castle which is made up of

heaps of rocks. When you come to the end, to the last, the tenth of these moats, you have again a cylinder, and a drop, but this time it is all ice. These waters that have come along in various forms, steeped with blood, cascading with a deafening roar, drop down now to freeze, and to form the well of Cocytus, which will be the last thing we'll read in the *Inferno*.

Dante launches out on his own about the inhabitants of *Malebolge*. He follows no example, and goes to extremes both in the venom of his invectives and in the general character of the representation. It's very hard to read except for those who know Italian; therefore we won't take it up in detail. The venom is provoked by a matter very close to his heart: betrayal of the traitors whose offense is the gravest because it most reduces the plenitude of love. In presenting various instances of fraud, Dante tries to organize them, articulate them philosophically. You can be fraudulent and traitorous as an individual, attacking the plenitude of' love simply as an individual, or as a group; and the groups may be of various sorts. But his two main attacks are against those who have destroyed the two great orders of society; one is the Church, the universal church, and the other is the State. The former, those who betray the love of the faithful are called simoniacs. They derive their name from the ancient magician Simon. Dante treats them with untold, almost inexplicable cruelty. It seems almost impossible or at any rate, difficult to understand how a Catholic who believes in the living presence of the Holy Spirit in the Church, who should be inclined to have a reverential regard for the popes of the Church, can treat some of them the way he does. Not only does he put the dead offenders in Hell, but he finds an ingenious way to put some of the living ones in Hell also. He treats them in a way which of course is symbolically significant, but which also serves to satisfy his desire for revenge. Why do you suppose Dante has it in for Boniface VIII? Why is this Pope made the first, not the first in time, but the first to be talked about in Hell, while he is still living, while he is still on earth? Nicholas, who has gone before him to his punishment, hears someone coming and thinks it must be the next pope and calls out to him. Dante corrects him on that score.

How are they treated here? In a very interesting way, symbolically. Instead of' being upright, as befits men imbued with the Holy Spirit, as popes should be, they are head down, their feet sticking up with fires biting at them. It reminds you of greasy pig's feet as they burn and wiggle up in the air. That's the punishment of the simoniacs. It's true that in those days there wasn't any dogma about the infallibility of the pope, but there were many other dogmas.

Boniface, of course, was the enemy of Dante's party in Florence, and Dante is bitter about it; but there is also perhaps a more noble reason than mere local politics. Dante's whole system of love-ethics is based on two groupings of men, united by love. These two groups are made up of the same individuals. The ones that constitute one group also constitute the other, although the activities of the one are far removed from the other. They are the Holy Roman Empire and the Catholic Church and both should be kept free and separate one from the other, in their activities. The pope should not interfere with the empire because he has no political capacity; and the emperor should not interfere with the affairs of the church because he has no ecclesiastical capacity. All the troubles in the world are due to the fact, and will continue to be due to the fact, that one interferes in the affairs of the other. Now that the empire has been destroyed, Dante blames everything on the Guelf party, or the Blacks, the descendants of that party: and for that reason, for the hatred that has developed through the years, because of his involvement in local politics and also for reasons very basic to his whole conception of things, he now explodes as he does.

It's strange that he should have kept up such heated concern for what were, in the eyes of most people, already dead causes. It was plain to see that the political supremacy of either one over the other was a thing of the past. The empire was finished; and even the religious supremacy of the pope was about to undergo great changes and to suffer at the hands of a worse enemy than the Imperial party. Shortly after the death of Boniface VIII comes the great Schism, the Babylonian exile. The Pope leaves Rome and goes to Avignon. Rome became a mere village, a village of robbers, and the pope for a while becomes the chaplain of the French sovereign. He who wanted to dominate the Holy Roman Emperor becomes a slave of the French monarch. The empire rises again as a kind of monarchy. Bat the glories of the Holy Roman Empire, the great exploits, like those of the great Henrys, of Barbarossa, of Frederick II, are gone forever. There's a loose organization that tries to keep together the German states and which in Italy serves only to give titles and recognize deeds, a very humble though honest purpose, as far as it goes.

Those who fail to recognize the political bond of these two groups united by love — one, the Church, the other, to which we ought to give our love but which so many seek to destroy instead, the State — those who betray that love are *barratti*, barrators. They are nothing more than grafters, as that word is used in English: those who for reasons of profit, like the others, the simoniacs, forget their obligations. In other words, both the offices of the Church and the offices of the State should be given for love and taken for love. Instead these simoniacs and grafters got their positions, became bishops, cardinals, popes, provincial rulers, monarchs, they became such by money; they bought those positions, instead of receiving them from and by the Holy Spirit. They received them for money. I say Holy Spirit because Dante uses the term here; besides, it should be clear that in the Sacred Scriptures the Holy Spirit means, more particularly, love.

One may wonder why the people in some of these circles are there. In the case of others, it is clear: we can see how their self-seeking diminishes the plenitude of their love of neighbor and love of God. Here, Dante becomes quite strong in his theology. He insists on this hollowing out of love that results from evil deeds, but he also projects a much larger view of the whole system of ethics that has love at its center. Some of these sins may seem rather odd: their connection with the general plan may seem strange. Why should we have the flatterers here, for instance? Dante is obviously leaning heavily on his personal experience. You can see that he had suffered at the hands of flatterers, that he has suffered also at the hands of simonaics and of barrators. Such people had made him suffer, as they made others suffer. But instead of representing them as malefactors because of the harm they have brought him, personally, he projects their

offences on a grander scale, as crimes against the great
institutions of Church and Empire.

What's wrong with flattery? Why is it a fraudulent diminution of love and why is it so serious? Unless
you look back to certain presidents who, aiming at a
kind of autocratic rule, have leaned backward or forward rather, to surround themselves with personal
counselors, the force of Dante's complaint may not be
clear today. Think back to the days of Dante, the
tyrants of his day, and the adventures he went through.
The flatterer who gets the ear of the sovereign is able to
do a great deal of harm to others. The power is not
theirs, but they wield it with their pretense. They are
the hypocrites (one might observe, correctly, that everybody for reasons of personal safety, personal interest,
is in some degree hypocritical). Dante follows here not
something peculiar to his day, but a classical trend,
which we see clearly in Cicero's writings.

In the eighth moat, or *malebolge* Dante shows us
the false counselors. The ones he focuses on are Ulysses,
and Diomedes. Ulysses is used to portray for us, to
describe to the reader the qualities of a historical
Ulysses, but of a historical Ulysses rebuilt along the
lines of those great adventurers, the Portuguese and
Italian navigators of the twelfth and thirteenth centuries. In other words he is not only the curious wayfarer
of antiquity but he is the great navigator, the prototype
of the great explorers who were to come, and some of
whom had already come. It's interesting to see how this
little mercantile Italy, unable to form a state with its
plurality of communes, in continuous rivalry — Venice
against Genoa, Pisa against Florence, Genoa against
Pisa — how most of these little city-states were either on
the coast or managed to build themselves a way to the

sea, so that even though situated in the interior they all had an outlet, all of them, and were therefore able to function as mercantile states. It is strange, I say, to see how these little city-states play such a big role in the discoveries of the age. Except for the Portuguese, all the big names are Italian. And not always Genoese or Pisan but also Florentine. Amerigo Vespucci, for one; and Verrazzano who discovered the river nearby long before Henry Hudson sailed on it.

It is that spirit that Dante portrays in his Ulysses. Some people have thought that Dante wanted here to describe the role of Ulysses as a false counselor, who urged his companions to go through the pillars of Hercules to their doom — a popular notion at that time. Dante here follows that popular view, that a captain should never permit himself to go beyond those limits. In reality, what was happening in their own days, actually from ancient Greek and Roman times, without interruption, was a steady flow of ships to and from Scandinavia, England, or, rather, Ireland, the northern coast of France, all around the Iberian peninsula, to Gibraltar and of course all through the Mediterranean. But the legend was there: you shouldn't go beyond the straits of Gibraltar. By the way, the first great archipelago discovered beyond Gibraltar was the Azores, known long before Columbus came into the world.

Another legend has to do with the unknown regions beyond. It's the belief that challenged the adventurous spirit. The desire to go to the land without inhabitants. That's the phrase that was used and that's the phrase Dante uses. According to ancient and medieval peoples, a quarter of the earth was inhabited. They spoke of the *quarta habitabilis* — the name given to it, in view of the fact that it was οἰκουμέτη, which means inhabited. The word *ecumena*, which is still used (you've heard of ecumenical movements, in recent years), referred to the fact that a quarter of the earth was inhabited. Of course there was something at the antipodes, but it was only water, no one lived there, and to go there was considered a crime. The Church maintained this view until the fifteenth century; eventually it was abandoned, even before the voyage of Columbus.

Before then, for centuries, this view of the antipodes was strenuously insisted upon. Many have concluded that it meant that the people in those days believed there were no antipodes. The Church did not deny that there were antipodes; it was perfectly aware that there were, but it insisted that they were not inhabited and not habitable. Of course connected with this strange thought was the religious question. If there were people there, nobody could convert them because they were in the hands of the devil. The point is that Ulysses here challenges the legend, defies the fulminations of the Church against the desire to go out beyond the limits of the inhabited earth. Therefore, according to some commentators, Dante, in depicting Ulysses as urging his men to sail there, to go out into the wastes of the Antarctic region, wanted his readers to see him as a false counselor, giving them false, fallacious counsel. Of course, apart from the nobility of the representation, Dante may have meant that. Dante does uphold the idea that there is such a thing as going too far in your investigations. But you can still see Dante's enthusiasm breaking through; he is not condemning but eulogizing the Tuscan navigators, in anticipation of the great voyages of discovery to come.

So this eulogizing of a sinner is to be explained here, as it is to be explained all along in this way: we have diabolical characters, sinners; once their sin is disclosed to the reader they are described so that you see a great deal in them to respect. We've met a few already. Farinata, for one. Not Francesca. She is *sui generis*; there is suppression not disclosure there. Dante is still in the mood of love. Brunetto Latini is another. Surely there's no possibility of ambiguity there. Brunetto Latini is in Hell for sodomy; but Dante depicts him with admiration, in spite of his ridiculous appearance, surrounded with shame. The result is a picture of the noble master, the good teacher, who loved to impart his knowledge to his students. So you have throughout the *Inferno* — very artistically worked, for it could become monotonous — a series of sinners who, once their sins are disclosed, are shown to be, in spite of that, worthy of respect. This is true in life, also. There is not one person, any sinner, of whom that is not the case. No one is wholly evil. I have known murderers, rapists, criminals, of all sorts, who were otherwise admirable people.

Dante of course recognized that. He avoids the two usual erroneous extremes. One is that false humanitarianism that wants to defend the criminal as if his crimes were not crimes, and would defend him against a society which doesn't want to be destroyed by the criminal. Or else, the other extreme: to do what we have done for so many years, identify them entirely with their crimes, represent them as completely vicious. Of course, philosophically, both positions are untenable. Dante tries to hold a just view.

When he looks down through the smoke, he

sees an array of lights such as you have along the
waterfront at night, where you see the highways illumi-
nated. Then, as he draws closer to the lights, the flood
of light destroys the contours of everything else. The
vision of the flame excludes the vision of the enflamed.
What Dante sees is a valley of flickering lights beaming
so intensely that nothing can be seen against the dazzling flash that comes from it. His initial description,
how he tries to describe this valley of the evil counselors, is interesting (Canto 26, l. 25). He gives us the
time of the day, the time of the year, the position of the
onlooker, with a little pastoral touch, in striking contrast with the situation. You are asked to put yourselves back on earth, in mid-summer, in the country-
side, in the evening, when the plowman, having worked
in the fields all day, as they do in Italy, goes back to the
hillside and relaxes. These farmers, relaxing in the
evening, looking down the plain, see all the fields
covered with fireflies, *lucciole*. Here, as on earth, Virgil
and Dante see these lights flickering and moving in all
directions like fireflies, "as many lights as the plowman
sees, the plowman who rests on the hillside, at the time
when he, who throws light on the universe, keeps his
face concealed from man for the shortest time," etc. He
who throws light on the universe is, of course, the sun,
and the sun conceals its face from us for the shortest
time in June, when the sun is in the tropic of cancer, at
the time of the summer solstice. Then he gives us the
time of day: passing from the lyrical to the humorous.

It is the time when the flies yield the scene to the
mosquitoes. There's an Italian proverb inspired by
deep pessimism, indicating how terrible this world is.
All day you're plagued by flies; and then at night, when
the flies stop, you go to bed and the mosquitoes begin

to bother you. The proverb is rather long-winded. As usual, Dante compresses the whole thing into one line: *come la mosca cede alla zanzara.* There is a great deal of humor and pathos in that line. "As many as the fireflies he sees down on the plain, perhaps right there where his vineyard is, where his fields are, so filled with flames was this eighth moat." He follows this with another image to tell us that the excess of light makes it impossible to see the contour of the lighted thing. Here he reminds us of a biblical scene. The scene is the chariot of Elijah, rising to Heaven in a triumphant blaze of fire. You stare at the light until all you can see is the flash of light illuminating all the universe. The horses of the chariot of Elijah were raised up into heaven erect: q*uando i cavalli al cielo erti levarsi, che nol potea sì con gli occhi seguire, ch'el vedesse altro che la fiamma, sola, si come nuvoletta, in su salire.* All that he could see was the flame alone, a line that seems to be taken out of the *Vita Nuova: si come nuvoletta in su salire,* "like a little cloud rising up," *tal si move ciascuna, per la gola del fosso, che nessuna mostra il furto, ed ogni fiamma un peccatore invola.* That is a masterpiece of rhetoric; but how to translate it? "Thus moved the flames along the gullet of the moat, for none of them shows the theft" — that is, the theft being enclosed in the flames, out-dazzled by the flame, and every flame steals a sinner.

You see, how elaborate a rhetorical construction Dante uses here to bring out the fact that the outline of the human figure is completely eliminated by the flash of light. In the next *terzina* Dante shows his anxiety; in the one after that, he requests Virgil to let him see who is in the flames. Virgil has told him that there are spirits in them. And Dante says: *"Maestro mio,*" "'I am certain of it, by hearing you say so, but I was already made certain of it by what I saw'." And then a further comparison, now localized to one or a group of these thefts, of these flames, some of which as they move along, coalesce. One group reminds Dante of two famous flames that would not merge because of the hatred of the two persons who were being burned. The reference is to what is perhaps the greatest tragic theme of Greek drama: the two were Eteocles and Polynices, sons of Oedipus of Thebes, who quarreled over the succession to the throne. In another, Virgil tells him, "'Ulysses and Diomed are tortured, and there they proceed together in pain as on earth they proceeded together in crime.'. . ." "'Within that flame is wept'," *si geme* means wept or grieved over, "'bad or false counsels, deceptions'." "*Dentro dalla lor fiamma, si geme*" false counsels.

Now comes a series of bad deceptions that are grieved over, regretted. First, the deception of the Trojan horse. Dante cannot resist, once again, the temptation of reminding us of his philosophy of history; namely, that Troy fell so that Rome might be founded. And Rome had to be founded in order to prepare the world for Christ, to provide one language, one law, for all the world, and a central see for the popes, "*l'aguato del caval che fé la porta ond'uscì de' Romani il gentil seme.*" Aeneus was able to escape, but he would not have escaped unless Troy had been destroyed. And Troy would not have been destroyed if Ulysses had not deceived the Trojans with his horse: "'within, in the flame, tears are shed also on account of Deidamia, who even in death sorrows for Achilles'" — "*si duol d'Achille.*" It is the sad story much romanticized by Dante. Deidamia was supposed to help Achilles while away his time disguised as a girl, and keep him from going to war. She finds him out, however, and falls in love with the noble young man. He had a child by this girl, so the story goes. But Ulysses learns of the matter and tears the youth away from the girl and the child. Achilles is torn away, obviously for *raison d'etat*; such a noble warrior as Achilles was needed at the front.

Another act of deception here lamented is the stealing of the Palladium, the stealing of the statue of Pallas, upon whom depended the fortunes of Troy. As long as the statue was there, Troy would not be taken. The enumeration of examples makes Dante press his request to Virgil to allow him to speak with the spirits inside the horned flame. Virgil acquiesces, in a mysterious line that explains and doesn't explain why Dante must not speak to Ulysses and Diomed — why it is Virgil who must speak to them and approach them in the name of their glorious exploits. "'O you who are in one flame, if ever I deserved anything of you while I lived, if ever I deserved much or little of you when on earth I wrote those lofty lines, don't move, but let one of you come, here in this desolation, lost in this world, let one of you tell us where you went to die'." Did Dante have access to the *Odyssey*? Obviously not. If he had, we might have missed this masterpiece; he might not have written it. *Lo maggior corno della fiamma antica cominciò a crollarsi mormorando*. . . . That is, a certain noise is made, there being no throat, or tongue; the place of the throat and tongue is taken by this flame: *pur come quella cui vento affatica* — the flame made a noise just as it does when it is belabored by the wind — then words come out: *indi la cima quà e la menando, come fosse la lingua che parlasse*, as though it were the tongue that spoke. That is, the soul within bestirs itself, and the top of the flame takes the place of the tongue in the living body: *gittò voce di fuori e disse*, "threw out a voice and said" — Dante very quaintly tries to show how you can get a voice from a flame, from an unsubstantial body — "'When I left Circe [the enchantress]'...." All this is mixed up, but the mixture has yielded a very beautiful picture. For a millennium Circe turned, and still turns human beings into beasts, made them into pigs, principally, but into animals, generally. Ulysses says he broke away from Circe. "*Quando mi dipartì da Circe, che sottrasse me più d'un anno là presso a Gaeta, prima che sì Enea la nomasse....*" Circe had kept him for over a year, at Gaeta (not then called Gaeta, the name it got when Aeneas went by). Dante is here making some changes. There is a spot near Gaeta, near the so-called Circean promentory, a very beautiful spot, which was supposed to have been the home of this enchantress. At any rate, the flame tells him that he left this mysterious Circe and went back home. The whole story is perfectly told: instead of remaining home, "*ne dolcezza di figlio, ne la pietà del vecchio padre*," "'neither the love he should have had for his son, and the reverence he should have had for his aged father'," "*ne il debito amore lo qual dovea Penelope far lieta*," "'nor the love due Penelope [his wife], which should have made her happy'" were enough to keep him home. In other words, the duties that Ulysses had toward his son, his wife, his father could not help him overcome his ardor — *ardore* — his passion, that blazing passion, "'that invincible passion to become acquainted with the world'," "*e degli vizii umani e del valore*," "'with human faults and with the good in men'." That being the case, not being able to quench his ardor, to put an end to his desire to see the world, he set himself on the high seas, "*misi me per l'alto mare aperto sol con un legno, e con quella compagnia picciola*," "'alone, in a single ship [*sol con un legno*], and with that meagre crew [his few companions]'." Of course, when Ulysses finally did get home from Troy, all his companions were dead; but Dante saves a few for this last great journey, a "*compagnia picciola dalla qual non fui deserto.*" In those days it was not usual for a ship to sail alone. Convoys were the regular procedure: two, three, four, and five ships at a time; but Ulysses sailed alone, "*sol con un legno*," "'with one ship, alone'." Then comes the description of the crossing of the Mediterranean.

15. THE EVIL COUNSELORS: ULYSSES; THE STORY OF UGOLINO

In this very famous canto Dante can't make up his mind whether to extol Ulysses or make use of him as a deterrent. Is he in this place as a false counselor or because of his inordinate pursuit of knowledge? St Paul speaks clearly on the latter. The notion of the antipodes never really frightened navigators. We should also note that Dante put Purgatory on earth, and he might be asked whether people still living might not sometime find the place and see the parade of souls ascending it. Perhaps he does this to indicate that it is in an inaccessible place. Perhaps he wanted to stir up admiration. Certainly the Church was a little disturbed by the spirit of the navigators. Down through the fourteenth century you hear cries that these Florentine navigators are going mad, not for profit but to see what hasn't been seen before. There is always that double pull: the desire on one side to know more and more, and on the other side the feeling that restraint is necessary.

There is something romantic in wanting to stir up admiration. Of course, by romantic — we do almost everything now according to Romantic criticism — by romantic I also mean the Hegelian school, the early Hegelian school of Italian critics, who gave the correct interpretation of the Paolo and Francesca canto, for example. They also put forth the disquieting and disconcerting theory that Dante was not aware of all that he was doing, yet he did it all the same. It is the notion

that the poet provides the primeval matter, and that
primeval matter is such that subsequent generations
are able to put upon it their own stamp.

The notion that Ulysses reached the antipodes
is peculiar to Dante. This is just one of the many
inventions about Ulysses. For some strange reason,
beginning with the fifth century B.C., Ulysses becomes
the object of strange loves and hatreds. And long
before Tennyson, long before Dante, people made up
strange tales about him. We know how ill he fared in
Greek tragedy. And if you happen to know how some
of the Church Fathers treated him, you might wonder
that Dante should want to take up his defense. The
whole story of Dante's Ulysses has nothing to do with
the story of Homer. Anyway the few lines that Horace
gave to him would be a sufficient basis.

The Romantic point of view, however, gives us
all the possibilities; it gives us any number of possibilities in that canto of Francesca; we can read into it all
sorts of things. The universe of discourse created by a
line like *l'amor che a nul amato amar perdona* was quite
different in Dante's time than today. All that has
happened in between affects us; we have the intermediary experience of the Romantic period, and we have to
carry it with us — the theory that every age recreates a
given text for itself. That's something that hasn't been
fully utilized by Anglo-Saxon criticism. Some day,
maybe, Americans will catch up with it, and something
good may come out of it. The multiple re-creation also
gives you a basis for distinguishing good from bad; the
bad is that which doesn't permit this re-creation; and
there's much truth in all this. When I was a boy, when
I was a young man, poetry meant a great deal. It was as
present to everyone as, say, television is today. There

was a great deal of it in the air, everywhere, even in politics. Newspapers, journals, all took it up; everyone was in one way, or another touched by the general enthusiasm. And some of the poets of the time seemed great because they expressed emotionally things which, because of their immediacy, seemed important, But things changed, time passed, and when those poets were looked at again, it was seen that the freshness was no longer there; and therefore the next generation refused to regard them as great poets. The example that the Italian idealistic literary critics gave in my day was that of Schiller and Goethe. They pointed to the gradual passing of Schiller, who had seemed so great when certain questions were uppermost in men's minds; and to the growing possibility of appreciating the genius of Goethe, the more time passed.

Someone should write a dissertation on the theme of Ulysses in literature. Many articles have been written; but no dissertation, with 500 pages, with 2000 notes, and 2000 blunders. Very touching these trembling, wavering effects of pious awe and sudden enthusiasm for the discoverer: this one is, I think, as high in the direction of lyrical representation as Dante ever went. "*Ne dolcezza di figlio*" (even musically the verse is magnificent) "*ne la pietà del vecchio padre, ne il debito amore lo qual dovea Penelope far lieta, vincer poter dentro di me l'ardore ch'ebbi a divenir del mondo esperto, e degli vizi umani e del valore; ma misi me per l'alto mare aperto.*" Notice how the rhythm changes with the new subject. "*Ma misi me*" (it's sort of a spondaic motion) "*per l'alto mare aperto*" (it's the high seas, without land, the landless seas) "*sol con un legno.*" We mentioned earlier the meaning of that stress.

The Scandinavians, the Norsemen, when they

started to come down, were very much amused and contemptuous and scoffed at the Italian or Latin convoys: the brave navigator always flashes out by himself and the Norsemen were brave. *"E con quella compagnia, picciola, dalla qual non fui diserto"* — they stuck by him, his many companions — *"l'un lito e l'altro vidi infin la Spagna."* "'I kept sailing, seeing now the coast of Africa, and now the opposite coast [Sardinia and Spain], *"fin nel Morrocco e l'isola de' Sardi, e l'altre che quel mare intorno bagna."* Of course, Dante knows that Morocco comes after the island of Sardinia but he is constrained by the rhyme. He goes on: *"Io e' compagni eravam vecchi e tardi,"* "'I and my companions were old and slow',", the line too sounds old and surely moves slowly, *"quando venimmo a quella foce stretta."* . . . It doesn't look so very *stretta*, so very narrow, when you pass through it — "'When we arrived at that narrow [*foce*]'" — here he treats the Mediterranean as if it were a river, and the passage at Gibraltar is referred to as the *foce*, the mouth of a river — *"quella foce stretta dov' Ercole segnò li suoi riguardi acciò che l'uom più oltre non si metta,"* where Hercules stamped his dread of what might happen if man goes beyond that boundary — *"dalla man destra mi lasciai Sibilia,"* "'on my right I had passed Seville; on the other [the left side] I had already passed Setta [or Ceta],'" more to the East. Now comes the critical moment: *"O frati, dissi,"* "'Brothers,' I said, 'who through a hundred thousand dangers have now reached the West',", *"a questa tanto picciola vigilia de' nosttri sensi ch'è del rimanente"* — that's a magnificent phrase — "'to that small residue of wakefulness that remains to your senses', *"non vogliate negar l'esperienza,"* "'do not deny the experience to this small residue of wakefulness'." Before death there is a little vigilia, a little period of wakefulness; let's make good use of that little period, "*non vogliate negar l'esperienza*" "'do not deny to this residue, to this'" *picciola vigilia*, the experience. In English, we don't say "experience," we would say, "discovery — here the possibility of discovery — of the other side of the world, by following the sun, "*di retro al sol*," the discovery of the world without people, the uninhabited fourth part of the world.

You have here what must have been in Dante's time, and as far back as ancient days, that curiosity about the uninhabited earth, for that imaginary region which the geographers had imposed on the mass imagination of people. Way back, from the third century BC, questions were raised; people have always wanted to know about it. And now, here's the chance to find out what there is in that part of the world that is not inhabited. Of course in that *senza gente* there is an obvious echo of the word for inhabited earth.

These lines are very famous. "*Considerate la vostra semenza*," "'consider the reason for which you were born','" consider what the potency of your seed is, *la vostra semenza*. You have a nature which has for its property — as Aristotle tells us in what is the most quoted line of all antiquity — the desire to know, *man by nature desires to know*. By nature. If you don't have that desire, you may look like a human being, but you will be one only apparently; in reality you will be some kind of beast. "*Fatti non foste a viver come bruti*," "'you were not born to live like beasts'" "*ma per seguir virtute e conoscenza*." You were made for the pursuit, not of happiness but of *virtute e conoscenza*, knowledge and power. Virtue in this sense surely refers to good qualities in the moral sphere, but it refers also to the application of knowledge in every sphere. "*Li miei compagni fec'io si aguti*," "'I made my companions so eager'," "*con questa orazion picciola*," "'with this brief speech'," "*che a pena poscia gli avrei ritenuti.*" "'After I had talked to them [delivered, my little oration], it would have been impossible to restrain them'." And now, with a sort of triumphant emphasis comes: "*e volta nostra poppa nel mattino*," "'we turned our backs to the known, our faces to the unknown'." We turned our *poppa* — our stern — to the East, and, therefore, our prow to the West, and "*de' remi facemmo ale al folle volo,*" "'and made wings of our oars for that mad flight'."

Here is the old and never-aging metaphor or simile, of the wings and the oars. It was already a commonplace in the third century BC. We made wings out of our oars, "*sempre acquistando dal lato mancino.*" They did indeed move out westward but always tending to lean southward — *mancino* — to the left, that's where south is when you are sailing westward. "*Tutte le stelle già dell'altro polo vedea la notte.*" Ordinarily, from our latitude we don't see the stars around the southern pole. Try to imagine the sphere of the heavens as you see it from here. In New York the polar star is up there, somewhere. And when you're near the equator, if you can see it, you will see it on the horizon. Below the equator, you can't see it at all. The poets tell us that simple Greek shepherds, on the mountain tops, pondered the matter; it was supposed to have been of interest to them. But, we're neither Greeks nor shepherds, and there are no mountains around here.

"*Tutte le stelle già dell'altro polo vedea la notte.*" Some here make *la notte* the object, but it's really the same in meaning, whether it be subject or object, "*e il nostro tanto basso*," and conversely "'ours [pole] so low'," "*tanto basso, che non surgea del marin suolo,*" "'so low that it did not emerge out of the surface of the sea'": in other words, it was on the horizon. "*Cinque volte racceso, e tante casso lo lume era di sotto dalla luna;*" "'five times I saw the light of the sun kindling the under surface of the moon'"; that is, I saw the moon passing from full moon to half to new moon, and so on. This process I saw repeated five times, which means five months had passed, "*poi ch' entrati eravam nell'alto passo,*" "'since we had entered into this deep'" — in literary Italian, as in ordinary Italian, the word *alto* means not only high but also deep — "*quando n'apparve una montagna bruna per la distanza,*" "'when all of sudden a mountain appeared before us, which because of the distance seemed dusky'," *bruna, "e parvemi alta tanto, quanto veduta non n'aveva alcuna."* That's a great deal for an Italian; they see high mountains often, they have the Alps. You don't even have to go to the Alps; the Appenines provide some very high mountains, ten to twelve thousand feet high. "*Noi ci allegrammo, e tosto tornò in pianto.*" The brevity of the solace is brought out by the rapidity of the line: "'our joy was turned to tears'," "*chè dalla nuova terra*" — this is rather interesting, *nuova terra*, new land; it's the Italian equivalent of Newfoundland — "*dalla nuova terra un turbo nacque.*" The proper word for *turbo* is tornado, a windstorm that moves not rectilinearly but circularly. A whirlwind, I suppose, would do. Tornado, of course, is technically correct. Cyclone won't do because of the dimension. "*E percosse del legno, il primo canto,*" "'and struck the first quarter of the ship'," that is, the prow; "*tre volte, il fe' girar con tutte l'acque.*" The whirlwind struck the prow and made it whirl around — not only the prow itself but the water under it — three times.

Dante wants to give the conditions for the sucking in of the ship: the whirlwind has generated a whirlpool. Three times it made it whirl with the water; *"alla quarta levar la poppa, in suso,"* "'the fourth time the poop, the stern is made to rear up'," *levar in suso,* as though it were a horse; *"e la prora ire in giù,"* "'and the prow rammed downward, as it pleased someone else'," *"com'altrui piacque"* — *altrui* means God of course — "'till the sea closed over us'."

After this exchange, Dante proceeds with Virgil on his pilgrimage through the two remaining moats of *Malebolge*. He finds interesting people like Mohamed and Ali; he finds great falsifiers, people who perpetrated all sorts of scams, people who transformed themselves into somebody else to draw up a false will, like Gianni Schicchi (unfortunately famous, not because of Dante but because of a poor opera), and Mirrha, who falsified her body for opprobrius lust. Then comes the tenth and last moat, and the wall that encloses the last; and beyond it, the ninth and last of these circles. Dante had been made aware of the approach to the eighth circle by a great roar, the roar of the stream rushing down the cylindrical concave wall which enclosed the eighth circle of Hell, down which wall he was carried by the image of fraud. Now instead of a deafening waterfall, he hears what sounds like thunder, stranger than any thunder he has ever heard; in reality it's the blowing of the horn of the giants who keep watch over the remaining sections of Hell.

This is another cylinder, within the larger one; only this cylinder, of the last circle, and the wall that surrounds it, is guarded by giants. These giants are so big that half of one of them is three times as large as any Frigian. Dante supposes his readers to know what he means by Frigians. They were a Germanic race, who were very famous even in antiquity for their size, and are still recalled today in France and in Italy. We call an enormous horse a Frigian horse. These men are at least six times as big as Frigian giants and stand like so many towers at the wall surrounding this last circle. To bring it before our eyes, Dante uses an image which was familiar until the last war: Monterreggioni, near Siena. The last war practically destroyed it. This wall, with these huge giants which in the dusk may have seemed like towers, reminded Dante of the towers of Monterreggioni.

The canto is full of references to many things which, fortunately, many of us have been able to see at some time. The giants are so big that their heads are as large as the pine-cone of St. Peter's. When people go to Rome, there are a number of useless things they are supposed to see. One of them is this cone of St. Peter. Brides, under Mussolini, used to be given a trip to Rome; and one of the things they had to see was that cone. But much more impressive than that poor thing, are the references to the Crusades, to Roland, to the *gestes* of Charlemagne, to the Oliphant, the famous horn of Roland. The epic poets described its sound as being so loud that the animals on both sides were frightened and ran away. And perhaps more impressive still: one of these giants has the task of doing what the beast of fraud had done in the other circle: that of lowering Dante to the next level. To help the reader visualize the experience he describes, Dante alludes to another tourist attraction: the Garisenda, one of the two towers of Bologna. The Garisenda is the one that is bent; the taller tower is more beautiful but the other is more interesting, an impressive spectacle. When the clouds move over these towers, if you stand on the side to which the tower is inclined, it looks as if it is falling on you. If you want to have a picture of a nightmare, go stand under the Garisenda when storm clouds are rolling over it.

In this last circle we come to the worst groups of love-killers: those who kill the love that unites those of the same country, of the same family. When Dante was writing the fifth canto, he must have had the whole thing worked out because Francesca there reminds Dante that because of her sin, she is there, whereas Caina attends the one that dispatched her from life. Caina is one of the compartments of this last circle, which is divided according to the different varieties of betrayal or treason. The punishment here has a very powerful symbolic presentation; the symbol here is ice. This not only represents the cessation of all life, but serves also to remind you that there is no fire, no spirit here, where there is no love. Love has been killed. We see this always against the symbolism of fire, the symbol of love.

The sinners in this ice are in different degrees of immobility: some sitting, some prone, some supine. Dante stops at a certain spot, where there are two Pisans known to everyone, made immortal because of Dante's poem: Archbishop Ruggiero and Count Ugolino. As you read these concluding cantos, you are disturbed by two feelings. When you consider how universal Dante can be — a man who can rise above local considerations, above time and place, to see things *sub specie eterne* — you wonder if at times you're witnessing a backyard Tuscan scrap. This feeling diminishes the universal power perhaps; yet these pictures of local affairs enable Dante to give us colors in poetry never seen before.

You see a man who is no doubt a traitor, and yet he is given a fine role because of the way he suffered; he is given a certain kind of redemption because of the cruelty of his death at the hands of the party of Ruggieri. The man is Ugolino, a Guelf, when the dominating party in Pisa was the Ghibelline. Here, in Canto 33, Dante comes upon the two sinners, and is reminded of Greek tragedy because of the cruelty of the characters. One is on top of the other, chewing the other's neck, which has no skin left on it.

Dante addresses the figure that is gnawing at the neck of the other, who, hearing the words of Dante, *la bocca sollevò dal fiero pasto quel peccator.* Dante has reminded us that this character is a sinner himself. He "raised his mouth from that beastly meal," *fiero pasto.* *Fiero* doesn't mean fiery; here is means simply bestial. Throughout this scene you have traits of bestiality. It has been so all along, since those giants appeared. "That sinner lifted his mouth from the beastly meal," that is, from the flesh, the imaginary flesh of the neck, *forbendola ai capelli del capo* — you can hardly translate *forbendola*; it's a verb that describes not the act of a man, but the act of a beast, the way a beast wipes his mouth on the grass. Dogs do it. That's the picture you get with *forbendola* — wiping the mouth on the hairs of the head he had torn from behind. *"Tu vuoi ch'io rinnovelli disperato dolor che il cor mi prema,"* "'You want me to renew my sorrow without solace'," despair without solace, "'the desperate sorrow that crushes my heart at the very thought of it'," *"già pur pensando,"* "'merely thinking of it my heart is crushed. But if my words are to be the seed to bear fruit of infamy for this traitor I am gnawing'"— remember, you are in Hell and revenge is Hellish — "*se le mie parole esser den seme che frutti infamia al traditor ch'io rodo,*" — in other words, he hopes his words will serve to heap infamy on the memory of this traitor (which they did) — "*parlar e lagrimar vedrai insieme,*" "'you will see me speak and weep at the same time. I don't know who you are'" — "*io non so chi tu sei*" — "'or how you came down here; but when I hear your speech, it seems to me, you are a Florentine'." Dante, you remember, gave himself away even to Farinata, earlier, for a Florentine, by just a few words. "*Tu dei saper ch'io fui Conte Ugolino,*" "'you must know that I was the Count Ugolino'." That's rather bold: you must know me; all I have to do is mention my name. "'And this is Archbishop Ruggieri'"; "*or ti dirò perchè i' son tal vicino,*" "'now I'll tell you why I have such neighborly feeling for him'," "*che per l'effetto del suo' ma' pensieri, fidandomi di lui, io fossi preso e poscia morto, dir non è mestieri,*" "'there is no need of saying that because of trusting him I was seized and executed; all that is well-known'." "*Però quel che non puoi aver inteso,*" "'but that which you cannot have heard'," which nobody knew, because it all took place in a secret dungeon, walled up forever, "'is how cruel my death was; that you will hear, and you will know whether he has treated me cruelly or not'."

Notice how effectively Dante gives us this account. The first thing that flashes before him, as he starts out, is the *breve pertugio*, the little hole, the narrow opening, within that mew, *dentro dalla muda* — apparently the tower was used for moulting birds — "*la qual per me ha il titol della fame,*" "'which has been named after me, the tower of hunger, and in which more people will have to be locked up'," "*in che convien ancor chi'altri si chiuda.*" "'This little hole had already showed me though its opening that the moon had renewed itself many times'," "*m'avea mostrato per lo suo forame più lune già.*" He didn't have a calendar; all he knew was that the moon had become new many times; that is, many months had passed, "*quando io feci il mal sonno, che del futuro mi squarciò il velame,*" "'when I had that evil dream that tore the veil from the future'." It was a dream that showed what the outcome would be.

16. FROM UGOLINO TO LUCIFER

Next to the fifth canto, the Ugolino canto is the most famous that Dante has written. Every child used to have to memorize it, in the old days; and I suppose that spoiled it for them, afterwards. Those few who haven't been forced to memorize it perhaps come to appreciate it more easily. Quite a bit can be preserved in the translation because there's a certain dramatic element that survives. Given good poetry, the possibility of translation varies inversely with the amount of lyricism in it; the more lyrical, the more difficult to translate — unless, of course, the translator is himself a great poet. But in this canto there are situations that of themselves excite the imagination.

The scene is infamous. The small dungeon, the family huddled together, the little hole, the meager light indicating the passing of time, the waxing and waning of the moon; all that sets the reader in expectation. Of course, an important element is also the musical quality of the passage. It's extraordinary how this hendecasyllabic line, which corresponds to our iambic pentameter, is made to produce such a variety of emotional effects. Anyone who knows something about metrics knows what I mean. With five feet, and only five or six possible variations of rhythm, and with quantity counting for very little in Italian as it does in French and as it does in English verse, it is a line that becomes heavy, except in the hands of gifted poets. Yet with all its handicaps, Dante has managed to keep it light so that it seems to have no weight at all, no heaviness. In this canto, as in the fifth, it becomes a vehicle for tragedy.

The little hole in this *muda*, in this mew was transformed into a jail; the tower had once been a moulting station, a place where birds, hawks, change their feathers (you can't imagine what hawkery was then; how important the hawk was in those days, as familiar as the dog is today). "'It has become known because of me, it has gotten the name hunger, because of me'," "*la qual per me ha il titol della fame.*" "*M'avea mostrato per lo suo forame più lune già, quando io feci il mal sonno,*" "'many moons had passed when I had that evil dream'" — evil in that it portends destruction — "*che del futuro mi squarciò il velame,*" "'that tore away the veil of the future'." This apparently was a morning dream. These poor people, in fact many from the time of Homer, thought that dreams that come at any old time are false, but those that come at dawn are true. And that's something you find in almost all the old poets: you find it in Lucan, you find it in Dante, and it was held by the populace too, which in many parts of the world still swear by the morning dream.

"'This one [this man here] seemed to me master and leader of the chase, pursuing the wolf and his whelps, to the mountain that prevents the Pisans from seeing Lucca'" — Pisa and Lucca are very close, but one cannot be seen from the other because of Monte di St. Giuliano which obstructs the view — "*al monte per che i Pisan veder Lucca non ponno.*" Rather beautiful this reminiscence. They were pursuing with *cagne magre* — not hounds, bitches. That adds a great deal; just as in the case of horses you have to stress sometimes that they are mares. The gender changes the character. People of the times believed that the females were more

keenly-scented, more vicious; and Dante shows here
that he thought so too. These bitches are *"magre,
studiose e conte"* "'lean, eager, capable'." *Conte* means
they were clever, they knew their business. The people
that led these hounds, these dogs, were the Gualandi,
the Sismondi and the Lanfranchi, three famous Pisan
families. When the tide of political fortune turned,
they led an exodus of families into exile — families that
became famous elsewhere, some settling in Switzerland, like the Sismondis — one of whom was the famous
historian. In a brief moment, *"in picciol corso, mi parean
stanchi lo padre e i figli."* The big wolf and the little cubs,
after a short pursuit seemed tired, *"e con l'acute scane mi
parea lor veder fender li fianchi,"* "'and in my dream I
thought I saw the sharp fangs of the dogs pierce
through their flanks'."

Dante, as you know. is rather generous with
dreams, as in the *Vita Nuova*. Little did he know that
the day would come when the analysis of dreams would
becomes not what it was for him, and for Homer, but
the thing the moderns have made of it. You have no
idea how these poor dreams of Dante have been tormented; how his literary biography has been recon-
structed. It's a wonder they haven't attempted to reconstruct his physical biography on the basis of these
dreams. That they haven't done; but, everything else,
the moderns say, is revealed through their analyses.
Well, here is the dream in which these great Pisan
Ghibellines are represented as hounds in a chase, the
hounds that pursued these miserable animals that are
prisoners here. "'When I awoke before morning',"
"quando fui desto innanzi lo dimane" — this tells us that
the dream is a true one; it's a morning dream —
"pianger sentì fra il sonno i miei figliuli, ch'eran con meco,

e domandar del pane," "'I heard my children crying in their sleep and asking for bread'." A pathetic touch. Apparently they had the same dream, but they are not awake yet. And there's an interruption here, a very dramatic one: "*Ben se' crudel se tu già non ti duoli, pensando ciò ch'al mio cor s'annunziava,*" "'you certainly are cruel [even at this early stage of the narration] if you are not already moved, considering what was being announced to my heart'." The coincidence of the dream and the hour of the day indicates that the thing will come true, and the painfulness of this foresight is as painful as that of the action itself, and so this exclamation: "'if you don't cry'," "*e se non piangi, di che piangi suoli?,*" "'what is it that can make you cry?'"

    Meanwhile the others have awakened, "*già eran desti.*" Notice the efficacy of the silence after that exclamation. Already they were awake, and the hour was approaching when food was usually brought in. They were expecting to hear the watchman come up, to hear the sound of his steps, the watchman who brings the food; instead they hear another sound, the sound of the key turning in the lock, or, more like the sound of nails being hammered in, to bolt or seal the door. The text might be uncertain, whether it is the turning of a key or the hammering of nails. But it is known that people condemned to death had to witness a certain ceremony, and the ceremony was the nailing of the outer door, indicating to those concerned both outside and in, that the end has come, the game is up: "*ed io sentii chiavar l'uscio di sotto all'orribile torre.*" Of course, the word horrible has been so transformed by misuse that it has lost its force, "dreadful tower" might be better here, "*ond'io guardai nel viso a' miei figliuoi sensa far motto.*" No words, no sounds; then the bolting, the nailing of the door, and then a glance exchanged between father and sons. "*Io non piangeva, sì dentro impietrai*," "'I did not cry, for within me I was turned to stone'."

To understand this, I suppose you have to keep in mind the genesis of weeping as explained by these people: their account of how one cries. Very briefly it's this: when you experience great emotions, sometimes sorrow, sometimes joy, a great deal of the air in the chest becomes compressed; part tries to come out in the form of sighs, another part turns to water and comes out in the form of tears, But sometimes the water congeals; and we say one has turned to stone, has turned to ice. That's what happened to Ugolino. The part that should have come out as tears was congealed. He didn't weep, but the others wept, "*piangevan elli ed Anselmuccio mio disse: 'Tu guardi sì, padre, che hai?*'" This rather meaningless line is perhaps the most beautiful of the whole canto. It brings out the despair, the infinite capacity for suffering. "*Però non lagrimai, ne rispos'io tutto quel giorno,*" "'but I did I not weep, and gave no answer all that day and the next night'," "*infin che l'altro sol nel mondo uscìo,*" "'until the next sun came forth upon the world'," "*come un poco di raggio,*" "'when a little light'" "*si fu messo nel doloroso carcere,*" "'when a meager ray pierced through into the grief-stricken jail.*"

It is now dawn. One of the ancient commentators makes the very interesting remark that at dawn you look at yourself in a mirror; here there are no mirrors, or rather there are four mirrors, the four young children who reflect in their countenance the grief-stricken face of the father — "*ed io scorsi per quattro visi il mio aspetto stesso,*" "'and I discerned my

aspect in their faces, and bit both my hands for grief'."
He could not speak. "'Thinking that it was because I
hadn't eaten, they jumped up and cried: 'It would give
us less sorrow, if you would take our flesh and eat it.
You clothed us with it; now strip it off and eat it'."
That, again, is a little touch of contemporary biology,
the function of the father in the building up of the
flesh of the children; the total absence of any significance on the part of the mother. "'You gave us this
flesh; take it back and eat it'." Rather diabolical; but
remember that the setting is Hell; all that is there is
diabolical, and so presented by Dante, except for the
sublimity of the few passages that seem to be taken out
of Hell, as in the fifth canto. *"Queta' mi allor per non
farli più tristi."* They had spoken little up till then,
except for this conversation which was a very sad one;
but the rest of that day, and the next, all of them
remained silent: *"lo dì e l'altro stemmo tutti muti."* Then
the dramatic exclamation: *"ahi dura terra perchè non
t'apristi?"* "'Cruel, merciless earth'" — he must have
looked up as he let forth this cry of despair — "'why did
you not then open up and swallow us? When we arrived
at the fourth day, Gaddo threw himself at my feet,
saying, 'Father, why don't you help me?'"

The earlier sense of sacrifice has given way to
the sense of helplessness. "'And there he died; and just
as you see me now, I saw all three die, one by one,
between the fifth and the sixth day. And I, already
blind'" — the science of the day taught that before you
die of starvation you became blind, and that goes back
to the science of the ancients — "'I began to grope over
each one'." In a way he wants to talk with them, and the
only way he can do so is by his hands; he can't see them,
so the way to establish some communication is by

touch. "'For two days I cried out to them after they died; then hunger proved more powerful than grief'," "*più che il dolor, potè il digiuno.*"

This is a line that has been tortured by commentators. And of course all it can mean to one who has followed this poem and has a sense of the artistry and is familiar with Dante's words is that grief, which should have killed him, doesn't kill him; that more vulgar thing, hunger, does. The other explanation put forward is that hunger made him eat his dead children. That's possible, providing he had begun to eat them at the beginning. But after four days, if you're starved to that point, not only can you not eat raw meat but you can't eat anything. If any of you have had in wartime any real experience with hunger, as some of us had at Caporetto, you can't start with raw meat; you can't even start with macaroni. Dante knew that; everybody knew it.

Quand'ebbe detto ciò, con gli occhi torti — note the musicality of the verse — *riprese il teschio misero coi denti.* You hear in that line determination, despairing determination; he attacks again the wretched skull with his teeth, gnawing the bone of the neck like a dog, *che furo all'osso, come d'un can, forti.* And then comes a curse against Pisa.

Nothing extraordinary. Dante has cursed every Italian city of any distinction. To have not been abused by Dante is really a bad sign; it means you're really obscure. You know what he says of Rome, what he says of Florence, what he says of Bologna — they're all attacked — but Pisa is the abomination of Italy: *Ahi Pisa, vituperio delle genti del bel paese là* — instead of saying "Italy" he follows the habit of the Middle Ages, which was to identify the country by the word used there to mean "yes" — *là dove il "sì suona."* *Oui* is the word for "yes" is northern France, *oc* is the word for "yes" in southern France, and *sì* is the word for most of the Italians. A little earlier he had described the inhabitants of Bologna as the people who used the word *sipa*. "Ahi, Pisa, abomination of the people of the beautiful land" *dove il sì suona*, "since your neighbors are slow in punishing you" — Pisa was one of the powers going down at the time; they had recently been defeated by the Genoese who were trying to break their power and had succeeded. Pisa was one of the great powers of the Middle Ages, and now it is dying — but it was not dying fast enough, according to Dante. That's pretty cruel. On the other hand, we might have to say of this cruelty on the part of Dante that he speaks this way because his vision of lower Hell has had a psychological effect on him. His vision of the devils that punish sin has made him a devil too — not in the commission of sins, but in his attitude toward the devilish punishment of sinners. "Since your neighbors are slow to punish you, let the Caprara and the Gorgona [islands] move from their cities toward the Arno and damn it up so that everyone in you drowns." Whether this is an indication of the growing severity of feeling against sinners, intensified as he goes along through lower Hell, or the usual practice, never belied historically, which has grown stronger and has reached its culmination in our days, which places the responsibility for public deeds on the whole population of an enemy, past and future, we can't be sure. The latter is likely, for it was common in the days of Homer, and no doubt before; Dante echoes it; and we have carried it to its extreme. Whatever a political regime does, all the people are responsible, and not only the living people

but those who come after. That may be Dante's idea
here. At any rate, he seems to be very eager to maintain
that thought. "'For if Conte Ugolino had the reputa-
tion of betraying you, you should not have put his
children to such torture'," *a tal croce* — here, *croce* of
course is not *croce* as the symbol of Christianity but the
pagan *croce* that had lived on through the Middle Ages:
the ordinary torture for the criminal. This episode
starts with a reference to the cruel infamy of Thebes
and ends rather artistically, to be sealed and unified by
the introduction of another glimpse of the horrors of
Thebes at the end. It's rather hard to reconstruct this
picture; it takes a poet to do it well.

In the last circle, we have traitors against groups,
not any groups but the two greatest groups — the
Church and the State. Dante has gone through the
ocean of ice and has seen the souls immersed in it and
has approached the Giudecca. The last lines of the
preceding canto are an invective against the Genoese:
Ahi Genovesi, uomini diversi d'ogni costume, e pien d'ogni
magagna, perchè non siete voi del mondo spersi? "Why
haven't you been scattered out there in the world?"
This Satanism is necessary; the cruelty is directed
against evil. After all, God gives man power, not to be
used at random, but to mete out justice.

The last canto opens with a quotation which is
one of the most impressive in the entire poem; *vexilla*
regis prodeunt, the great processional hymn of the
Church, intuned at the approaching of the Cross: "the
banners of the King advance." All the poetry which is
heard when this hymn is sung is turned upside down
here, it is all changed by the addition of one word:
inferni. You have to be very clever, when you read this,
to bring the effect out with your voice. With that last

word, you have to take back all that you have said before. The voice is raised to heaven first — *vexilla regis prodeunt* — then drops back to Hell again: *inferni.* They are coming toward us, therefore look ahead, says Virgil; see if you can discern them. Dante looks and sees a sort of murky atmosphere and in it a windstorm, *come quando una grossa nebbia spira, o quando l'emisperio nostro annotta.* In other words you can see very little, except what can be seen through the darkness, such as you have when a thick fog blows over or when our hemisphere is covered by the darkness of night. "What I saw in the distance looked like a windmill," *par da lungi un molin che il vento gira, veder mi parve un tal dificio allotta.* Not only does he see this windmill through the darkness, but he even feels the cold blast of air it produces; *poi per lo vento mi ristrinsi retro al duca mio,* "because of the wind, I pressed up behind my guide" *che non li era altra grotta,* "for there was no other cover."

"I now reached a spot (and with fear in my heart I put it into verse) where everyone was covered over." Until now some parts of the bodies of the sinners were sticking out of the ice; but here they are all covered, *transparean come festuco in vetro.* The reason you can see them is the same reason you can see a straw in a glass receptacle, "like a piece of straw in badly formed glass," a quaint image for human beings imbedded in the ice; *altre sono a giacere,* "some are lying down"; *altre stanno erte,* "others are erect"; *quella col capo e quella con le piante,* "this one has its head up, and this one its feet up;" *altra, com'arco, il volto a' piedi inverte;* "others bent in a kind of arc that turns the face back to the feet," twists them around.

Quando noi fummo fatti tanto avante, ch'al mio

maestro piacque di mostrarmi la creatura ch'ebbe il bel sembiante, "when we had reached so far ahead that my master saw fit to show me what had been the fairest of things created" — Lucifer, once the most beautiful of all created beings — "Virgil made me stop, saying, 'Behold Dis,'" "*Ecco Dite,*" "'the place where it behooves you to put on the armor of fortitude'." Dante had passed beyond the perils of fire into the blast of this icy wind. *Com'io divenni allor gelato e fioco, nol domandar, lettor, ch'io non lo scrivo, però ch'ogni parlar sarebbe poco.* "How I froze to death, how I lost my voice, reader, do not ask." He froze at the sight and could not speak — and don't ask me how that happened because anything I may say would be too *fioco,* falls far short of reality.

Dante here begins to work on the development of an anti-trinity, a trinity of evil, as you have, above, a trinity of good. And as he develops that trinity of good, above, so he develops this trinity of evil, below. The good trinity is ineffable; so is this one. The experience of the trinity above had been described as an *ecstasis*; here too he experiences an *ecstasis*, but an *ecstasis* before evil. What happens when you have an *ecstasis*? You are drawn out of yourself. All sensations except the sensation of sight go out of you. But that is metamorphosized because an *ecstasis* is usually accompanied by a vision, in such a way that it's not really you who see, but some higher power. You're really dead to reality; but unlike being dead, you return to life. *Io non morrì, e non rimasi vivo: pensa oramai per te, s'hai fior d'ingegno, qual io divenni, d'uno e d'altro privo.* "Think for yourself, if you can [if you have the intellectional power to do so] what I became, being neither one nor the other."

Dante stresses this *ecstasis* to concentrate your

attention on the fact that he means something more than a mere phrase. And just as he had done for the heavenly trinity, he concentrates his power in a double capacity. In the beginning of the *Inferno* God is the Emperor of the universe but King of heaven; just as the Roman Emperor was emperor of the world and king of the Romans (the Romans being the Germans; the Holy Roman Emperor merely a fiction, but very much adhered to). Here you have *lo imperador del doloroso regno*, "the emperor of the dolorous kingdom," *da mezza il petto uscìa fuor della ghiaccia*, "projected out of the frozen lake from the middle of the chest up," the other part apparently immersed in ice. As for size: "I am in size closer to giants than giants are to his arms." In other words, he's pretty big. "See for yourself," *vedi oramai quant' esser dee quel tutto, ch'a così fatte parti si confaccia*, "what the whole must be, that is proportional to such parts."

And now you see why he had stressed at the beginning of the canto that once he had been so beautiful; he had been the most beautiful creature in the universe and to know how great his beauty was, we have only to consider in reverse his present ugliness. If one who was given the maximum of beauty could lift his brow against his maker, surely all ill must come from this: *ben dee da lui procedere ogni lutto. O quanto parve a me gran maraviglia, quando vidi tre facce alla sua testa!* "What a marvel [how astonished I was] when I saw three faces attached to his head" — here is the evil trinity — *l'una dinanzi e quella era vermiglia*, "one in front, and that was crimson," one aspect of the holy trinity, love, is represented pictorially as crimson too; *l'altre, eran due, che s'aggiungieno a questa sopr'esso, a mezzo di ciascuna spalla, e si giungieno al loco della cresta,* "there were two others joined to this one over the middle of each shoulder, coming together where the crest of an animal should be." They are divided at the shoulder, but at the top they came together as one. To show their bestial character, Dante calls the crown of the head, the crest.

Doré's illustration is very accurate but not very poetic. Artists often used three heads for the Holy Trinity; an art that became discredited, but something of it survived to some extent into the sixteenth century.

17. LUCIFER / SATAN, THE GREATEST BETRAYER

Dante's primary interest at this point is in startling you with some comments on the physical properties of the position he has reached. All along here, he hasn't given very much thought to the moral significance of events, as they have unraveled before us. He has been primarily interested in painting and modeling. Elsewhere, he has shown us the graded cruelty of punishment. Now he has succeeded in showing us the sinners with an almost infinite capacity for suffering and practically no actuality. You have worms so constructed that they can suffer *ad infinitum*, but nothing more. Until now, Dante has described sinners as bad but stressed that they have remaining traces of goodness. There's nothing good to be said, however, for these three worms and this beast from which all evil flows. Here, once you have indicated the sin, that's all that can be said. The devil is devoid of all dignity. This is not Milton's Satan. You know what a fine fellow that devil of Milton is; you could easily fall in love with him. And the shame is, many have. Here there is no dignity, nothing attractive. Everything diabolical for Dante has to be revolting.

Dante's Satan is, like all the other devils we have met, grotesque and ambitious — which means, they have to be forever trying to assert themselves, yet impotent. This combination of qualities makes them grotesque. They are ambitious, they want to do things, but are impotent; and ambitious impotence is always a source of laughter. At least Dante creates that effect.

The scientific principles Dante is amused to consider in this canto are principles that could be gotten from any text book or could be reasoned out by plane and solid geometry. First of all, the center of the earth is such that no matter in what direction you turn, you can't go in any direction but up. Dante, who has been sliding down, clambering down the matted hair of the devil, between the body of the devil and the edge of the crust of ice, finds, at a certain moment, all of a sudden, that he has to begin to climb. And you can't climb up by keeping your feet in the same direction. He has to turn his head where his feet were so that he can climb. Another point is that, at the center of the earth, relative to the outer universe, you can have any time you want. If you look this way, you have noon, if you look the other way you have midnight. Dante doesn't describe it quite in that way. He describes it, to make it more familiar, by considering the situation not quite at the center but on the surface of a very small sphere concentric to our earth's surface. Virgil says: it's dusk, evening, night is coming; and after just a few seconds he says: it's dawn, let's get going. What has happened? They have measured the lapse of time not according to the surface of the earth but on the surface of that little sphere with its diameter of a few feet. These observations amused Dante; he set them down in magnificent lines.

The colors of the three heads of the monster, of Satan, have given much trouble to the commentators. We can't do much about that. The symbolism of colors is such that unless the author gives us some clue, it's pretty hard to determine. Black, of course, is pretty clear; but red sometimes connotes the best, sometimes the worst: it can be the symbol of the holiest, purest love, but also the color of the harlot's lust. *Sotto ciascuna uscivan due grandi ali . . . .* Two huge wings come out from under each of these three heads, wings befitting a bird of this sort. They were larger than any sails he had ever seen, *vele di mar non vid'io mai cotali.* These wings were not made up of feathers; they were like bat's wings, veined, *e quelle svolazzava.* He can't, doesn't fly with them; *svolazzare* is the flapping of a bat's wings, *sì che tre venti si movean da elle,* so that, three winds were started up, *quindi Cocito tutto s'aggelava,* cold blasts from the wings of Satan, of Lucifer, that have frozen all of Cocytus, which, as we pointed out earlier, is the last manifestation of that single river which is Acheron and Phlegeton, in turn, running and boiling and cascading to the center, where it freezes because of the flapping of Satan's wings. Notice how geometrical and arithmetical he is in this kind of schematic description.

"He wept with six eyes, and down three chins streamed tears and bloody froth" — *bava* is a special kind of foam, froth; "spittle" in English isn't quite right. *Da ogni bocca dirompea coi denti un peccatore, a guisa di maciulla.* In each mouth he chewed with his teeth a sinner like a *maciulla* — *maciulla* is a terrible instrument; you used to see it on every farm, but even in Italy it's disappeared. It was used to tear, to break up the stalks of hemp. It had very, very, sharp teeth. The effect of its cutting is awful. Those who have ever seen human beings mangled by it would know what Dante means here, *dirompea coi denti un peccatore, a guisa di maciulla,* like someone breaks hemp. *A quel dinanzi il mordere era nulla verso il graffiar* "the biting was nothing compared to the scratching." Notice how low Dante sinks, to the lowest level in describing this biting and scratching: *che talvolta la schiena rimaneva della pelle tutta brulla*, "so that at times the back remained stripped of all skin." *Quell'anima lassù che ha maggior pena*, "that soul up there who is suffering the greatest pain" — Dante is here looking up to the grotesque figure of Judas — that one can't do anything, his head is being chewed up; outside he can only wiggle his legs. *Degli altri duo ch'hanno il capo di sotto, quei che pende al nero ceffo*, "of the other two who have their heads out, the one hanging from the black [*ceffo*]" — *ceffo* is the worst kind of word we have in Italian for head. We have fifteen or twenty, but this is the one that arouses the greatest revulsion. To describe such things is an art, isn't it? In Italian there are over three hundred words to describe death, three hundred ways to say "to die," and, according to the character of the person, one chooses the proper one. The choice of the word expresses your appraisal of the person who has died. Of course, social conventions restrict your choice in practice to fifteen or twenty different expressions; but in the various strata of society the full range of expression is covered. So here is Brutus, hanging from the mouth of the black *ceffo*. All he can do is twist his body, nothing more; he can't utter a sound, *non fa motto*. The other is Cassius, who here seems *membruto*, corpulent, not the lean and hungry-looking Cassius we're familiar with.

One thing is certain: this is a striking place, and Dante wants to get out of it quickly. This is brought out by the rapidity of the descriptions: *ma la notte resurge*, "night is rising." Dante has a very special definition of night. He defines it for us in the *Convivio* and conforms to that definition in the *Divine Comedy*. By night he means the point which is diametrically opposite to

the point which is the center of the sun: when the sun
sets, night, which is a point of no dimension, is rising
on the eastern horizon. *La notte resurge. Risurge,* you
see, just as the sun rises. "*Ed ormai è da partir che tutto
avem veduto,*" "'and now we have to leave, for we have
seen everything'." *Com'a lui piaque,* "as he wished, I
clasped his neck and he, at the proper moment" *ci prese
di tempo e loco poste,* temporally and spatially he was on
the look-out, you see. *E quando l'ale furo aperte assai,*
"and when the wings [of Satan] were wide outspread,"
appigliò se alle vellute coste, "he took hold of the hairy
ribs."

   Notice how precise all this is. At this point he
begins to go down from one tuft to the next, between
the thick mat of hair and the frozen crust. He climbs
down, as one would in mountain climbing; only, instead of clinging to rocky ledges, as in mountain
climbing, he clings to something much safer, the tufts
of the devil's hair. He is lowering himself in the space
between the devil's body and the walls or banks of ice,
which is the frozen crust of Cocytus.

   "When we reached the point [on his body] where
the thigh turns on the large part of the loins [*sul grosso
dell'anche*]", that is, when we reached the middle of the
body, where the body joins the legs, "my master, with
toil and panting, turned his head where before he had
had his feet, and turned to grapple on the hair," *come
uom che sale,* "as a man who climbs, not as a man who
descends easily, so that I thought we were verging back
to hell." There is pathos in that line: *sì chè in inferno io
credea tornar anche,* "I thought we were turning back to
go to hell again." "*Attienti ben,*" "'hold on'," "*che per sì
fatte scale,*" "'for by a ladder of this sort° said my master
panting like a man exhausted," "*conviensi diparti da*

tanto male," "'is the way to leave behind such evil'."

For once, we have a touch of powerful morality. When you have reached a certain level of evil, you have to pant to get out. For Dante, of course, it's not a matter of getting out of a sin, but the experience of purification by the sight of the consequences of sin. *Poi uscì fuor per lo foro d'un sasso,* "then he came out through the opening of a rock and put me on the edge [of a hole] in a sitting position," *appresso porse a me l'accorto passo,* "then he turned toward me his careful [that is, his watchful] step." He deposits Dante on this ledge and then walks up to him. "I raised my eyes thinking to see Lucifer as I had left him, but I saw him instead with his feet up in the air; and if I was disturbed, troubled, uncouth people [*la gente grossa*] can imagine, who do not understand what point that was through which I had passed." "'Get up,' [*levati sù*], says my master: on your feet'." He just put him down and now tells him to get up. *"La via è lunga e il cammino è malvagio,"* "'the way is long and the path is hard'."

The climb ahead is rocky, difficult, and steep; already the sun is at *mezza terza* (half third). We know by now that the day was divided into two parts, the hours of daylight and the hours of night; and each part, regardless of the season of the year, was divided into twelve hours; and these were the so-called canonic hours. The first of the daylight hour was the hour of dawn, and the twelfth hour was the hour of sundown. Therefore the *terza,* at this season of the year near the equinox, would be about nine o'clock; and *mezza terza* then is about halfway between six and nine o'clock. A little while before, Virgil had said that night was rising, it was evening; now the sun is above the horizon. Of course, these terms, like *mezza terza,* awakened in the mind of the reader — not the reader today, but the reader of those days, even in some people who lived only fifty years ago — a certain image. I'm afraid, it's an image in the depths of a memory rapidly dying out. When people of another time heard these words — *terza, sesta* — they heard bells. Bells were rung to mark these hours. Some (I hope) still exist, in Italy at any rate. They were the three *angeluses* of the day: the one at dawn, the one at midday, and the one at sundown. They are the three moments, the three times when you pray to the Virgin Mary. Well, there was one also at *mezza terza*. Dante heard it and he reminds you of it now.

Non era caminata di palagio: the path, he says, was no *caminata di palagio*, it was not beautiful smooth pavement, not a palace hall. There was no palace hall where we were, *ma natural burella*. The *burelle* in Florence were the ruins of the old amphitheater. I don't know if they are still there; they were horrible things, dangerous, filled with bats and serpents. This place was like the *burelle* of Florence but, unlike the *burelle* in Florence, these were natural. The others were made by the Romans; these *avea mal suolo, e di lume disagio*, "were hard to walk on and hard to see." These natural *burelle* had an uneven surface, not smooth like that of the *cammino di palagio*, and there was an absence of light. "'Before I come out of the abyss,' I said, when I had stood up, 'tell me, say a few things to clear away my error'." Until then, he had been sitting down where Virgil had deposited him. Now he asks. "'Where is the glacier? And how is this one imbedded upside down? And how come that in so short a time the sun has passed from evening to morn?'" "And he to me: 'you think you're still at the center, where I took hold of the hair of the worm [*del vermo reo*]'."

Here again we have to note the moral language; this is a very important line: "*del vermo reo, che il mondo fora,*" "'of the evil worm that pierces through the world'." The line deserves a great deal of thought. "'You then passed through the point to which all weights are drawn'." Of course, it's a pretty awkward translation for that very *schnelle* line: *il punto al qual si traggon d'ogni parte i pesi.* You are now under the opposite hemisphere, that's why the time has changed by almost twelve hours. When the ancients used the word hemisphere in this connection, they applied it not to the surface of the earth but to the outermost sphere of the heavens, to the *primum mobile*, or at any rate, to the eighth sphere. That explains the awkwardness of some of our phrases; we think of the tropic of Cancer and the tropic of Capricorn as if they are lines on the surface of the earth; when in reality they are lines passing through constellations of the eighth sphere, projected against the ninth.

We are now at the point beneath the hemisphere opposite to the one that covers the *gran secca* – that's a Biblical term — the great dry land, the *arida*, meaning by that, the part of the earth that is inhabited — inhabited because it is not submerged in water but dry. That *secca* extends, they thought, 180 degrees. The point that is located over the middle of this hemisphere, according to Dante's cosmology, is half-way between the extremes of the major arc of this *gran secca* or *arida* and plumb over Jerusalem. The religious morality of the geography of the *Divine Comedy* is built around it; more precisely, around the vertical piece of the cross on which our Savior was crucified. From that point there are supposed to be 90 degrees to the Ganges and

90 degrees to Gibraltar. Of course, his geography is all wrong, but it is for him a moral construction.

Dante speaks of the hemisphere over the *gran secca*, the hemisphere that extends over these 180 degrees of dry land, as the upper part of the surface of the ninth sphere. The mid-point of it is the line which goes from that point to the surface of the earth, where Jerusalem is, where Calvary is, to the vertical bar of the Cross, projected through the center of the earth, emerging at the opposite side, at the *antipodes*, where Purgatory is. So, we have now arrived at the central point beneath that hemisphere which is opposite to that which covers like a canopy, like a vault, the great dry land, the *arida*. Beneath that point "*sotto il cui colmo ... consunto fu l'uom che nacque e visse senza pecca*," "'was undone the man that was born and lived without sin'," that is, Christ, who was born, naturally, without sin and lived without sin. "*Tu hai li piedi in su picciola spera che l'altra faccia da della Giudecca.*" Before you were in one hemisphere of this little sphere, and now you are on the other, opposite to it. Therefore, like on the sphere of earth above, on one side, here, it is morning, while there, on the other side, it is evening; although down here, the one side is only a few steps from the other. This would be so, that is, if the sun could be seen. Actually you can see nothing above, but if you could, you would see this phenomenon. "'And this one here, who served as a ladder for us with his hair, is still impaled as before. He fell from heaven on this side'."

Again, this is a traditional part of the cosmology, of the religious cosmology. Lucifer fell down from heaven — *cadde giù dal cielo* — and reached the earth in the southern hemisphere. It's a very old idea.

And the land that used to be above the surface, here, has shifted. Dante now wants to explain this mythological geography of his. There is no land in the southern hemisphere, in those three quarters we mentioned. There was, but it moved away frightened, when Lucifer fell, *"per paura di lui fe' del mar velo."* The land that once rose, through fear of him, made a veil for itself of water, and came to our hemisphere. And perhaps to escape him, the part that is hollowed out now rushed up above the surface to form the mountain of Purgatory.

Here musically, there is a very sharp reversal. *"Luogo è laggiù da Belzebu remoto tanto, quanto la tomba si distende."* This is a hard nut to crack. What is this *tomba?* Probably, on this little sphere of Giudecca, there is a place removed from Beezelbub, a distance equal to the radius of that little sphere, a cavern, discernible not by sight but by sound, the sound of a rivulet, which runs down through a hole in the rock corroded by the flowing water (*che egli ha roso*) with its curved course, which winds about and is barely inclined. "My master and I [here he proceeds more rapidly]," *lo duca ed io per quel cammino ascoso entrammo a ritornar nel chiaro mondo; e senza cura aver d'alcun riposo salimmo suso, ei primo ed io secondo, tanto ch'io vidi delle cose belle che porta il ciel, per un pertugio tondo; e quindi uscimmo a riveder le stelle.*

There is definitely a change of sound here. "My master and I, through this hidden, dark, path began to make our return to the world of light without taking care for any rest; and we climbed up, he leading and I following, till I saw the beautiful things that heaven bears." Until now, their eyes have been darkened, made dirty by the filthy soot of Hell, now they see *le cose belle che porta il ciel.* "I saw the beautiful things of heaven through a round hole; and hence we came forth to see the stars again."

18. THE ENTRANCE TO PURGATORY; CATO

It's not very hard to appreciate the artistic effort of Dante in this second canticle, because *Purgatorio* is built primarily on contrasts. After the gloom, inertia, the groping in the heavy atmosphere of the *Inferno*, we suddenly have an outburst of clarity, of purity; a sharp contrast of life against death. Dante is very careful to let you feel that this entry into Purgatory is a coming back to life after infernal death. He stresses this, sets the stamp of death on what has gone before, with phrases like *l'aura morta*, "the dead breeze," and not just physical things: poetry too is dead in Hell, *la morta poesia*; here there is a sudden renascence of vitality, of motion, of life; it is a veritable resurrection. The trip up is very quick and very steep following the course of the little river that was formed by the water that had washed off all the sins of the souls of Purgatory, after having initially served to restore the memory of all good and to wipe away the memory of all evil. It is one of the two great hydrographic systems of the *Divine Comedy* that meet at the center of the earth: the one that flows through Hades and this one that comes down from Purgatory.

When Dante emerged from this steep climb up from the center of the earth, it was two hours before sunrise. Dante doesn't tell us in these words; he talks about the constellation of the Fish, which is the one that immediately precedes Aries. At the beginning of March, the sun is in Aries, so that if the constellation of the Fish is now on the horizon; it means that in about two hours Aries will be there. He fills in the natural time with this picture of astronomical time. He give us this information, representing graphically the temporal situation by saying that the light of Venus was so strong in the eastern sky that it out-dazzled all the stars around it, which were the stars of the constellation Fish. In other words, Venus, the *bel pianeta*, is now the morning star. It's the one star you can't mistake, the one most easy to identify. It's so bright, its light is so strong that it casts a shadow. It's probably not much seen in the morning because most people are still in bed. But in the evening, when Venus appears in the West, it's brilliance is unmistakable. And here the brilliancy of it is brought out by the statement that the Fish were dimmed out of sight by the splendor of it.

Dante has emerged in the southern hemisphere at the *antipodes*, at the mountain where Christ was crucified. He tells us that, he tell us we are deep in the southern hemisphere because we no longer see the *Wain*; the whole thing with the Polar star has disappeared from view, in the north. What he sees corresponds to the *Wain* in the southern hemisphere, and that is the so-called southern cross — very beautiful stars, very prominent dazzling stars. The problem is: did Dante invent them or had he actually heard of them? Of course you have to go pretty far south to see these stars, you have to go at least as far as the Canary Islands. In any case they are there and very brilliant. Dante may have heard of them; but in connection with this matter and also with reference to the mountain of Purgatory — which reminds us of a very famous mountain which many people have seen — in all this we have to go by what we know of their knowledge; and what we know is often very different from what *they* knew. Many things, which at one time we thought they didn't know, we later have found out they did know. We have been proved wrong so often that we should know better. That doesn't mean that the converse is true: because *we* know a thing doesn't prove that *they* knew it.

Dante needed four stars to represent the four cardinal virtues. Here, in this life as it is, you can get virtue only through effort. But that isn't the way God at first made man. Originally man could make himself virtuous as naturally as he breathes air and drinks water. In man's original state, temperance, prudence, fortitude and justice dominated human conduct in the same way that the sun and moon dominate the tides. Now that no longer is the case. The pursuit of those four virtues in our time involves things that are not very dear to most of us, at least not until you have already made considerable progress in your moral education. At the start now you are reluctant to go the way of these four cardinal virtues; not so when man was in Eden. Eden was and is on the top of the mountain of Purgatory. Eden therefore was the home of man as originally created, where he was meant to be naturally virtuous. Dante will describe the beauty of life in Eden before the fall, when man naturally did what is now often his painful duty to do; when the *libitum* was the *licitum*, which is rarely the case now. Most of us do what we have to do, feeling the burden of duty; only the rare, noble souls, the more beautiful ones, as the romantics called them, are able to do so, without that feeling.

So Dante sees, as he emerges, these four beautiful stars, about which he may have known something. We know that we are not going astray in the identity of these stars because, at the end of Purgatory, when the reunion with Beatrice takes place, the four cardinal virtues that attend her say: here we are maidens, while in the heavens we are stars. In other words, he gives a stellar aspect, a stellar essence to the virtues; the initial motive force, the initial power of virtue is in the stars. It conforms with the main tradition of teachings back to the days of Plato. These beautiful stars that showed their beauty to the people that dwelt under them, the original people, Adam and Eve, infusing virtue, now shine on one man, and who that one man is, is a source of great surprise for us.

Artistically it's something very beautiful that we have here. The light is still very dim; all you see is the flash of light of the stars. It illuminates the bearded face of an old man who we are told is Cato. The Cato who shaved daily is presented to the reader very anachronistically like a Longobard king; with hair so long that it is brought forward and down to mingle with his beard. A strange figure, worthy to be depicted by the most powerful brushes, except that it's a beauty that defies painting. Try to picture it, this figure in the dim light of the stars. That it is still dark is confirmed by the fact that Cato doesn't see that Dante is alive but thinks he is an escaped soul. These people in Purgatory, all along, will discover that Dante is alive only in the daytime, by the fact that his body casts a shadow. And that proof that he is alive is not apparent here.

It is surprising, or should be, this presence of Cato as guardian of Purgatory. We know he is guardian because Dante shows him in that role, and he solemnly affirms it later, so that he give us confirmation that is both *apodeictic* and dramatic. Naturally this arouses the indignation of some fervent believers, indignation that the ecclesiastics can ease perhaps, by saying that this is, after all, a fiction. We must not suppose that he is theologically really interested in redistributing the souls. He is writing a poetic fiction of the nether regions. Still, here is this Cato, who is a pagan. Did he die before Christ? Obviously he died before Julius Caesar, and Julius Caesar died on the Ides of March. But here he is in Purgatory, Cato, who is a suicide, a Stoic of the best or worst order. To that rapidly disappearing species — those few poor dodos who read the classics — to many of them Stoicism appears noble, but it is a nobility which to a Christian presents a very jarring contradiction. That jarring contradiction means nothing today because people know almost nothing about Stoicism. If anyone has read the Church fathers, knows anything about St. Augustine, he must know how he, especially, argued the attribution of any virtue to Stoicism. And Christianity generally has upheld that view.

What is wrong with Stoicism? After all, they taught and practiced tight moral conduct, chastity, moderation; as we see here, all the cardinal virtues shine upon Cato, and it may be said that no philosophical school has more thoroughly extolled the cardinal virtues than the Stoics. What's wrong with Stoicism, then? One is tempted to say: nothing. But that would be heretical. We can cite a famous quotation from St. Augustine, which is often repeated and deserves to be quoted again. He speaks of the state of mind of a nun who exults in her practice of virtue, how she resists temptation, keeps herself unsullied, and so on. St. Augustine comments that a nun who exalts her virtue has fallen into greater sin than had she succumbed to fiery lust. Why? Because all those virtues cease to be virtues unless they proceed from a certain root, and that root is *humility*. I'm reminded of a map I saw in a little school in Italy in my childhood days, a map of the tree of virtue. There were four trunks, or rather major branches, and some very lively heads of persons embodying the virtues, heads of persons like St. Catherine of Siena. But at the top was a big stocky trunk — it was an inverted tree — and engraved above it, where the root began, were the words in Latin: The root of all virtue is humility. Augustine says: who cannot be brave? (Of course, that's exaggerated; if you've lived long enough you see many cowards in this world.) Who can't be brought around to some degree of moral virtue? The difficulty is to sustain virtue out of humility. What's wrong with Stoicism is that it lacks humility.

Dante faces these three difficulties by putting Cato in Purgatory as its guardian. To get by the first difficulty, Dante can say that it's possible, since God can do anything, to save Cato even though he died before Christ. People can be saved apart from Christianity. The Patriarchs lived before Christ. We may say that most men are saved not *per gratia Dei* but *per gratia Christi*; still what happened to the Patriarchs could have happened to some of the Gentiles.

What about suicide? Well, Dante had it easy there, because, somehow, or other, going back from St. Thomas to Plotinus, many arguments were brought forth in defense of Cato. It's easy enough for us to understand their attitude, not being Stoics. Reading them, one sees they're all very tender on this subject: they're all willing, or very nearly willing, to pardon Cato. Of course Dante's intention is to make a dramatic situation out of this. Suicide is a damnable thing; it's tolerable only on one count; it is in a sense justified

when it's done to insure Freedom. Dante belongs to
that verbal school, instituted by the Greeks, pushed to
great heights by the Romans, echoed straight through
Western history, and which is now ready to receive its
last rites. He is very happy to have the occasion to give
voice to that school. Suicide, damnable in itself, is
justified only by love of liberty. He takes up the old cry
of liberty to turn a negative into a positive value. It's all
bombast — always has been; but even as we talk, knowing it is all bombast, one feels a certain fervor. That's
how Dante gets over the second difficulty.

The third difficulty can't be thrown aside so
easily. Cato was a Stoic, and he was proud; as a Stoic he
had to be proud. The formula is often cited. The true
Stoic must be fearless in the face of everything: *si
fractus inlabatur orbis, impavidum ferient ruinae.* If the
whole world breaks up — that is, if an atomic bomb falls
— when all the ruins, all the fragments, all the world
begins to fall on him, the Stoic will not move, he will
not bat an eye. On the other hand, every child knew
what was written on the top of that map or chart that
depicted the virtues: you couldn't be a Christian and
be proud, for the root of all Christian virtue is humility. Dante knows this and ends the *Divine Comedy* with
an exaltation of the virtue of humility in the Virgin
Mary.

Knowing this, what does he do? He converts
Cato, makes him humble. The symbol of the Stoic's
fortitude was the mighty oak. Who cares how strong
the storm is? This trunk withstands all of the blasts,
whether they come from the south or the north. The
Stoic is the sturdy oak; that's the symbol for Stoic
fortitude. But here that is done away with. Cato teaches
Dante that you can stand the storms of this world

without breaking — not by the stiff oak-like strength of pride but because of the pliability of an ordinary plant. The oak is replaced by the *giunce*, the weed, the rush.

Before he can begin his own purification, Dante must let Virgil bind his brow with a *giunce*. It is a recantation of the power of the oak. The *giunce* is able to stand where every other plant must perish, because it is able to bend; whereas plants that harden would inevitably break under continuous buffetings. It's an impressive change from the Stoic symbol. Dante has to begin his purification by letting his heart be convinced that you progress nowhere morally, except through humility.

Well, times change. Anyone interested in the appreciation of poetry has to read Dante and every other great poet in this way. Not that you can ever retrace the complete elaboration of all that goes into the formation of a poetic line; for that goes back through the entire range of emotional and intellectual experience of the poet. But you have to frame it in a world of aspirations, of emotions, of experiences, which in turn has to be placed in a larger frame of cultural experience and thought. You cannot read this with the dictionary on one side and yourself, with all your personal appetites and interests, on the other. You have to get out of yourself and move through history, and then come back to yourself — for always you remain in the present — but you come back to yourself magnified by the itinerary, enriched by the history of the thought and passion or emotions of several centuries.

As in the *Paradiso* so here in *Purgatorio*, we find the image of navigation as a symbol of the poet's experience. You have the *piccioletta barca* at the beginning of the *Paradiso*, and here you have the *navicella del mio ingegno*. In the beginning of both canticles Dante feels it useful to establish a *rapprochement* between the experience of the navigator who crosses difficult seas and the journey of the soul of the poet. Even in the *Inferno*, he uses the image of navigation: *e.g.* the image of the shipwrecked man who, when he has finally attained the safety of the shore, turns to look back on the waters in which he almost perished.

Per correr miglior acqua alza le vele omai la navicella del mio ingegno, "the little ship of my talent." *Ingegno*, everywhere in Dante, everywhere systematically and coherently, has a very precise meaning: it means the capacity to discover things unknown, originality not merely in a mechanical sense but any kind of originality; it's the capacity to do or understand something new; to discover, but always with originality. That little ship *che lascia retro a se mar sì crudele*, "which leaves behind it such a cruel sea" — the world of Hell is now compared to a stormy relentless sea.

In this second canticle, *canterò di quel secondo regno dove l'umano spirito si purga e di salire al ciel diventa degno*, "I will sing of the second realm where the human spirit is purged and becomes worthy to rise to heaven." Of course, this indicates that whereas the ethics of the first canticle, of the *Inferno*, was pure ethics, having almost nothing to do with religious ends, the ethics that has to be applied here, that limits, that delays the souls here in their progress toward redemption, is a Christian ethics. Occasionally Dante seems to forget this and stresses the pagan aspect of ethics even here, but generally it is Christian.

Ma quì la morta poesia risurga, "here let dead poetry rise again." "*O Sante Muse*," "'O Holy Muses, since I am yours'" — that's what you have here: "*poichè vostro sono*," "'since I am possessed'." It's the technical word, and has been at least since Plato, who was not quite the first to speak of poets as being possessed by the Muses. You don't reason poetry, you let a higher power get into you, and you faithfully let it operate in you like an automaton. Dante describes this process when finally, after having allegorized about the Muses, he comes to tear away the veil and replaces them by naming the power which has really operated all along, namely, the Holy Spirit. He is the one that possesses the poet's soul. But for the time being we can speak veiledly of the power of the Muses. "*O Sante Muse, poichè vostre sono.*" Notice the boldness of calling them *sante*. Of course the last time Dante asks for inspiration, in *Paradiso*, he no longer calls upon the Muses, no longer calls upon Apollo, but calls upon God Himself.

[E] quìCalliope alquanto surga, seguitando il mio canto con quel suono, di cui le Piche misere sentiro lo colpo tal che disperar perdono. "Let Calliope accompany me here with that music, whose power the magpies felt, such that it made them despair of pardon." Those beautiful girls, the Pierides, who challenged Calliope, were so badly defeated that they thought they could never ward off the punishment to be inflicted on them for their defeat, the punishment namely of being converted into magpies. To understand the relevancy of this comparison, think of a magpie and a blue-jay. That's what became of the sweet-voiced girls who tried to vie with the Muse of Song. The voice of the magpie can hardly disturb us today, with the harsh sounds being offered as music all around us. If you lived in Naples, constantly surrounded by sweet-singing voices,

you would be disturbed by the harsh sound. Sweet color — *dolce color d'oriental zaffiro* — this oriental is not an ornamental, not a poetic device; it's a technical term which has remained technical down to the nineteenth century. Jewelers still speak of the three orients: diamonds, sapphires and emeralds. "Sweet color of oriental sapphire," *che s'accoglieva nel sereno aspetto dell'aer puro infino al primo giro* "which was lathered in the serene countenance of the air which was pure as far as the first circle." That is, the entire sphere of air up to the first sky, the sky of the moon, was cloudless. There are no clouds, Dante will tell us eventually, down in the southern hemisphere. That sweet color of the air that goes up to the first circle *agli occhi miei ricominciò diletto*, "recreated joy to my eyes," brought joy again to my eyes, that were veiled in purple, so to speak; now joy begins, is resurrected again, and that joy is the oriental sapphire coloring the heavens.

Tosto ch'i uscì fuor dell'aura morta, "as soon as I had issued forth" — *aura* means really a breeze, so that there is here, in the phrase *aura morta* a sort of oxymoron — from the motionless breeze "that had filled with sadness my eyes and my chest," *ch'avea contristati gli occhi e il petto. lo bel pianeta che ad amar conforta faceva tutto rider l'oriente, velando i pesci ch'erano in sua scorta.* This beautiful dark blue, sapphire color, tells us we're still far away from the light of day. And now, *lo bel pianeta*, the beautiful planet that invites us to love, Venus, *faceva tutto rider l'oriente*, "spread a smile over the entire eastern zone." In other words, the brilliancy of Venus was such that the whole oriental zone was lit up with a smile so brilliant that the Fish that were in her retinue were veiled. "I turned to the right and tried to see the other pole," *l'altro polo*, that is, the south pole, *e vidi quattro stelle*, "and I saw four stars never seen by anyone except the primal people." The Garden of Eden was in the southern zone and, according to Dante, on this mountain of Purgatory.

Goder pareva il ciel di lor fiamelle, "the sky seemed to rejoice in their flames;" they are very beautiful, these stars; like little flames. That corresponds to the descriptions given of them by navigators. Of course Dante is more interested in the derived meaning than in the pictorial meaning; he wants to impress on us that from that brilliancy there emanates a power that showers upon mankind all the virtues; and virtuousness is the root of all joy, the only source of real joy.

O settentrional vedovo sito, "O widowed north," widowed because bereft of seeing them, "when I had moved myself," *com'io dal loro sguardo fui partito — loro sguardo* is objective genitive, that is, "when I had turned my glance away," *un poco me volgendo all'altro polo, la onde il Carro già era sparito*, "turning somewhat in the direction of the north pole, where the Wain had already disappeared" — it had not set, it had never risen for the people of that southern latitude — when I did that "I saw near me an elderly man, alone, worthy of such reverence," *degno di tanta riverenza, in vista, che più non dee a padre alcun figliuolo*, "worthy of so much reverence at the mere sight of him" — all you had to do is look at him to be filled with such reverence — "that no son owes as much to any father. Long was his beard white like the locks with which it was mingled flowing in a double mesh [*doppia lista*] to his chest." The rays of the four holy lights *fregiavan sì sua faccia di lume* "trailed his face so with light, that I could see him as if the sun were upon him." In other words, here is a pagan who has not seen God, the sun, but who has seen at their utmost power the four stars, the four virtues that lead to God.

Then, abruptly: "*Chi siete voi,*" "'Who are you'," "*che contro al cieco fiume,*" "'going against the blind river'," the blind river that flows down into the nether regions — blind because lifeless — "'who are you, who, running against the lifeless river, have escaped from the eternal prison'," *diss'ei movendo quell'oneste piume.* This is a very graphic touch; his face is so covered with hair that as he speaks you can't see his lips moving, only his hair; his hair stirs with speech, *movendo quell'oneste piume,* "stirring those honorable feathers."

Of course, *piume* doesn't mean feathers, it's a generic word that includes feathers, hair, plumes. With the word *onesto,* of course, Dante wants to remind you of that great moral construction, the *Honestum* — which does not mean honest and which was the creation of the Stoics. And of all the Stoics the one that loved the *Honestum* most was Cato. What was the *Honestum?* There are three motives for doing a thing. You do some things not for utility, but simply because you get pleasure doing them. Or else, you do a thing because it is useful. You don't enjoy it, but yon do it because you know something good will come out of it. Pleasure and utility are the first two. And finally you do a thing, not because it's pleasant or useful but because you *should* do it; it's you duty. If you're a Christian, you have to do it to conform to God's will. This last is the *Honestum.* In the old days, when Latin was still generally studied, this word *Honestum* was often put down as one of those to be explained by candidates for degrees.

19. DANTE'S TRANSFORMATION OF CATO; HUMILITY AS THE FUNDAMENTAL CHRISTIAN VIRTUE

Dante is now at the foot of the mountain of Purgatory which, as we explained, is at the *antipodes* of Jerusalem, of Calvary. It was the close of night, two hours before dawn, still dark except for the light that is shed down on the scene by one planet and four big stars, Venus and the stars of the southern cross, which Dante imagines to be those stars which, like Venus (encouraging us to love) and Mars (encouraging us to be brave), urge us in the direction of the four cardinal virtues. Dante is made to kneel; through the whole scene he remains in a kneeling position. It is the humble beginning, after which Virgil will let Dante go, so as to conquer salvation for himself — first by examining what happens in *Purgatory* and later by noting what the reward will be in *Paradise*.

In reading the *Purgatory* one has to become accustomed to the symbol or analogy of the sun, Of course, by Dante's time, it was a commonplace: it was already ancient when Plato used it. Analogously, as the world of matter is to the world of ideas, generally, so the physical sun is to the spiritual sun. For Plato it is the sovereign good, the symbol of the Idea of the good. Dante consistently, but not monotonously, elaborates the symbolism.

And if the sun has a moral significance symbolically, night too must have a significance. So he makes of the night a time when no intellectual comprehension, no moral progress can be made; all spiritual activity must cease at night because truth and what guides the way to truth has disappeared. It might be worthwhile for those interested in these matters to read what Dante has said about Cato in the *Convivio*, where he makes of him the representative of God — like God, and becoming God, as far as a Christian can. It's a notion that Dante must have gotten through contact with Cicero and Lucan, the attitude of the Stoics toward God. For them, a deification like that which Dante now effects for Cato, was very possible, because God, according to them, was a growing personality. Every progress made by a Stoic increases the divine stature of' Jupiter. In the old days, God was less than he is now. Jupiter owes to the wise man as much as the wise man owes to Jupiter. We have lost their sense of the progress of mankind, whereby man evolves into a deity as a result of this progressive deification. Nonetheless it is startling to find Cato here functioning in this capacity.

Virgil now reminds us: "'I have shown him [*la gente rea*], the guilty people . . . and now I intend to bring before his eyes those spirits that purify themselves under your [*balìa*]'." *Balìa* is a word that ought to be carefully interpreted, because it is perhaps the most forceful word we have in the Tuscan language to indicate complete political power: sovereignty in its executive capacity. It's the same word I suppose the philologists will tell us give us "bail" in English. The meaning has changed quite a bit in the interim. "'How I have led him here is a long story: from on high comes a power'" — *virtù*, virtue, in the writings of all these people, has the significance of power; always, in the ancient authors, it meant that — "'a power that helps me to guide him to see and to hear you'." That's quite a tribute. Dante's progress with help from above, from heaven, has been progress toward the understanding of Cato. "'Now may it please you to welcome him: he comes seeking liberty'," "*libertà va cercando, che é si cara.*"

This is perhaps the most famous line in Dante; and yet those who quote it do not do it justice because the thought that Dante had, and his contemporaries had when speaking of liberty is different from what those who have quoted the line in recent times had in mind. Dante's conception is different and much higher. "'He goes looking for liberty, which is so dear, so precious'." For some, the image may be spoiled by the connection which may be made with the soap-box orator and his usual bombast about liberty. The best way to get rid of that picture is to remind yourself that the Stoic, when he thinks of liberty, doesn't mean civil liberty or physical liberty but liberty that is self-imposed, which nothing can take away. You can be free, though in chains. It's a conception so powerful that when the Christians had to face the fact of slavery and wanted to reconcile Christian freedom with it, they could do nothing more than to borrow the words of the Stoics: "Of course, you want to do away with slavery; slavery is wrong. But what really counts is not slavery of the body, but slavery of the soul." So don't think that Dante is here just beating his breast in speaking of liberty: those men had risen to a very spiritual conception of it.

In this whole speech, there is a tendency to mold Cato on the poetry of Virgil. I don't know if it has been sufficiently noted. He goes on seeking liberty, which is so dear, "'as he knows who'" "*per lei vita*

rifiuta," "'as he knows who rejected life for its sake'."
"'You know it, for, in behalf of liberty, death was not
bitter to you, death was sweet to you since you faced it
for the sake of liberty'." Cato died in Utica (Africa), for
the liberty of Rome. "'In Utica where you left the
garment [your body] which will be so resplendent on
the great day'," *"la vesta che al gran dì sarà sì chiara."*
Dante wants to be sure you understand that Cato will
be among the blessed. When Cato gets his garment
again — when the flesh is resurrected — it will be
resplendent.

　　　This is quite different from the condition of the
bodies of the suicides in Hell. Dante forces you, his
poetry is so constructed, that he not only facilitates
such skipping back and forth but makes it inevitable.
"Non son gli editti eterni per noi guasti," "'Hell is Hell
still, the laws of Hell are not broken';" they are what
they have always been. "'This man is not yet dead',"
"questi vive, e Minos me non lega." Virgil is in the first
circle and therefore not subject to the laws of Minos —
not the law-giver, but the executor of the law, the judge
— "'Minos does not bind me'." Minos meets the sinners, as judge, on the ledge that divides the first circle
from the second. The spirits in Limbo are not under
Minos' sway.

　　　"'I come from the circle where the chaste eyes of
your Marcia [Cato's wife] who as one may plainly see'"
— here comes again a little bit of flattery which will be
rebuked by Cato — *"in vista ancor ti prega,"* "'who still
yearns for you, O sacred heart'," *santo petto*. The phrase
is almost sacrilegious, but of course the apparent
impiousness of it is removed when you remember the
Latin from which it is translated: it's the very pagan
sacrum poetus Catonis of Lucan, so that it's not quite as

sacrilegious as one might think. "*'Ancor ti prega o santo petto, che per tua la tegni'.*" "'She still wants you to consider her your own'." She had been divorced, repudiated by Cato, and later in her life had been reunited with him. Dante, in the *Convivio*, elaborates these biographical details as a wonderful allegory. "'She begs you that you hold her for your own. In the name of her love therefore'," "*a noi ti prega,*" "'hearken to our request. Permit us to go through your seven kingdoms. I shall bring back to her'," for Virgil has to go back, "*grazie riporterò di te a lei, se d'esser mentovato laggiù degni.*"

The compliment is very pretty, quite in the manner of the Provençal poets. But Cato will reprove him for it. "'I will say pleasant things about you to her, if you deem it worthy to be mentioned down there'." That's what Virgil says. And Cato answers: "*Marzia piacque tanto agli occhi miei*" — that's pretty hard to translate — "'was so pleasing to my eyes'."... Of course *piacque*, that famous *piacere*, both in the language of the poets and the language of the philosophers, means sometimes, but rarely, *placentia* but more commonly *complacentia* — not *attraction* (the *effect* is attraction), but something much richer, not *affinity* either. This reciprocal attraction in Dante, as in the Provençal poets, as in Plato and St. Thomas, is not what the Romantics have made of it. It's a laborious process. In other words: here is a woman who is beautiful (this is Plato), here is this beautiful person who, because of her beauty, *piace*. That beautiful thing does not just send out its power; that's not enough. It's up to the other person to respond, to see that reciprocity takes place. The arrow is not in one direction but in both. How is it done? Plato says θεράπεία which translated literally into Italian gives you *servente* — the service of love. That word *servente* has lived through the ages. Unfortunately in our modern Italian it has been killed by its application to one kind of love. Think of the *cavalier servente* of the eighteenth century. It's interesting, this evolution of θεράπεία from Plato to Goldoni. It began as the act of the lover that forces requital; but in the eighteenth century it became purely ridiculous. Mind you, the *cavalier servente* is not a panderer. It's a respectable enough role. It was accepted that a woman should have three persons devoted to her: one is the husband, the second is the *bien aimee*, and the third is the *cavalier servente*. He opens the umbrella, he holds the door, even for the lover when he calls, and stays outside to keep watch to see that nothing happens to disturb the lovers. That's the *cavalier servente.*

   "*Marzia piacque tanto agli occhi miei, mentre ch'io fui di là,*" *diss'egli allora,* "*che quante grazie volse da me fei.*" Dante is not a bit careful to avoid sacred words like *grazia* in connection with this worldly pagan situation. Of course, Dante is very — shall we say — unorthodox? Every time he uses the word *grazia*, pious persons tremble. "'All the graces she wanted she received from me. But now that she lives beyond the evil river, now she can't move me any more, because of that law that was made when I issued forth from there'" — that is, when Cato got out of Hell with the Patriarchs. For Dante there is not one sacred people before Christ, but two. He treats the Romans just as he treats the Hebrews — the sacred books and the sacred law: a perfect parallelism. If you find him quoting the Psalms, there's always something from a Roman author also. No one has studied the matter thoroughly in Dante; but it would be easy to do, to search out the parallels between the two chosen people. Of course, you can see why he does it: his political preoccupation is clear enough.

But, "*se donna del ciel ti move*," if not my wife, but *donna in ciel* moves and guides you, as you say, "*non c'è mestier lusinghe*," there is no need of *lusinghe*, flattery. This indicates that he is aware that Virgil is flattering him. Flattery is not necessary; to ask me in her name is enough. "*Va dunque, e fà che tu costui ricinghe d'un giunco schietto*," "'go'," he says, to Virgil, "'and see that you bind this man with a smooth weed or rush and that you wash his face so that every trace of filth is removed'," "*sì che ogni sucidume quindi stinghe*," for he would be totally unfit, with eyes still confused by some mist, to go before the grand minister — the prime minister — of the host of Paradise. That is, from now on your eyes must be clear to receive the splendor that comes to you from on high, from the host of heaven. "*Questa isoletta*," notice how the tone changes, almost idyllic, "*questa isoletta intorno ad imo ad imo*," "'this little island, all around, down at the very bottom'.". . . They are at the bottom, but not quite at sea-level. They have come out through a hole on the side of the mountain, on a little plateau that slopes down to sea-level. Above this plateau is the mountain proper. This *isoletta* down there, where the waves beat on the shore, "*porta de' giunchi sopra il molle limo*," "'bears reeds on its soft mud'." Mud is rather a bad word here. *Limo* isn't mud. *Limo* is vegetation that has been putrified and sinks. This is a picture that suits much more the conditions of a lake, than the sea shore. It's hard to find limo on the sea-shore. Anyone who has traveled to the lakes of Europe must have seen these lake shores, the slopes of which bear rushes like the ones Dante has in mind. No other plant — here the allegory becomes very transpar-

ent — no other plant, that puts forth leaves or forms a
trunk, could exist there, because, *"però che alle percosse
non seconda,"* because the blasts from the wind are so
strong that you can't hope to survive them, to beat
them by resisting, but only by yielding to them. You see
how suggestive morally the picture is. *"Poscia non sia di
quà vostra reddita,"* "'then don't come back here'," *"lo
sol"* — and here comes the first indication of the guidance of the physical sun, indicating that God Himself
is the guide — *"lo sol vi mostrerà, che surge omai."*

You notice how time has passed. The sun will
show you, for it is about to rise, how to *"prender lo
monte,"* "'how to climb the hill'," *"a più lieve salita,"*
where the grade is least steep, where the ascent is
easiest. Having said this, Cato disappears. All through
this Dante has been kneeling. I wonder why no painter
has ever thought of representing this scene? It's magnificent. I suppose it's a picture to be realized more
perfectly with the imagination than with the brush. "I
stood up without speaking, and drew back toward my
master, my guide, and fixed my eyes on his countenance." Notice how Dante is very much moved by the
events; that's what these words are intended to indicate. He began: "'My son'," *"figliuol, segui i miei passi,"*
"'follow my footsteps: let us turn back!'" Before they
can begin to climb they have to do some descending,
"for it is here that the plateau slopes down to its lowest
level," that is, to sea-level.

It's not quite sunrise. The sun is winning its way
upon the fleeing breeze of the advancing dawn. In
other words, just before sunrise — and this is constant
whenever there is warm air settling in — you have a
breeze on the seashore; that is a phenomenon that
occurs only on the shore. If you go ten miles inland, it

ceases, and if you go ten miles out, it ceases. You have this breeze; then, all of a sudden, when the sun comes up and begins to heat the atmosphere, it dies. This is what you have to keep in mind when you read these lines: the breeze was dying. You don't feel it any longer on the shore, but you can still see it as it proceeds outward: you see it in the ripples of the water moving away from the place where Dante is. *L'alba*, the sunrise, was overcoming the moving breeze, receding in front of it, *sì che di lontano conobbi* — Dante now with the increase of light is able to see something in the distance for the first time — *di lontano conobbi il tremolar della marina*, he was able to see something of the trembling of the sea. It's pretty flat said that way. But in Italian it's really beautiful. "We were going through the solitary plain," this descending plateau — and now comes the expression of a sentiment that is quite dear to Dante: the sorrow experienced by one who has lost his way. It comes out most movingly as the experience of the pilgrim, who, after he has started to go back home, loses his way, and regrets so losing his way that, all the time he is lost, instead of advancing, he wears himself out with sorrow, until he gets back on the right way again.

"We went along the solitary land, like those returning to a lost path who seem to move in vain till they have found that lost path. When we came where the dew fights hardest against the sun," *la ruggiada pugna il sole* — not at this particular moment but where the dew remains for a long time. Why? Because it is in a place which is shadowed. The dew remains dew; it is not dissipated by the sun's rays because it is in a shaded place. In other words, there's plenty of dew here. The rising sun, which usually dispels the dew, does not do

so there. "My master put his hands outspread upon the tender grass," *soavamente... ond'io che fui accorto di su' arte, porsi ver lui le guance lagrimose.*
     Try to visualize the scene. Virgil puts out his hands on the dew, spreads them and presses them. Dante seeing him do that stretches his neck, brings his head close, to make it easier for Virgil to wash away the stains of pity and sorrow that had been imprinted in him by his experiences in Hell. You can't proceed up the mountain of Purgatory if you still have commiseration and pity for the damned sinners of Hell: *ivi mi fece tutto discoperto quel color che l'inferno mi nascose.* "And so he uncovered entirely, brought out to light again, that color which Hell had closed over." *Venimmo poi in sul lito diserto,* "and then we came upon the deserted shore." *Lito* here, *lido,* does not have its technical meaning but simply means, as in classical Latin, the seashore, *che mai non vide navicar sue acque,* which never saw a man navigate over its waters that could afterward experience the trip home. No one that comes here, or rather, of all that come here, no one ever returns home; only the ghosts of those who have died and are to go through purification come here. "There he bound my head," *quivi mi cinse,* "as he had been directed by the other [Cato]. *O maraviglia!* The wonder of it was that *qual egli scelse l'umile pianta, cotal si rinacque subitamente la onde la svelse,* "as soon as he plucked the humble [lowly] plant immediately another rose in place of the one plucked."
     Here the symbolism is, again, very light. All this is a chant; we can call it a magnificent hymn to humility, because it's sung by the man who was the proudest of men. As we've already seen, Dante now becomes more and more Augustinian as he goes along in this.

Humility, as we already explained, is the antithesis of human pride. Human pride consists in acting as if man is the artifex, the artisan of his fortune. He has free will; he has genius, he can make all kinds of things; he has the power to fight wars, to shape the course of history — none of which things, St. Augustine reminds us, is true. Mankind has power, but it is power which is twisted around to bring about the will of the real Author of things, which is often the very opposite of what we generally want. So here we have a dramatic contrast along those lines in the figure of the proud man contrasted with that of the humbled one — but it's the humility of one who does things with his mind fixed on God.

This humility consists in knowing that we can't do anything by ourselves; the confession that we don't know where we are going, that the goal we are seeking may not be, is not, the one toward which God is directing us. In this kind of humility, the fundamental attitude is not merely to say, I am a humble man, but to say, I am an insignificant man — to say it and mean it. This is the first indication of the Augustinian doctrine Dante introduces here and which he will develop in the *Purgatorio* and complete in *Paradiso*, where he will give it its full spiritual amplitude. The power, the wealth, the greatness that men strive for — all that is such that the more you have, the less the other fellow has. My riches represent the impoverishment of someone else.

Of course someone will tell me that Bacon has done away with this; and yet the doctrine of St, Augustine remains as true as ever, because, it's not the attainment of material things as such, but in the proportion of them relative to others that satisfaction of material desires is sought. No matter how much you increase the total, no matter how much you're able to multiply it at any moment, it remains a finite amount: there is only so much; and if some have more, others have less. So we must have the kind of wealth that is such that as the number of people who share in it increases, the satisfaction of each increases. These are, of course, the spiritual goods. And we will see later how perfectly Dante develops this line of thought, how the virtue or means which is the *sine qua non* for developing the taste for the kind of wealth which is such that the share of each increases as the number of the partakers increase is *humility*. Humility is the basis for the building up of this kind of spiritual economy.

20. THE ANGEL OF PURGATORY; DANTE'S MEETING WITH CASELLA

Dante begins the second canto of *Purgatorio* with the usual astronomical — what shall we call it — adventure? No matter what he writes, he seems to have a nostalgia either for what goes on in the heavens, for the phenomena of the stars, or for the phenomena here below that correspond to the astronomical phenomena: shadows, reflections, sunlight and moonlight, the contours of mountains, and so on. And it's not just pure fancy or fancy for a subject of remote interest, because he himself tells us in another place, in speaking of the avaricious, how those people lose their souls trying to get hold of earth, or the things extracted from earth; looking for metals with their eyes always earthbound. And he asks, how could they lose themselves thus, when all they had to do was to lift up their heads, raise their eyes and they would have seen things infinitely more precious than all the metals in the world.

It's a thought that came down from antiquity. You find it also in Kant's beautiful book, *Critique of Pure Reason* in spite of the complicated style. It's something that stays with you once you've read it. If you have a moral conscience already, it will deepen it for you; if you haven't, it may help to get one started in you. Two things, he says, have the power to fully excite the soul of man; one is the spectacle of the celestial bodies, the stars above you, and the other, contemplation of human freedom within you.

But even if Kant had not lived to say it, Dante long before had spoken eloquently of these two great subjects, the movement of the stars above and the spectacle of the freedom of man, of the freedom within us. There's a bit of pedantry here, and also something that most people feel, whether they're cultivated or not, and that's a certain nostalgia when you try to find your way through earthly phenomena by looking above at the heavenly movements. All one has to do is read any Italian poet, especially in the eighteenth century, to see how consistently they love to follow the celestial movements, reflected in commonplace occurrences here below. (There's one very pretty poem about an Alpine village, the aspect of which, its colors and shadows, are seen to reflect the state of the heavens.)

Dante is not just trying to show off his knowledge when he brings before you these astronomical pictures, as at the beginning of the second canto — which is rather gay, with good humor, joy even, for those who have to be purged. "The sun had already reached the horizon," that is, the eastern boundary of our hemisphere; he always gives us the astronomical horizon, not that horizon that marks a circle that is only twenty or thirty miles wide — not the horizon you see from the top of the Empire State Building — but the great circle that divides the celestial sphere into two parts, two hemispheres. There is in Dante also the special horizon from the Straits of Gibraltar to the mouth of the Ganges, and which, therefore, should measure 180 degrees from Gibraltar to Calcutta. Of course, in reality it's not so; his contemporaries know it, but Dante had to give spiritual significance to his cosmology, and so he alters the facts accordingly. In this view of spiritual cosmology, this hemisphere has as its middle point the city of Jerusalem. In other words, there are 180 degrees from Gibraltar to the Ganges, and 90 degrees from Gibraltar to the mountain of Calvary. At the *antipodes* of this mountain of Calvary is the mountain of Purgatory.

What are the *antipodes*? Two places are said to be *anti*: when their latitude is the same — in one case north, in the other case south — and their longitudes are 180 degrees apart. In other words, if you are in this hemisphere, and you go down to a place that is 42 degrees south and your place is 42 degrees north, you would not be at the *antipodes*; you have to go all the way around. The two places have to be the end points, in other words, of a diameter of the terrestrial sphere. So we are told at this point that the sun has reached the eastern horizon. It's no longer dawn, it's sunrise. In the previous canto the sun was still two hours below the horizon, so that you couldn't see it. Now the sun is on the horizon, so it's sunrise on the mountain of Purgatory. Keep in mind: Dante called night not a period of time but a point; a point diametrically opposite to the center of the sun, so that when the sun is rising on the mountain of Purgatory, the night which circles opposite to it, was coming out of the Ganges — which is the *antipodes* as we said, of Gibraltar: *e la notte che opposita a lui cerchia, uscia di Gange fuor con le bilance.* The sun was in Aries, and night which is opposite to it would be in the constellation opposite to that one, which is the Scales, *le bilance.* After Aries you have Taurus, Gemini, Cancer, Leo, Virgo and then Libra: that's half way around, opposite Aries. "Night was coming forth from the Ganges with the Scales, which fall out of its hand" when that month is over, or he says, instead, "when it passes over." Until now the sun has been in the south, until it attains its position in Aries; now the position is reversed — it is the point where the sun moves north.

That's what was happening all over the world: in six lines Dante encompasses the Ganges, Gibraltar, Jerusalem, and Purgatory. And now he leaves the astronomical and comes to a local description: "so that the white and rosy cheeks of Aurora through aging were becoming orange" — in other words, as the sun rose, the colors changed rapidly on the horizon. Dante has given us an accurate description of that change to orange — *rance*. "We were still on the seashore, like people with nothing else on their mind but the way that lies before them, people who, while not moving with their bodies are already running with their souls." Quite a bit of pathos there. Anyone who has ever experienced such things knows what he means. Then he sees a light, and a dazzling white something around this light. It's the boat that brings the souls to Purgatory from the mouth of the Tiber, the souls that are not damned. The allegory is quite simple. The grace of God saves these people and sets them on their way. God saves, *but* — Dante is here not in any Pelagian mood — *but* it's got to be done within the limits of the Catholic Church. The saving grace has got to come through the agency of the Bishop of Rome. So Dante gives us here this rather interesting description: "Lo! as, near the time of dawn, the planet Mars [which is pretty ruddy at all times] appears particularly ruddy through the thick vapors" — Of course this part is low down, on the sea, so Dante compares it to a star that's on the horizon. And the star that he picks out is Mars because it's always ruddy anywhere in the heavens; its pretty fantastic, but particularly at dawn; and especially in climatic conditions like those in the Mediterranean at sunrise, or sundown, when it's very brilliant, deep colored and even ominous. One can understand why it was picked out by the ancients as the star of war. There is nothing of that in Dante, however. Here you have only what it looks like through thick vapors when you see it at dawn on the horizon, *per li grossi vapor Marte rosseggia*. Why are there more vapors when you see it on the horizon than when you see it overhead? Since the strata of vapor are concentric with the earth, the passage through the accumulation of vapors from here to the horizon is longer than the passage through overhead. That's clear, *cotal m'apparve*, "just as Mars appears on the horizon, so it appeared to me — still now as I am writing I have it before my eyes — a light coming so quickly over the sea, that no flight can compare with its motion. And when I had turned my eyes away to question my guide, I saw it more resplendent and becoming larger." *Poi d'ogni lato ad esso m'apparìo, un non sapeva che bianco*, "on either side of this appeared to me I know not what whiteness, and under it little by little another whiteness came out." *Lo mio maestro ancor non fece motto*, "my master still said not a word," nor did Dante say a word until the first white things showed themselves to be wings. Then he put an end to his silence about the pilot, *galeotto*, a word that impresses upon you the fact that words have a history, they change in meaning. The word *galeotto* has come to mean someone in jail — jailbird or jail-keeper; it's original meaning is gone. It doesn't mean panderer, either, as in the Francesca episode. But what has not gone is the meaning of jailer, which derives from the fact that galley oarsmen were often slaves in chains. But of course there's none of that in Dante. To grasp Dante's picture, we have to make an effort to destroy that other meaning, and give to the word *galeotto* the old sense of helmsman, pilot.

"My master cried": "*Fa, fa che le ginocchia cali: ecco l'angel di Dio.*" Notice how excited and jerky Virgil is; he too is aroused by this approaching sight. Here is the angel of God, "*piega le mani,*" "'fold your hands',", clasp your hands, "'from now on you will see such'" *ufficiali.* Functionaries? Ministers? "*Vedi che sdegna gli argomenti umani.*" "'See how he disdains human instruments, so that he relies not on oars nor on sails other than his own wings'," "*tra liti si lontani,*" "'coming across the expanse of the ocean'," that is, coming from the mouth of the Tiber to a shore so far removed. See, "*vedi come l'ha dritte verso il cielo,*" "'notice how straight they [the wings] point heavenward, beating the air with those eternal feathers'," *penne,* plumes, "'which do not change as mortal feathers do'." Then, they near that divine bird, *uccello.* In Italian *uccello* can suggest something exalted, dignified; but in English it seems to be just the opposite. So much so, that to avoid sounding ridiculous you often have to search out a synonym of some sort.

The closer the *uccello* came, the more resplendent it appeared, so that the eye could not endure it, *per chè l'occhio da presso nol sostenne.* When it got to be nearby, the eyes could no longer endure its splendor. "Not being able to look, I lowered my gaze. And he came to the shore with a boat so quick and light," *un vasello snelletto e leggiero tanto* — I suppose we'd better stick to the old meaning of the word *snello.* The word came to mean slender, but it went through a series of phases to get there. It had to come from the German, but the question is, when did the meaning change? You still hear *schnell,* meaning *quick, hurry up,* in some parts of Italy. Here it is translated as *swift.* Of course, slender won't hurt the picture very much: *un vasello snelletto e leggiero, tanto che l'acqua nulla ne inghiottiva.* It had no draft; in other words, its lead was such that it skimmed over the surface, naturally, there being no heavy bodies in it. At the stern stood erect the celestial pilot — *nocchiero* of course is a more satisfactory word than *galeotto* — *tal che parea beato per iscritto,* "such that he seemed a written image," a graven image of beatitude, *e più di cento spirti entro sediero,* "and more than a hundred spirits sat within."

You have to get accustomed to the incongruities of these spirits that occupy no space and are not material or substantial in any physical sense — incongruities that consist in making them move around in space and talk and even touch. They touch and can be touched in Hell, as you remember. Here, in Purgatory, Dante adopts a very conventional way of dealing with them. These spirits, as far as Purgatory is concerned, are totally devoid of matter, but they consist of a sort of visible film; so that if you try to touch them, you touch nothing. Of course when you come to *Paradiso,* even the film disappears, and there is only light, the soul becomes a light; but, by flashes, it communicates in such a way that you can comprehend its acts as if it had a body.

"*In exitu Israel de Egitto,*" *cantavan tutti insieme ad una voce.* As they landed, they sang this Psalm, all of them in unison. Why this Psalm? Dante is very fond of it; he explains its meaning more than once, and, of course, explains the allegory. It's one that's very familiar. It was familiar to the ordinary people and not confined to those who learn from books. Even monks who were barely literate, not schooled in theology, knew that it meant the liberation of the flesh from the corruption of the body. Egypt — not only here, but again and again in the Old Testament — Egypt was taken to mean corruption. Israel was the soul. Just as the Israelites succeeded in getting out of Egypt, so the souls of all men are saved by getting out of the flesh.

It's very effective, this psalm. You hear it often at funerals, at solemn celebrations of the dead; and it serves to relieve those occasions of great sadness, it takes away a great deal of the pain. That, I suppose is one of the great ends served by the Catholic ceremonial — to take the sting out of death. Here, they sang in unison as much of that Psalm as is thereafter written. *Poi fece il segno lor di santa croce,* "then he [the angel] made the sign of the cross," *ond' ei si gittar tutti in su la piaggia, ed ei sen gì come venne, veloce.* Notice how quick the action becomes. First the singing of *In Exitu Israel de Aegypto,* then the sign of the cross, the unloading of the passengers, and the quick departure of the celestial boatman: *ed ei sen gì, come venne, veloce,* "and he left as quickly as he had come." *La turba che rimase lì, selvaggia parea del loco,* "the crowd that remained there seemed" *selvaggia. Selvaggia* is very common in all the Latin languages — meaning, not savage but unfamiliar with, shy, reluctant. What does *sauvage* mean in French? When a girl is said to be *sauvage,* she doesn't scratch your eyes out, she's shy, timid, backward — the word is not connected with the other sense except etymologically. The translation here has "strange," but we should find a better word than that — *rimirando intorno come colui che nuove cose assaggia,* "looking around as one who is assaying [taking in] things before unseen."

That word *nuove* of course has been worn down

almost to nothing; but Dante manages to make it appear as a shiny new coin. With his use of it in the *Vita Nuova*, with his use of it to mean good as opposed to *vecchio, antico* in the sense of sinful, so that the two are opposed as virtue and vice; with all those devices, with all these uses, Dante made of the word *nuovo* something other than the insignificant word it had been and has come to be since. *La turba che rimase lì, selvaggia parea del loco, rimirando intorno come colui che nuove cose assaggia. Da tutte parti saettava il giorno lo sol.* I wonder if you can feel all through this the change of music. Usually, of course, it's a passage from minor to major. This last passage I just read was in the minor but now it's definitely very much in the major. *Da tutte parti saettava il giorno, lo sol.* Now the sun is free of the horizon. It's high up, it shoots its rays in all directions. *Da tutte parti saettava il giorno.* "The sun was hurling daylight, in all directions," *ch'avea con le saette conte di mezza il ciel cacciato il Capricorno.* "The sun had, with its arrows driven Capricorn away from its place in the middle of the sky." Capricorn of course was three constellations away; so that when the sun rose, Capricorn was at the zenith, and had been visible at the zenith until then, *quando la nuova gente alzò la fronte ver noi.*

The word *nuova*, as used here, carries a very common meaning in Latin, especially in the Latin of the Holy Scriptures. In St. Paul you have *nuovo* in the sense of good, in the sense of purified. Not just a change, a new look; it's no doubt a change, but a change for the better. So that, just as the word *vetus* has the contour of evil, *novus* has the contour of good. It was the popular meaning. There is nothing abstruse about it. These new people ask, *"se voi sapete,"* "'if you know it'" — this is a little bit of humor, two blind people trying to get help from one another — "*se voi sapete, mostratene la via di gire al monte,*" a line that has become proverbial in Italian, "'if you know it, show us the way to the mountain'." Virgil answers: "'Perhaps you think we are familiar with this place, but we're strangers here, like you. We arrived here just before you came, from another way, which was so rough that climbing will seem pleasant, even though it will be very steep'." Of course, the souls wouldn't know from Dante's appearance that he is not dead, because they too have the contour of the body; but they see that Dante's throat gurgles, which is something that they do not do. They have bodies but no breath. "The souls who had become aware of my state, that I still lived, by the way I breathed, became pale in wonderment."

To understand what follows you have to conjure the vision of what happens when someone comes from Jerusalem, where he has gone on a pilgrimage; as proof of his having been there, he brings back a spray of olives. And when someone appeared with a spray of olives, everyone in the town would run to that person and hear the news. It's similar to what happened here. These souls find that Dante is still alive, so they rush to him, to hear what has happened, as when people crowd around a messenger bearing the olive, for news of Jerusalem. That sense of the presence of Jerusalem and of the pilgrim from Jerusalem, which was such a familiar thought in the twelfth and the thirteenth centuries, and which continued a while longer, is completely dead now. People don't go on pilgrimages any more; today, of course, there are obstacles, but even when it was easy to go — in the recent past — people didn't go. They have lost the desire, just as they have lost that terrible longing for the Veronica, for the image of our Lord. People used to travel long ways to go to Rome; many died on the way, starved, to see how our Savior's features were formed. Dante's age was a time when these things were familiar.

In this scene, *di calcar nessun si mostra schivo*, no one seems to be a bit hesitant to press forward, *così al viso mio s'affissar quelle anime fortunate tutte quante*, "so all those fortunate souls gazed fixedly on my countenance." Of course, St. Augustine would scold Dante for using the word fortunate here. They don't get here by fortune, but by good deeds and providence. All these lucky souls gazed at me because I was alive, *quasi obbliando d'ire a farsi belle*, almost forgetting to go on to *farsi belle* — purposely used here, for the sense is playful in many respects; we still say something like that today, "doll yourself up," that's what it means. Only here it applies not to the body but to the soul. "Almost forgetting to make themselves beautiful."

Now comes the well known encounter with Casella, a great musician and composer, a friend of Dante. He had set to music, apparently, some of Dante's songs, and particularly one that Dante asks him to sing here. We have no idea of the real lyrical quality of these songs because we read them, and they weren't meant to be read but sung. Of course they are beautiful in themselves as poetry but it was poetry organized into the charm of music: "I saw one coming," *io vidi una di lor trarsi avante*, "I saw one of them coming forward to embrace me with such great affection in his countenance that I was moved to do likewise." That sentence is one of the reminders of Dante's theory of how love, affection, is communicated. "*O ombre vane*," "'O unsubstantial shadows'," unsubstantial in everything except their appearance. To the eye, they're real; to the other senses, they're not. "Three times back of it I clasped my hands, and as many times I ended up clasping my own chest." *Di maraviglia, credo, mi dipinse.* The expression here is designedly forced: "I was painted all over with astonishment," *per che l'ombra sorrise e si ritrasse*, "wherefore the shadow smiled and drew back," *ed io, seguendo lei, oltre mi pinsi*, "and I following it, moved a bit further." *Soavemente disse ch'io posasse.* Here we have to be careful to give the word *soavemente* the right meaning. Dante so far has not recognized Casella: he embraces him, because the affection openly displayed by this soul had so moved him that he had to do likewise. "But now when he told me so sweetly that I should rest, I knew who he was," *allor conobbi chi era e'l pregai che per parlarmi un poco s'arrestasse*, "then I knew who he was and prayed that he might linger a while to talk to me."

He answered: "*Così com'io t'amai nel mortal corpo, cosi t'amo sciolta*," "'just as I loved you when in my perishable body so do I love you now, when [my soul is] freed from it'," "*però m'arresto*," "'that's why I stop; but you, why are you going through here? You're not dead'."... "*Casella mio.*"... This is a very beautiful line, this and the one that follows. Preachers often use it, for it is very appropriate. "*Casella mio, per tornare altra volta là dove son, fo io questo viaggio.*" "'I take this trip now to be sure I'll take it again'." He will take it again, when he dies. If he doesn't take this trip now, he may have to take the other trip, in the other direction, "*ma a te com'è tanta ora tolta?*" Casella had been dead some time, so Dante says, why have you been made to wait so long? "And he to me:" "*Nessun m'è fatto oltraggio*," "'no injury is done to me, when He Who takes up when and whom He pleases, more than once [*piu volte*] has denied to ferry me to this place'." That is, the embodiment of divine justice cannot be contrary to justice, because His will is made out of the will of Justice. "*Veramente da tre mesi egli ha tolto chi ha voluto entrar con tutta pace*," "'however, in the last three months, without objecting at all, he has taken on everybody and everyone who wanted to come'." It was then the 25th of March; the Jubilee of Boniface had been going on from the 25th of December, and in the last three months the angel has taken up everyone who wanted to come.

Dante is here in a very Catholic mood. "*Ond'io che era ora alla marina volto, dove l'acqua di Tevere s'insala, benignamente fui da lui ricolto*." "'And so, I who was there at the mouth of the Tiber, was kindly taken on by him, who has now turned his wing again there'," "*però che sempre quivi si raccoglie qual verso d'Acheronte non si cala*," because everything that doesn't flow down to Acheron is gathered at the mouth of the Tiber. In other words, everyone who is not destined for damnation has to go through Rome, not the city of Rome, but Rome as the symbol of the Roman Catholic faith.

And now Dante asks Casella to sing. Music, he tells us here, takes you away from whatever pains or sorrows you have in this world.

21. THE MEETING WITH MANFRED

The second canto is a very lovely farewell to the world. Here is the last pleasure, the last mundane pleasure that these souls will partake of. From now on, there's nothing but punishment, suffering and penitence in order for them to reach a higher, an infinitely higher degree of happiness, which will come when they finally enter Paradise. So that Purgatory is enclosed, encased between the last lure of the world and the lure of the summons of Paradise. And the honor of representing the world in this highest ultimate degree of allurement falls not to painting, not to poetry, but to music. This isn't the only time that Dante speaks this way of music, in the old Platonic and neo-Platonic tradition, placing music on such a high level. This exaltation of the supreme beauty of music, whether Dante was aware of it or not, is distinctly neo-Platonic. The power of music is a power that acts on the senses, but because of its infinite purity it transforms the materiality of the senses and inwardly integrates the soul. Dante writes elsewhere of music, *che l'anima integra*.

This tribute to song begins with the line: "'If the law of the new land does not strip you of the memory or the faculty that you have for song, and the singing of love'" — Nearly all these *canzoni*, or nearly all, the great majority of them, are songs in one way or another connected with love. *Donne ch'avete intelletto d'amore*, is the one that begins the new poetry: "Women, who have intellect of love . . . ." Dante seems to look back to that first *canzone*, which is the first of the *Vita Nuova*, with a great deal of admiration. Of course we don't know exactly what he saw in it, but surely with the phrase *intelletto d'amore* he means to have you understand that he is dealing with a new kind of love. It is love that comes not through the desire of the sense but through the desire of the mind. *Intelletto d'amore*, in other words, is contrasted with *senso d'amore*. In the first *canzone* of the *Convivio*, the song *Voi, ch'intendendo il terzo ciel movete*, addressed to the movers of the sky of Venus, which is the planet that induces love, you have a similar notion; they move it, he says, *intendendo. Amor che nella mente mi ragione*, that's the next *canzone* — "love that comes to reason within me." Again, *nella mente* — not in the senses, but in the mind. After the initial period, love is something that has to do with an activity of the spirit that leads the lover and the beloved beyond the *mundus sensibilis*, the world of sense, to the *mundus intelligibilis*, the world of ideas, where love, as Plato says, is aroused first by physical beauty, here seen (though it does not belong to the travesty of reality) to lead us to its home, to the place from which it has come, the realm of ideas.

In connection with beauty, we might hint at the question of the priority of music over poetry. There is much to be said for poetry, and Plotinus and others have; but for beauty of form, music is surpassed by no other art. There is the question also of the supremacy of one sense over the others. That sense, in Plato, in Plotinus, in St. Thomas and in Dante is not the ears — not hearing — it's not touch, but sight, the sense of the eyes. It's the sense that sees and therefore understands; it's the closest to the mind. So this *amoroso canto* — Dante, isn't speaking of a particular song but of the general quality of love-singing — this *amoroso canto*, coming from the voice of Casella, "*che mi solea quietar tutte mie voglie*," "'which was wont to soothe all my longings'," "*di ciò ti piaccia consolare alqanto l'anima mia*," "'may it please you to console me somewhat with this music'," "'console my soul'," "*che, con la mia persona venendo qui, è affannata tanto*," "'that has been fatigued, together with the body it carries, coming up here from the middle of the earth'."

And then Casella begins to sing that *canzone* which was discussed and interpreted in the third tractate of the *Convivio*: "*Amore che nella mente mi ragiona*," "'love that discourses within me, in my mind,' he so sweetly began that the sweetness of it still, now," after all that I have seen and heard, after all of the experiences I have had in Hell, Purgatory and Paradise, "'resounds within me'." *Lo mio maestro ed io e quella gente ch'eran con lui parevan sì contenti, come a nessun toccasse altro la mente.* "My master and I and all those people that were here with him seemed to enjoy this music as though they had no other care," as if they were not a bit concerned about anything else, as if their only task were this. Their true care, their only real source of satisfaction should have been something else — purification. Instead, they were content standing there, listening, as if nothing else touched their mind. *Noi eravam tutti fissi ed attenti alle sue note,* "We were all fixed, intent on listening" to the music of Casella when suddenly, the *veglio onesto* — again it's very hard to translate *onesto*, the *honestum* — righteous perhaps, if the word had not been so abused — shouts "*Che è ciò, spiriti lenti?*" "'What does this mean, sluggish souls. What negligence is this?'" "*Correte al monte*," "'run to the mountain to cast off that crust, that [*scoglio*] that makes it impossible for you to see God'."

The reference here is to the belief, the old doctrine that proper understanding is conditioned by moral living, by just and pure living. Plato has it; Cicero makes a great deal of it; St. Augustine too at one time said that you can learn nothing until your mind is cleansed of all filth and made morally pure. But then he retracted it and said something like what Dante here says: you can learn mathematics and other subjects like that fairly well without a purified soul; but you cannot approach the highest knowledge without moral purity. In other words, ethical life becomes an element in speculation only at the high source.

At this point, as very often in Dante, the canto closes with a humorous touch; sometimes, in the *Inferno*, it is a sarcastic touch, but not here. The touch of humor in this instance is the description of the rapid flight of these souls, their rush to scatter. As we noted earlier, according to Cicero the man who runs makes himself ludicrous except if he has to run to pursue the enemy in battle. In every case, running or moving rapidly robs the mover of dignity. Again and again, you find the ancients stressing that running makes a man ludicrous. So now, after the scene of the joy to be found in music, you have this laughable scene, where the souls run for their lives at the reproof of Cato. They are compared to pigeons who spend their time strutting and showing off until their hunger is aroused; then their only concern is to eat, or until something else comes to take the place of hunger, namely fear. The image dramatizes the reaction of these souls at the approach of Cato.

As when, *cogliendo*, "picking up," culling? gathering? wheat or straw, pigeons gather together to eat in quiet, without showing their wonted pride" — pride isn't the word, boastful isn't right, either; they're strutting, showing off. What do you say to describe a man or woman that walks into a room as if to say, "look at me, how beautiful I am." Perhaps conceit is the better word. *Senza mostrar l'usato orgoglio;* they forget all about parading their pride — a very neat touch — and *se cosa appare ond'elli abbian paura, subitamente lascino star l'esca.* Notice the quick rhythm of that line: "then suddenly stop feeding because they are assailed by a great fear, so I saw this band leave off singing and move toward the sloping hillside as one that goes on but does not know where he will come out; nor was our departure [his and Virgil's] less sudden."

In the third canto we have a series of encounters with people who have not begun as yet the process of purification because they had waited until the last moment of their lives to make their peace with the Church; they died in the wrath of the Church, though not in the wrath of God. Some of these encounters are very beautiful indeed, very impressive. There is the case of one who, not being able to do anything else, makes a cross with his dying arms; and another who calls out to the Virgin Mary with his last breath, in the very last instant, and is saved. The only punishment for their delay is that they have to wait here for the length of time they delayed, multiplied by thirty: that is, thirty times the number of years they have been outside of the Church, or in the wrath of the Church. That's one of the problems we face here; another is how suffering is mitigated, shortened by prayer. That is a purely Catholic doctrine: through prayer, in the bosom of the Church, the intensity and the length of punishment in Purgatory is diminished and reduced. Actually, it's not the prayer that does it — prayer is only the instrument — it's the love of the living that does it. Dante says it, and many before and after him have said it: through love there is unification. Love is a unifying power. When love becomes full enough, the distinction between the lover and the loved one disappears. This is the doctrine of *suffragium*, of suffrage — not in the sense of the vote, of course. This is the suffrage of the dead, as when you have masses said for the dead. Memorial? Intercession? In the Latin it's *suffragium*, but I wouldn't recommend the use of "suffrage" here, because of the ambiguity with the other meaning.

Here Dante is obviously in a mood to stress his pious regard for the Church. On the other hand, we'll soon see his love for the enemies of the Church, when he takes the side of the Holy Roman Empire against the Holy Roman Church. His love for the emperor makes him say some very harsh things against the Church, which he otherwise exalts. Here we find many of the traits of allegorizing of the Old Testament, particularly of the Orphic utterances of antiquity, made use of at the beginning of Purgatory. One of them is that the ladder is, at the beginning, very hard to climb; but it gets easier as you go on. Which means that the way of purification is very hard at first but becomes easier as you go along; and at the end the punishment becomes the source not of suffering but of joy. The other — how the paths of evil are very broad and those of purification are very narrow — comes up again and again in the course of Purgatory.

The closing lines of the canto are the exaltation, the deification. the apotheosis of an otherwise terrible person, Manfred, the illegitimate son of Emperor Frederick II, who was not elected to the imperial office and did not really inherit it, but managed to cheat his legitimate brother, Conrad, out of it, to become King of Sicily. His opposition to the popes, his constant siding with what you might call the Ghibelline party, brought on his ruin at the hands of the new ethnic group invited by the pope to establish itself in Italy, namely, the armies of the French led by Charles of Anjou, which eventually put an end to the Hohenstaufens, overcoming their rule in Italy — a rule which had started with Henry VI, Frederick Barbarossa, and Frederick II after him. Sicily was soon lost, but not southern Italy, where they left their imprint for a long time. The French infiltration in southern Italy was not limited to the Anjovines. Before the Norsemen, or Normans had come in to drive off the Moslems, before they came to Italy, they lost all vestiges of their Norse descent and had become what we must call true Franks, bringing to southern Italy the civilization of France. The French defeated Manfred, they killed him at the battle of Benevento, a city which has become somewhat famous recently in the annals of the Second World War.

These people have made a sign to Dante and Virgil — those who have to wait their turn before proceeding toward purification — a sign that corrects their orientation. Virgil, who was so competent, so helpful redirecting them in Hell, here is rather helpless; he has to rely all the time on the directions given by others, on what the inmates of Purgatory tell him, and on the light of the sun, which is another way of saying, on the inspiration of God. They have told Virgil to go back and try another way. Then one of them speaks to Dante: "*Chiunque tu sei*," "'whoever you are, turn your face toward me, look at me, and tell me if you ever saw me in the other world, if you ever saw me in the world below'." Dante couldn't possibly have seen him. Why this curiosity on the part of Manfred, whom Dante here has deified? "I turned toward him and looked at him fixedly." *Biondo era e bello*, "he was fair-haired," — *biondo*, because he was a Suabian, a Hohenstaufen. He was fair-haired and beautiful and noble of aspect. He came from perhaps the greatest of all the royal families of the time. Dante calls him, or rather calls the last one after him, the last breath of Suabia, Germany. In the old days in certain neighborhoods of Brooklyn, one could see the designation on the signs of German stores. In Germany and in Austria too. With Franconia, and Saxony, Suabia was one of the three great divisions of medieval Germany.

[L]*'un de' cigli, un colpo avea diviso.* "A thrust of the sword had cut one of his eyelids." This is not said to indicate that his beauty is diminished, but to show that his beauty was increased. French German nobility used to make much of this insistence on the power of a scar to beautify. Even in our day rather ridiculously, not in this magnificent way, Germans love to get scars on their faces in duels, when they can't get them on the battlefield. *Quando io mi fui umilmente disdetto d'averlo visto mai*, "when I had humbly answered I'd never seen him before, he went on" — this is said almost apologetically; Dante wants to make clear that this spirit especially deserved to be known. That's not all: "showing the pride he had in his wounds he said, 'Look here,' and he showed me the wound of the sword high on his chest." All these are wounds that have been dealt from the front. Until modern times, it was considered dishonorable to have wounds except on the face and breast. For a soldier to have wounds on the back meant that he got them running away. Of course that's no longer dishonorable now. The scene, therefore, becomes meaningless if you don't recall how things were at that time. "Then smiling he said," — smiling with a certain kind of contempt, condescension — "'I am Manfred'." "*Io son Manfredi*," "'grandson of the empress Constance'." Constance was the wife of Henry VI, who was the father of Frederick II, who was the father of Manfred. "*[O]nd'io ti prego che quando tu riedi*"; this is who I am and this is where you find me and therefore when you go back to earth, set the reports straight about me, and "*vadi a mia bella figlia, genitrice dell'onor di Cicilia e d'Aragona, e dichi il vero a lei, s'altro si dice.*" "'When you go back, go to my beautiful daughter, the mother of the glory of Sicily and of Aragon, and tell her the truth, if other things are being said about me'." Dismiss the rumor that having been excommunicated, his ashes scattered to the winds, and his bones having been removed with torches overturned, he couldn't be saved. Dante is telling us that he *was* saved. "*Poscia ch'io ebbi rotta la persona,*" "'After my body had been put down'" "*di due punte mortali*" — both his wounds were deadly — "*io mi rendei piangendo a quei che volentier perdona.*" Here the phrase is beautifully put to indicate that he who had fought to the end, who, already dying had refused to surrender to the enemy, did surrender to God, who gladly pardons. All he had to do to reconcile himself with God was turn to Him with tears. "*Orribil furon li peccati miei,*" "'truly my sins were horrible'," "*ma la bontà infinita ha sì gran braccia che prende ciò, che si rivolge a lei,*" "'but the infinite bounty, generosity of God, has such widely extended, long arms, that it embraces everything that turns to Him. And if the

Bishop of Cosenza who to my pursuit was set by Clement [Pope Clement IV]'" — no longer the pursuit of the warrior but the pursuit of the dead body, which ended when they burned it and scattered the ashes by the order of the Bishop of Cosenza. Throughout, the language of this warrior is insistently military, the language of a soldier. *Caccia* is not the hunt, but military pursuit. Here, however, it is not the pursuit of an enemy by cavalry, which is what it means technically, but the pursuit of a dead body. "'If the bishop of Cosenza had well read this side of the face of God'," that is, not the face of justice, but of Mercy, "'he would have left the bones of my body to lie at the bridgehead near Benevento'.'"Again the military man speaks out. He doesn't fight just anywhere; he fought where valiant warriors fight — at the bridgehead. That's where noble soldiers fight, holding the line of defense at its most dangerous point, its critical point. If you know anything about military art, you know what Dante's talking about; if you don't, I don't think it's worth the time to explain it. *"[L]'ossa del corpo mio sarieno ancora in co' del ponte presso a Benevento, sotto la guardia della grave mora."*

These are very solemn lines. His bones would still be at the bridgehead which he so valiantly defended, near Benevento, under the guard — again we have a military term: the tomb is not said to cover the body, it guards, like a sentinel, *la grave mora* — "'of the mountain of stones cast there by his soldiers as they passed by'." *"Or le bagna la pioggia e move il vento."* Now his bones are not protected, guarded over by that stony sentinel, they're exposed: the rain wets them, and the wind scatters them, *"di fuor dal regno."* Again, regret: he was king of the two Sicilies, yet now not even his bones are allowed to remain protected in the land which was his kingdom, over which he had ruled. There is pathos in this: "'outside the kingdom'," "*quasi lungo il Verde,*" which is part of the river that is called the Garigliano, "*dov'ei le trasmutò a lume spento*" "'where those bones were transferred with extinguished lights. But in spite of their curse'" — that is, the curse of the Church — "'in spite of their curse, the eternal love is not so destroyed, lost, for a man's heart, that it cannot return'." It had been lost because of his horrible crimes, but it has returned. You can always hope, as long as you live. Or, as he says: as long as there's hope, as long as there are green blossoms, as long as life is verdant with hope.

"*Vero è,*" "'true it is that anyone who dies [*in contumacia,*] rebellious to the holy Church, even though he repents at last, the condition is that he must linger here, he must wait here a time proportional to the time that he has remained outside of' the Church'," unless "*tal decreto più corto per buon preghi non diventa,*" "'unless this sentence is not shortened, pardoned in part, as the result of good prayers, the prayers of the good'." In every canto there's an insistence on this; the *suffragium* must be good, must come from the hearts of good people, must be such that will kindle the flame of love. "'Now see if you can make me happy by revealing to my good Costanza [his daughter] my condition, that you have seen me here; and tell her also of the delay'," "*che quì, per quei di là, molto s'avanza.*" "'that here, through the help of those down in the world much profit [gain? advantage?] can be made'."

22. THE COMING OF NIGHT; THE POET SORDELLO AND JUDGE NINO

With the eighth canto, we have reached the end of the first day in Purgatory. Dante describes the approaching sunset, which in his scheme calls for a halt. The climb must stop after sundown. The meaning of that is rather obvious. We have reached a point where human reason cannot of itself rectify conduct. The only power that can do so now is God. Dante, as many people before him, uses the sun as the symbol of God, the symbol of a higher reason, a divine reason and guidance. The Church, of course, prefers to see the representative of God in that role; Dante prefers most of the time to indicate that it is God Himself who inspires directly with guidance. And that is symbolized by the presence of the sun.

In this canto, Dante reminds us almost violently that this is not a mere story, not a mere fiction he is giving us; it is the duty of the reader to pierce the veil of fiction and get to the truth — particularly here, he says, where the veil is so thin that you can easily pierce through it. Dante has reached, when this canto begins, the last people who are wandering around unable to begin purification because they delayed until the end their reconciliation with mother Church. And, as is fitting, this group is made up of rulers, sovereigns, those over whom there is no higher political authority. Of course, Dante would be much disturbed by this statement: for him there's only one ruler that has such authority. The rest depend on him, the one supreme emperor, for their authority. But with that limitation in mind, these may be called sovereigns.

They have gathered for protection against the night in a little hollow glen in the mountain, protected on all sides save one, where Dante and Virgil enter. Here they find the great spirits of those who have ruled the earth. Dante is brought to this cove by one of these great rulers, who in Dante's mind, had one advantage over the others, just as Virgil had an advantage over Aristotle. The advantage that made Virgil preferable to Aristotle as a guide was that he was a poet. Here we have Sordello. If Frederick II had been available he, perhaps, would have served the purpose, for he was a poet as well as an emperor, and therefore most suitable to serve as a guide. But Frederick, unfortunately, is in Hell. Despite his admiration for him, as Emperor, Dante in fairness put him in Hell. So we have Sordello here, not particularly famous for his poetry or for his political keenness, but made immortal by Dante for the fierceness of the famous invective that comes from his lips against Italy. It's the fiercest thing that has ever been written by anyone against any people.

Those defects that Dante records here are the defects that have marked all the people that have inhabited that peninsula throughout the ages — not the Romans, of course, who had their own defects; but they weren't these. Throughout their history, the Italians have shown themselves weak along certain lines; Dante picked up those lines and enumerated them all in what is perhaps the greatest condemnation in all Italian literature. It begins: *O serva Italia* — "O slavish Italy," Italy is not a sovereign but a slave, *di dolore ostello*, "hostel of grief," *nave senza nocchiero in gran tempesta*, "a ship without a pilot in a destructive storm, "not as you boast [his is the old imperial pretension], mistress of provinces, [the provinces being the rest of the empire] but a brothel." Dante calls Italy a brothel, then proceeds to enumerate the faults, beginning with the incapacity to stay together: how Italy is divided, region against region, city against city, each city divided within itself with one faction against another, one family against another, even the inhabitants of the same house divided against one another, separating themselves by walls in the same house, because they are ferocious enemies. Then he speaks of their propensity for law-breaking. The Italians are not the only ones, of course; but the point is that, as many historians have pointed out, the course of Italian history has taken the shape it has, to a large extent, because of certain characteristics of the Italian people; and the qualities historians have dwelt on are the very qualities Dante brings out here. Sordello was not really capable of such indignation; he is here just as a voice for Dante.

The relation between Sordello and Virgil, between one poet guide and the other poet guide is very prettily made. Of course, both are from Mantua. Well, Virgil was not from Mantua but from a little village near-by. And when asked where his birthplace was, he begins with the famous words of the inscription — no doubt apocryphal — on his so-called tomb in Naples, the tomb which has been transplanted again and again, every time the city expands. Virgil is said to have died in Calabria, his bones brought to Naples, and a very beautiful tomb raised there with the inscription: *Mantua me genuit; Calabria rapuere; tenet nunc Parthenope. Cecini pascua, rura, duces.* When Sordello, a poet and a great admirer of Virgil, hears Virgil begin to reply to his question with the word Mantua, he therefore responds with an echo of the first line of that inscription. That reveals the situation; the two poets embrace one another, the one destined for Paradise and the other to Hell; but for the time being they can embrace on this common ground.

The allegorical veil that we must pierce, what's back of Dante's mind here — the Virgin Mary, the devil, the hymn of St. Ambrose, the rather cheap dig against women — all this indicates that Dante is interested in a certain phase of purification which very briefly can be explained as follows: there's something we do and should not do, not because of any defect in our spiritual constitution, but because of some diabolical temptation or influence. Until now, the treatment of moral matters has been all quite pagan; almost everything that Dante says can be found in the Greek philosophers. But in this there's something very new, very different. The Greeks had their daemons, but they were rather beneficent. We all know the daemon of Socrates, which, every time he did something wrong, stopped him, and urged him in the right direction. Here — and this is quite an innovation — is a diabolical power that tempts you always to go wrong. The only protection you have is prayer. And your great ally in this, your great support — just below God — is the Virgin Mary.

The Virgin Mary is here exalted as the protectress of mankind, as it is being attacked by diabolical temptations. Of course, these diabolical temptations have to do with something; and that something is the cupidity (if we can use that word) of the senses, carnal cupidity. The protection of the Virgin Mary against diabolical temptation is especially needed at night; for, under the cover of darkness, we are moved to do many diabolical things that we would not do in the daytime. Not only that, but there is a phase of night life which we loathe and despise, certain experiences which our reason cannot control and for which it cannot be held responsible. They are to be avoided with the help of the Virgin Mary, to whom we appeal with the hymn, of which only the first line is here quoted. It's a hymn St. Ambrose wrote, which was taken over by the Benedictines shortly after and used as their hymn of *compline*, the last hour of the day, just preceding sunset. And they sing this song, this hymn of St. Ambrose that begins, "*Te lucis sante terminum.*" "'Now that night is coming, we pray that we may be spared pollutions of all sorts that night brings." Dante does not quote the whole of it but tells us that the whole was sung.

To indicate what more than this first line there is to this hymn, a dramatic situation develops: the devil appears and the angels of the Virgin Mary, dressed in green, move to rout him. Of course, it's all allegory; the angels, according to the Church, are not dressed in green; or in white, or anything else. The Church insists there are angels, but they are spirits. What they can do to us is something analogous to what the soul does to our body. When a child in the old days asked, how can an angel do the things he does, how can an angel affect us? the teacher would explain: think of your body as it is just before and just after you're dead. After death it's the same body, but it can't do the same things it used to do. What has gone is the soul. The soul disappears at death; the body seems hardly changed but there's nothing to move it from within. The angels operate, act upon us, in a way analogous to the action of our soul on our body.

This is what you might call the allegorical setting. All this makes up the veil of fiction, the picture — the devil, the snake, the swords, the waving garments, the green raiments, the blonde hair. Not surprisingly, Dante quotes the familiar line of St. Augustine on allegory, which indicates what his intention was. It is a statement to the effect that in an allegorical poem, or allegorical prose composition, the details do not, must not be all allegory. Only a part should be allegorical, the part that has to make a point; all the rest is support, just as — says St. Augustine — with a plow, an *aratrum*, not all the plow cuts, only the blade. But all the other parts have to be there to hold the blade that does the cutting. So here, all this apparatus we have mentioned is not allegory, but it is there to give vitality to the part that *is* allegory. And this is the canto that illustrates best Dante's system of allegory.

Night has come, it's time to sing *compline*, the last of the hours in the Benedictine orders. Dante begins: *Era già l'ora che volge il disio ai naviganti*, "it was already the hour that turns the desire of seafarers" — *volge il disio* in Italian, is very beautiful, but it cannot be easily translated. This whole system of desire and love is based on a conception of the intellectual faculties, a conception of the appetitive and apprehensive faculties in which desire is represented as inclination. There's an object before our understanding, and we are affected by that object. If favorably affected, we turn to it, inwardly. And that turning toward an object is called an inclination. We spoke of it before — how common that idea is, of love as an inclination, as a *penchant*, as a leaning of some sort. And it's because of that inclination that Dante here uses the word *volge*. Of course, if you use *arouse* or some such word, you get the sense but not the picture — "turns the desire in the sailor's heart" — not sailor, necessarily, but seafarer, *e intenerisce il core lo de' e' han detto ai dolci amici addio,* "and moves the heart to tenderness, the day on which they have said farewell to dear friends." That is, when you've left those you love, you're particularly sad when night comes, *e che lo nuovo peregrin d'amore punge, se ode squilla di lontano, che paia il giorno pianger che si more.* The newly departed seafarer is pierced with love of home if he hears the tolling of bells from afar which seem to be weeping, crying, for the day which is dying. It's the evening bell. The tolling of the bells which you hear at *compline* is the third of the *Ave Maria,* it's the third *angelus,* the *angelus* of the evening. It is something that has attracted the attention of poets and non-poets for centuries and has been frequently described the way Dante does here. Someone has published an anthology, a small book of poems on the melancholy of the evening *angelus,* including poems of Manzoni, Byron, Petrarch and many others. We don't really need poetry; anyone who has ever heard the bells of evening has surely felt the emotion Dante describes here.

People have wondered how you could hear these bells, from out at sea; and some, therefore, have tried to change the sense of these lines suggesting that in the first *terzina* you have Dante speaking of seafarers on the sea, while in the second *terzina* he speaks of a wayfarer on land. Dante does say *naviganti* first and then *peregrin*; but *peregrin* does not mean pilgrim. It's the man who is, or is about to be, away from his home, his country, one who goes abroad to become a foreigner abroad; and in that sense it very often is rendered best by "traveler." In any case, we don't have to reject the old explanation. After all, navigation in Dante's days, at least in the Mediterranean, among people of that part of the world, was coastwise. One way was called *capotaggine*, which means that you go from one headland, one promontory to another. Which means, in turn, that the only time you leave sight of the shore is when you are between one headland and the next. Anyone who has traveled in the Mediterranean knows that the promontories are often high mountains. On the very top, there usually are churches dedicated to the Virgin Mary — Santa Maria della Guardia, among others; one in Marseilles, two in Genoa, ten or twelve in between. In these churches on the headlands, dedicated to the Virgin Mary, were bell-towers; and in the evening, as you sailed by them, you could hear the tolling of the *Ave Maria*.

It was that hour *quand'io incominciai a render vano l'udire*, "when I began to render vain the hearing and to gaze fixedly upon one of the souls, that had risen and which with its hands" — notice how hieratical the whole description turns out to be, "was lifting up his hands, asking to be heard, asking for a hearing." The next line is characteristic of the service of *compline* as it's still done by the Benedictines: "It clasped and raised both hands, fixing its eyes toward the east," the particularly characteristic gesture of this hour, not infrequently represented in painting, "as if it said to God: this is all I care for."

All this soul cares for is the return of the sun. On the western horizon the sun has set, but it will rise in the east. *"Te lucis sante" sì devotamente le uscì di bocca.* This soul that asks for a hearing now sings, *"Te lucis sante,"* the hymn of St. Ambrose, in which one begs to be spared the things which so often assail us at night.

"Te lucis sante" "so devoutly came from the lips, and
with such sweet music that it drew me out of myself,"
that is, it made me forget myself, "and the other souls,
after it, devoutly, and sweetly followed it for the entire
hymn [*l'inno intero*] keeping their eyes on the celestial
revolutions," the revolutions of the stars. "Sharpen
here your eyes, O reader, sharpen your gaze toward the
truth." When you look at something which is not very
easy to grasp, you sharpen your eyes. "Look for the
truth now, for the veil here is so thin that going beyond
it is easy."

Now comes the fiction. *Io vidi quello esercito
gentile* — *gentile* in Dante means noble in the feudal
sense of the word. Although, in the *Convivio* he tried
to prove that real nobility has nothing to do with
family, with what you inherit, that it is a matter of
personal worth, here he could not go against the
usage. He calls them *gentile*, these sovereign rulers, the
noblest of nobles. "I saw that noble army," *tacito poscia*,
"silently after this, gazing upward," *quasi aspettando*,
"as though expecting, pale and humble;" *e vidi uscir
dell'alto e scender giù due angeli*, "and I saw emerging
from on high, and coming down, two angels with two
flaming swords, truncated," that is, harmless, deprived
of their points. *Verdi come fogliette pur mo' nate, erano
in veste*, their garments were green, the green of leaves
just sprouting; they trailed behind them as they were
fanned by, fanned and moved by, their green wings or
feathers. This line is extraordinarily fine in the Italian,
depicting with matchless beauty these effects of motion. As the air moves them, these green garments swell
out and trail behind.

"One came and took his post a little above us,
the other descended on the opposite bank." We're in

this little cove, in the side of the mountain, closed in on three sides; the angels take their places on opposite sides, *sì che la gente in mezzo si contenne,* "so that these people here were contained between them," protected, in other words, by the angels. *Ben discerneva in lor la testa bionda,* "I easily discerned their blonde hair" — why blonde? I suppose for some reason or other poets always have had a predilection for blondes; not only do gentlemen prefer them, but poets as well. As far back as the days of Homer, heroes have been represented as blond. Virgil, Ovid, Catullus — Dante, naturally, doesn't get it from Catullus, but perhaps from Ovid, perhaps from Virgil. *Ma nelle faccie l'occhio si smarrìa,* "but my eye lost itself in their countenances," the light of their countenances out-dazzled all else. He could not see anything more than you can see anything when you gaze at the sun. Invisibility is caused by two things, lack of light and an excess of it, *l'occhio si smarrìa come virtù che al troppo si confonda,* "like a power [power, in the psychological sense; power of hearing, power of see-ing] that out-dazzles in the same way that any power is nullified not by lack but by excess." Too much light cripples the power of seeing. "*Ambo vegnon del grembo di Maria,*" "'both come from the lap of Mary'."

The word *grembo* is purposely chosen; "Mary's bosom" is quite wrong. The connotation of the word *grembo* in Italian is protection, the mother who nour-ishes her child. The *grembo* is the lap, symbolizing protection. "'Both come from the lap of Mary', said Sordello, 'to guard this cove because of the serpent which is about to come in'." Apparently this was a recurring scene that always terrified. And here too you have to break through the veil. *Ond'io, che non sapeva per qual calle,* "I who didn't know from which way the serpent would come," *mi volse attorno*, "turned around, and drew close, chilled with fear, to the trusted shoulders of my guide. And, again, Sordello: 'Now we can go down'."

All this time they have been on the ledge of the ridge that protects the cove, from which they could see all around, looking down on the rulers gathered below. Now that the singing is over and the talking begins, Sordello says: "'Now we can go down among these mighty shades, and we shall converse with them, and it will be very pleasing to them to see us'." "I think," says Dante, "that I descended only three steps." These three steps mean more than the obvious. The idea of their having stood all this time on a level only three steps raised above the cove, when they could have chosen a more elevated point of vantage, from which they could have seen more, is very strange. "I stepped down only three steps, I think, and was below, and I saw one who looked at me as though he were about to recognize me." *Tempo era già che l'aer s'annerava*, "It was already the hour when the air was becoming dusky." An hour or so after sunset, the air becomes dark, but *non sì che tra gli occhi tuoi ei miei non dichiarisse ciò che pria serrava*, "but not so that as I drew nearer the air failed to reveal, though darkening, what passed between his eyes and mine;" (a rather roundabout way of saying it was dark but still there was light enough for him to distinguish me and for me to distinguish him). *Ver me si fece, ed io ver lui mi fei*, "he came toward me and I toward him." "'O noble judge Nino'" — here, judge is not the title of one who sits with a robe on the bench to sentence men for crimes, or to acquit them of charges; it was one of the many names then given to the sovereign ruler. So this title, *giudice*, here means ruler.

Of course, ruler is generic, and *giudice* is specific. We still make use of that idea with regard to the land ruled over by the *giudice*. But *giudice* for the person of the sovereign, as the title of a person, has not been retained.

"'O noble judge Nino, how pleased I was to see that you were not among the damned'." *Nullo bel salutar tra noi si tacque* "no noble greeting was left unsaid between us; then he asked, 'how long has it been since you came to the foot of the mountain across the wide expanse of ocean?' 'O, I said to him, I come here not across the wide expanse of the sea, but through the dismal regions," [*lochi tristi*]; I came this morning and am still in the first life, though even as I travel now, I am acquiring the second'."

Again, Dante tells us this way of purification is for him the way of salvation. *E come fù la mia risposta udita*, "and as soon as my answer was heard, Sordello and he drew back, as persons that are of sudden bewildered." Not even Sordello was able to see that Dante was still living because, when he first saw him, the sun had already set. We know by now that the only way the fact that Dante still lived could be revealed was by the casting of a shadow. The sun was down: no shadow; so Sordello could not know that he was still alive. *L'uno a Virgilio, e l'altro ad un si volse che sedea lì, gridando*, "One said to Virgil and the other turned to one seated near by crying: 'Come, come, see what God in His grace has decreed'."

This was Conrad of the Malaspina family. Dante was, after this time, or rather after the time here assumed, which is 1300, to be an honored guest in the house of the family of the Malaspina. They still show tourists the room where Dante slept. Of course, you know how that works out; everybody slept everywhere, great men of all times. *Poi, volto a me,* "then turning to me: 'in the name of the extreme gratitude which you owe to Him, [namely God]'," *"che sì nasconde lo suo primo perchè, che non li è guado",* "'who so conceals his first cause, his first motive, so that you have no way of knowing it'," *"quando sarai di là dalle larghe onde,"* "'when you will be again beyond the broad expanse of the waves, tell my Giovanna, my daughter, that she invoke my name there where the innocent are heard'." *"Non credo che la sua madre più m'ami."* I am asking you to tell my daughter because I do not think my wife, her mother, still loves me, "'now that she has cast off her white veil'" — that is, she married again — "'which veil she will long for in future wretchedness and regret'."

In other words, this Visconti, Giudice of Pisa, had married this Giovanna, who, after his death, married Galeazzo Visconti of the Milan Visconti family; then things happened — of course Dante knew it, when he was writing, but they happened after the time Dante here assumes, which is 1300 — things happened, which made her regret that she did not remain a widow. Dante pretends to prophecy. "By her example it may easily be understood how short-lived in woman is the flame of love if it be not frequently kindled by sight or touch." Love is soon forgotten if the beloved is not felt near by or at least gazed upon. Of course, Dante might have said more fairly, this holds not only for woman, but also for man. He himself wrote a little book to show how forgetting the woman you love when she is gone can be justified. *"Non le farà sì bella sepoltura."* The *giudice* is sure she will regret having changed her status — this is something very medieval and oriental — because she would have had a much better funeral if she had remained a member of his family rather than the wife of him for whom she changed her status. But, instead of being said like that, it is put in terms of the coats of arms of the two families. The coat of arms of Nino is the cock, the rooster; the coat of arms of the Visconti of Milano, the viper. "'[S]he will not have such a beautiful burial at the hands of the viper that bears the Milanese into battle as she would have had at the hands of the cock of Gallura'." The viper on the standard, of course, was used to bring together the Milanese forces in the field.

23. NIGHT AND TEMPTATION; THE EVIL SNAKE

The description of the last human light that Dante gives us in the eighth canto is very beautiful. Of course, Dante was not primarily interested in the poetic lyricism that we love so much. His intention is to give us a scheme, an allegorical scheme that settles things. But for us it's very hard to see what he is driving at. The setting of the sun is the setting of the light of the mind; the absence of physical light symbolizes the absence of spiritual light, of divine inspiration. We read it and it moves us; yet how to interpret Dante's allegory, here, remains a mystery. The attempt to solve the allegory, with the absence of more direct personal historical information is fruitless. Anything can be said and everything sounds plausible. Each commentator has his own interpretation. It's an exercise in futility. At best, all but one must be wrong.

We have reached the scene of post mortem jealousy. It is very medieval; its importance was based on the fact that it was considered a divine duty — a duty in the eyes of God and men — that one of the most important things you can do for those departed is to show them your respect with a great funeral. For some of us today this seems shocking; for some it's essential. Judge Nino thinks very highly of it. He measures the difference between himself and the Milanese Visconti by the difference in the funeral their families could furnish the lady. Of course, the Visconti of Milan were not able to do much at the time here presupposed. The woman died in 1302, so, in his fiction, Dante shows himself to be a prophet. Because of the calamities in the family, the funeral had to be very meager indeed.

"So he said, marked, stamped with the imprint of his aspect," *di quel dritto zelo* — "zeal" for *zelo* is completely wrong. In Dante's time *zelo* meant "jealousy." It's the meaning the word has in the Bible; wherever the sense of the original was jealousy, St. Jerome used the word. And you have it clearly enough from the etymology of the word *gelosia* in Italian. In other words, etymology, for once, has been faithful according to the meaning. So apparently there's a *dritto zelo* as there is a *dritto* in everything else. *Zelo* is supposed to be one of the extremes which are vices compared with the mean. It cannot be *dritto* any more than cowardice can be *dritto*. But we are taught otherwise here. Jealousy, apparently, can be right or wrong. It is possible for a jealous man to hold a right mean between two extremes — excess and deficiency. Nino has a proper or right jealousy because his wife was not faithful to him after death. And fearing that you might have missed the point, he repeats it in the next line: *di quel dritto zelo che misuratamente in core avampa*, "the righteous jealousy that burns in the heart in due measure." *Misuratamente* means "not too much." So you learn that Dante believed there could be too little and too much jealousy.

Of course, like all great artists, like Plato, Dante may have taken the liberty of setting forth dramatically the convictions of another person with sympathetic ardor; that always can be said, and should be said. "My eyes eager.". . . The phrase is greatly strengthened by the word *ghiotti*. Dante loves these transfers: to make it more intense he passes from the eyes to the belly, from sight to the appetite of the glutton. His eyes are gluttonous, voracious. It's very effective. I don't think it works in English. Yearning expresses the idea, but the force of the image is lost. "My yearning eyes were again turned towards heaven" — apparently, Dante gets tired of this conversation, and turns to another matter, a sort of recurring motif in Dante, in all the Purgatory — "there where the stars revolve slowest." The stars move most slowly in that part of the heavens where we see the least rapidly moving stars, not the eighth sphere. There is one kind of motion there, which is slow, from west to east, but Dante is here thinking of the motion from east to west.

What he refers to here is the motion of stars near the pole. At the pole itself the motion is zero. A point on the equator completes in twenty-four hours a motion of the size of the great circle of our sphere — the equator is a great circle — about 24,000 miles. A circle near the pole, parallel to the equator, may be only a few inches around, and yet the time that it takes to revolve is the same as for a point on the equator. To make it clear Dante passes from solid geometry to plane geometry, from the sphere to the circle. And for the circle he gives us the picture of what all people had before their eyes, namely the wheel. Just as the sphere, the celestial sphere, revolves most slowly at the pole, so a wheel revolves most slowly at the hub. At the center there is no motion at all, even if the wheel revolves very rapidly. Of course, the hub is made up of more than the exact center, so you have to be careful about using that comparison. He turned his eyes "where the stars move slowest, just as a wheel at the point which is closest to the [*stelo*]." Instead of axle, or hub, he says (whether the rhyme forces him, or he likes the picture) *stelo*, by which he transforms the wheel into a flower, a beautiful flower. The criticism of mixed metaphors cannot be applied to Dante; he knows what can be done with them and thereby shows his great artistry, often startling the reader to open his mind's eye and enter into a world which he has never seen before.

"And my master said: 'Son, what are you looking at up there? Why are you ignoring so rudely this man with his lesson as to why women should love their husbands even after they are dead? What are you looking at up there?' 'I'm looking at those three blazing torches'." Dante and his contemporaries, and many others just after them, loved to say that the further south you go the more brilliant the stars become. It's the old traveler's yarn. The air is purer the further south you go, and so on. Anyway, it serves Dante's purpose here. These are three very extraordinary stars, *di chè'l polo di quà tutto quanto arde*. Whether he uses the word *polo* in the medieval or scientific sense, or in the classical sense, the picture is beautiful. In the one it means the point directly to the north or south; in the other, which is the classical sense, or Virgilian sense, it means the whole sky. The picture is, perhaps, more beautiful in the Virgilian sense, as if these three stars kindled the whole evening heaven.

Dante is here showing you how the four cardinal virtues must give way to the supernatural virtues. In the daytime, when reason works, the virtues that operate on reason are visible. But when night comes, and your reason ceases to function, then you have to rely on something else — something supernatural; and the power that acts, that has to take the place of a moral virtue, is the power of the supernatural or theological virtues: faith, hope and charity. In the revolution of the stars from east to west, the revolution which has brought on the night and therefore made it impossible for men to use their reason, the place of the four moral virtues which make it possible for men to live right, is now taken by the three theological virtues; and it is a change for the better.

Com'ei parlava, e Sordello a se il trasse dicendo: "Vedi la 'l nostro avversaro." This is very effective. No sooner have the theological virtues been mentioned, when the attack of the devil occurs. No matter what you believe, and no matter what all these people may have said about the devil, there was always a commonsense meaning underlying their thoughts, whatever the particular, imaginative opinion might have been. What is the devil, for someone not interested in metaphysical theology? Have you a right to speak of the devil? We have all, I'm sure, had the experience of finding that, after carefully calculating and planning everything, a power greater than ourselves upsets all the calculations and we do perhaps the very thing we were bent on not doing. The preacher would say, the devil has gotten into you. Psychologists are interested in such matters, today; but the ancients and the medievalists were also interested. It's rare, this experience, but it does happen that, contrary to reason, contrary to all your intentions, on occasion something seems to take hold of you, and you find yourself doing things that horrify you. I have had people, very correct and pious, tell me that at the moment, the most awe-inspiring moment of a funeral, they wanted to shriek with laughter or do something obscene, against all reason. Freud may have written all about it; but these people said it was the devil.

"Vedi là 'l nostro avversaro;" e drizzò il dito, perchè

in là guardasse. That's an Italian construction. You
have it in English, also, of course; but the professor
would probably mark it wrong and give you a "B" for it.
It's very common, the Irish do it all the time in their
colloquial speech. "Sordello drew him close saying:
'See there our enemy'; and pointed out with his finger
where he wanted me to look, where the little valley has
no protection."

This glen of the kings was protected on all sides
except one, and there the devil appears. What the
allegory is, I don't know. What the protection against
the devil the sides of the cove could afford is hard to
say. Dante stresses the fact that the devil came the easy
way, but he could have come the difficult way: "a snake,
perhaps the one that gave to Eve the bitter food," *tra
l'erba e i fior venìa la mala striscia.* This is a terribly
picturesque line: instead of calling it a snake, he calls
it "the evil streak," it's a *mala striscia* "coming along,"
*volgendo ad or ad or la testa e'l dosso leccando come bestia
che si liscia,* "turning its head from time to time, licking
itself like a beast [*che si liscia*] smoothes itself, licks
itself;" animals do that, even cats do it, lick themselves.
What is Dante aiming at here? This snake in certain
eyes must be rather attractive. "I did not see, and
therefore cannot tell how the two celestial falcons
[*astor celestiali*, the two eagles, hawks] moved, but they
did. And the serpent, hearing the air being pierced by
their green wings, fled."

Again, Dante here forces the running together
of the senses: he wants to throw some color into the
picture, so he says "green wings": *sentendo fender l'aere
alle verdi ali.* Of course, the symbolism of *verde* is
pretty obvious. "The snake fled," *fuggì il serpente,* "and
the angels returned to their posts. The shadow that

had drawn up close to the judge when he'd called, in all this assaulting action never for an instant stopped looking at me." He never for a moment released his gaze from Dante, as though he were spellbound. And then comes a construction which is rather hard and which always Dante repeats in couplets; it's the predicative *se* the Latin *sic* which has nothing to do with the Italian *se*. It means: "so may." "So may the light that guides you on high" — but to get the meaning of it more easily you have to invert the construction, you have to stress the beginning of the next *terzina*. "'So' — he began — 'if you have true news from Valdimacia.'. . ." Valdimacia is a valley not very far from Tuscany, on the border of Tuscany, where this Malaspina who is now talking, comes from, "'If you have true news from Tuscany or the neighboring district, tell me'," "*che già grande là ero*," "'tell me, for once, formerly, I was [*grande*] mighty there'." Notice the construction. After the "if" *terzina* comes the "so may" *terzina*: "'so may the light that leads you upward'," this line affirms that it is a supernatural power that moves Dante up, "'find in your free will [*arbitrio*] sufficient energy'." Only, instead of saying sufficient energy, he continues the simile of light, saying, "'so may it find as much wax [*cera*] as is necessary to reach the highest enamel'." Dante at the top of Purgatory will make a big point of this *smalto*. *Smalto* is green; the *sommo smalto* is the highest meadow. So may Dante find enough "*cera*" "'as is needed to complete and perfect the process of purification. I was called Corrado Malaspina'." Of course, he wants to make it clear that this is not the great Corrado who signed the famous treaty between Barbarossa and the Longobards; he is not that Corrado. "*Non son l'antico, ma di lui discesi*," "'I am not the

ancient Corrado, but a descendant'" — "descendant" in
Italian might be one who is related back through a
grand-uncle, but in Dante's time it means direct descendant — "*a' miei portai l'amor che qui raffina.*" That's
a very famous line: the love he brings here is not love
of fatherland, or love of God; it is a certain amount of
family egotism which needs purification here. "'O,' I
said to him, 'I have never been to your region'." Dante
didn't always speak so well of the Malaspina family.
Elsewhere he speaks harshly. But when he wrote this,
not at the assumed date, but when he wrote this, he had
changed his mind.

At the time of the events here described, Dante
was their guest for a time, in Valdimacia, on the west
coast, on the Tyrrhenian coast, half-way between Pisa
and Genoa. "*Per li vostri paesi giammai non fui;*" "'I have
never been in your part of the world, but where in all
Europe is there anyone who is not aware of your
merits? The fame which honors your house, your
dynasty proclaims the [*signori*]'." *Signori* is a hard
word to translate. It was the common word in Italian
for sovereign. The rulers who *superiore non reconoscens*
are the *signori*, the supreme political masters. In a
democracy, the executives are the *signori*. So great is
the fame of your family, as sovereigns, so widespread
is it that even those who never were there would know
of it. "And I swear to you" — now comes an echo of that
predicative *sic* that came before; it is an amoebean
construction, you start off with a certain construction,
and it's repeated several times, responsively, though
here only once — "*ed io vi giuro, s'io di sopra vada,*"
"'and I swear to you, so may I proceed upward'," to the
top of Purgatory, "*che vostra gente onrata non si sfregia',*"
"'that your honored family does not [*sfragiarsi*] strip

itself'." Of course, the phrase is a feudal one, one of chivalry, rather, used when you strip the emblems of a knight from his armor, "*si sfregia del pregio della borsa e della spada.*" *Spada* and *borsa* refer to the two virtues which you should have in consequence of which you cannot be stripped of the emblems of nobility: magnanimity and magnificence. If you are magnanimous, you're ready, for a good cause, to cast your life away; and if you're magnificent you're ready to cast your wealth away for a good cause. "*Uso e natura sì la privilegia,*" "'good habits and nature give it such privilege that'" — and here is a very anti-Guelf line — "*che, perchè il capo reo il mondo torca, sola va dritta, e il mal cammin dispregia,*" "'so that, for all that the evil head leads the world astray, it alone goes on the straight path and despises the evil road'." The *capo reo* is the head of the Church. This has been said before and will be said again. "And he: 'you can go now, you have told me enough; but the sun will not rest seven times'" — again, the astronomical picture: the sun is in Aries, and Aries is the ram. Around these stars of the constellation the figure of a ram can be traced with its tail and its paws. It's very common, this figure of the ram. For the month of March, and for a period near March, it's the habitat of the sun. What Dante is saying is: the sun will not again lie down to rest seven times in this bed which the ram covers — bestrides — with its paws, before this courteous opinion shall be nailed to the midst of your forehead with greater nails than the mere words of other men, if the course of judgment is not stopped. In other words, this will happen, unless I'm mistaken.

    The sense is perfectly clear; we all know the zodiac. The sun, for a whole month, stays here in this *letto* and then passes on to another constellation. Aries bestrides this *letto* particularly marked by its paws. It's interesting, how they were able to imagine these various figures in the constellations. The last line here must be read carefully, otherwise you will make Dante contradict himself. The man he meets is no prophet. He is no scientist; he can't read God's mind. But he knows that Dante will go to Valdimacia and he knows that by the *corso di giudizio*. The meaning of *giudizio* in this sense is kept in English in the phrase judiciary astrology, the astrology that draws a horoscope. The horoscope is the *giudizio*. It is the *giudizio* in this sense: the judgment according to the course of the stars.

What follows, in the beginning of the ninth canto, is a famous description, but there is much disagreement as to its meaning. It can, obviously, be understood in two senses; but it's beautiful in both senses, so it doesn't much matter. *La concubina di Titone antico*, "the mistress of ancient Tithonus" — concubine, here, means nothing more than mistress; Dante knew the legal sense in Roman law — "the mistress of ancient Tithonus was already becoming white on the ledge of the east." The reference is to Aurora. It's a very beautiful story, the tale of this magnificent girl, this goddess who, having fallen in love with Tithonus, son of King Laomedon of Troy, obtained immortality for him but forgot to ask for eternal youth. In time he became more and more wrinkled, smaller and smaller. She was the only one who could kill him, but she wouldn't. So he grew older and older, smaller and smaller, until he had grown so small that one day she inadvertently walked over him, stepped on him, and killed him. So, this Aurora, rising, was becoming white "*s'imbiancava*," and the white of dawn will be followed by crimson red and yellow — *già s'imbiancava al balco d'oriente, fuor delle braccia del suo dolce amico*, "leaving the arms, the embrace of her sweet friend." The myth has it that this beautiful woman spends the night with her lover and then leaves him at dawn and drives with her chariot across the horizon — a very beautiful picture; *di gemme la sua fronte era lucente*, "her forehead glittered, was resplendent with gems set in the form of the cold animal," the stars which surround the glow of Aurora, the cold animal that strikes with its tail. Now the sun is in Aries and therefore Aurora comes before, in the constellation immediately preceding, that of the Fish, and the Fish are represented as cold animals.

The picture, so far, is very clear. The fish may well be the cold animal which, with its tail, strikes people, but the question is: how come it was sundown only a few moments ago, and now it is dawn? This is not the center of the earth, where simply by moving a few feet you pass from one side to the other. Purgatory is on the surface of the earth. Some have tried to explain this apparent contradiction of an aurora at about eight o'clock at night by saying that Dante is talking here of the lunar aurora. Of course, there never was an Aurora who had an affair with Tithonus. A lunar aurora, celestially, would fit the situation, but the mythology would be very strange. If it was the lunar aurora, then the constellation is no longer the Fish but Scorpio, which is considered, usually, a warm animal; but, as in all things, you have some interpreters who hold otherwise. Still, it doesn't seem to match the rest of the picture.

How can we keep the beautiful image of the

lovers, Tithonus and the Aurora? By recalling that
many times Dante begins by speaking of heavenly
phenomena as seen from where he stands as the writer,
and then drops down to the point of view of his story.
He begins by saying, "where I am now it would have
been dawn," and then says, "but there, where I was, the
night had already taken two of the steps with which she
climbs and already was binding its wings for the third."
That is: two hours of night have passed; they have
talked and now it's the third hour of night. According
to Dante's calendar, there are twelve hours of night
just as there are twelve hours of daylight. Usually the
hours of night are not of the same duration as the
hours of day — except two times in the year, at the
vernal and autumnal equinoxes. Now it is the vernal
equinox. The whole thing makes sense that way. It was
two hours after sunset here, at the mountain of Purgatory, and it was two hours after sunrise in Italy, when
something happened, *quand'io, che meco avea di quel
d'Adamo*, "when I, who had in me that [the flesh] of
Adam" (the others hadn't), *vinto dal sonno*, "overcome
by sleep, bent over on the grass, where all five of them
had been sitting." The whole night is skipped over;
Dante has fallen asleep.

The next thing you know it's dawn and we hear
the chirping of swallows. *Nell'ora che comincia i tristi lai
la rondinella presso alla mattina, forse a memoria de' suoi
primi guai*. To understand this you have to remember
the story of Procne and Philomela, the story of the
tragedy of their lives, why Philomela is the nightingale,
Procne the swallow. The chirp of the swallow comes at
dawn. You know what the poets have said in all languages — Greek, Latin, Provençal, French, Italian;
Petrarch, Shakespeare and all the others — they have

played on this theme. It is dawn, therefore the nightingale stops singing, and the swallow begins. The singing of the nightingale ceases with dawn, for the night of love ends; not so the chirping of the swallow: *e che la mente nostra, peregrina più dalla carne e men da' pensier presa, alle sue vision quasi è divina.* At dawn, our mind, far away, far removed from the flesh, therefore less seized by preoccupations, less troubled by cares, is almost prophetic in its vision. And that's quite true; the ancient doctors spoke of it and Dante must have gotten it from them. After the turmoils are worked out in the course of the night, the slumber that comes at the last hour of dawn is very pure, very peaceful. And any dreams you have at that time are almost "divine" — Dante uses the word *divina* in the sense of prophetic. And now comes the vision of the dream of Lucia as an eagle, who in a flood of light and fire that almost kills him, snatches him up and carries him aloft, scorching him so that his slumber is broken.

24. PURGATORY PROPER; THE SCENES DEPICTED ON THE FIRST TERRACE

Lucia carries Dante into Purgatory proper. What he means by this is pretty hard to say. Surely it has little to do with the Catholic Church and Catholic practices, although he shows considerable regard here for what Catholics would want to know. There is a clear reference to the Church and to the practices of the Church in the three steps that lead to Purgatory, the three conditions for the beginning of purification, and the role of the gatekeeper, who gives Dante some instruction, gives him a kind of blessing and explains to him the function of the keys. What are these keys? There are over one hundred cities that have the two keys as part of their civic emblems. A textbook I once came across, said that one is to open and the other is to close. The obvious explanation is given in Catechistic instruction, and it is that the Church has two powers, given it by God, the power to care for, to scrutinize, to assay the conscience, and the deeds of the culprit, and that is the silver key; the other, the golden key, represents the authority which the Church alone has, after having examined the state of a man's conscience and conduct, of deciding whether or not to open the gates of salvation. One is dearer, says Dante; the other requires a great deal of knowledge of human deeds and their motivation.

But while Dante here makes clear the great function the Church has in all this, the inescapable element of humanism also appears. Dante introduces an orphic motif: the angel that opens the gate for Dante tells him to go in but never to look back. Of course, morally and allegorically interpreted, this applies to all religions and not particularly to any phase of the Catholic Church or Catholic practice. It recalls the story of Orpheus and Eurydice: Eurydice was warned not to look back; when she did, she was lost forever to the love of Orpheus.

The structure of Purgatory — the famous painting of Michelino in the Cathedral of Florence helps to visualize it — is that of an ordinary conical mountain, such as you frequently find in nature. Its base is very steep, making a difficult access. Anyone who has traveled, especially in Italy, must have seen how often cities were built on just such mountains, with a cliff-like base, making it hard for a hostile army to get up to the city. So here, the lowest part is hard to climb, it is very steep and rough; and, as often in mountain climbing, to make your way you have to find a cleft in the mountain and help yourself up with your hands and feet.

This mountain is divided into seven terraces, where the seven sins are purified. We start in inverse order, with the gravest sin, which is pride, on the bottom, and on the top the lightest which is lust. Protestants, or anyone brought up in the ordinary Protestant atmosphere, may find this hard to swallow, or at least, surprising. Only the latter, lust, is a sin, some may think: pride is the best thing a person can have; man is nothing without it. Dante, of course, doesn't go the whole length that St. Augustine goes, where St. Francis *always* went, which is the demolition of individual being for the greater glory of God; which means to bring down, as far as possible, the kingdom of heaven to this earth; or, by annihilation, bring on the deification of man. Dante has some of this. Often he forgets it, but occasionally he goes to the furthest extremes, opposing all political constructions of power. He is a champion of the Holy Roman Empire, but he would seem to want that political construction for one sole reason: to keep peace for the protection of ethics, for the protection of morality.

After these seven terraces, where the sins are purified, you have a sort of plateau, and that again is something nature gives us frequently. Many mountain peaks in the Alps and in Central Italy have a plateau on the top. You go up this almost sheer lump of sugar, up the side of this mountain which is nothing but barren rock, and then suddenly there is a level ground, all green, with streams and fountains gushing forth. So Dante, on the top, finds water, but no ordinary water. The source of such water usually is a higher mountain, off in the distance. Dante has a different explanation. The water he finds here has a different source. This plateau, at the top of Purgatory, was Eden, the original abode of man. Dante is furious at Eve when he sees how beautiful it is, and that man could have been enjoying it all this time, had he not been deprived of it by this lady.

The ascent is hard at the beginning, but the further up you go the easier it becomes. The difficulty of climbing gradually diminishes, and at the top it's actually pleasant. Here, the entrance is very narrow, because if it were broad, it would not lead to salvation but to destruction. So Dante, by some real Alpine climbing, finally gets to the first circle which is a terrace in the mountain side, with a sheer drop down to the plateau, or plain, which Dante had left and where he had found Cato. Here the proud are purified.

They are purified in one of the two ways, which are fairly orthodox or Augustinian at any rate. One is to make of those pleasures which drew you away from God, into sin, the source of your punishment. How? When Dante wants to punish the avaricious, those who have sought to store up wealth, he distinguishes between the avaricious man and the miser. The miser wants gold or land for its own sake; the avaricious man wants to use it in a different way, to secure other pleasures. In dealing with the miser, who wants to store up wealth, we have to acknowledge two sources of wealth: one is land and the other is metal. So, in connection with the avaricious, the punishment is brought about by making the source of their sinful pleasure the source of their punishment. They wanted land and now they have all the land they want. They stick their faces in it, they swallow it, and they are buried under it. They would like to look up to enjoy the sight of the revolution of the heavens, but instead they have their noses in the soil. That is one way. The other is rectification by a contrary action. This is the one that is found in the last circle of Purgatory. The proud who go about contemptuous of others, looking down on all, as if they owned the world — I'm trying to recall the description of Cicero — who strut on earth, are punished by being so crushed by the weight of their pride that their chins almost touch their toes. You'll find this conception not only in Dante but everywhere in the representations and teachings of the Catholic Church. Dante compares them to an architectural structure, a caryatid. They used to be all over, when there were still some people who thought there was value in the imitation of classical art, before we arrived at the U.N. ideal of pencil box architecture. The proud

look like caryatids, those muscular figures bending
down and holding up the massive weight of an archi-
trave on their shoulders. The name originally desig-
nated female figures. Atlantes, were the male figures,
but the latter name has gone out of use. Caryatids hold
up the entablature, like columns.

The punishments in Purgatory are all organized
in one of these two ways. Then there is the indication
of a pleasure which is the opposite of the vice that is
there purified, and the anticipation of that pleasure is
always accompanied by a reference to the Virgin Mary.
You know how often in the twelfth, thirteenth, fourteenth centuries you find sermons that have for their
theme the seven utterances of the Virgin Mary. She is
supposed to have spoken seven times in the Gospel.
Here we find examples which are supposed to be the
very opposite of the seven sins being purged, representations of the virtue that should have drawn you on
earth, taught to you not only by the Virgin Mary and by
the Saints, but even by — and here is the humanist
coming through again — by the example of illustrious
pagans, the ancient moralists and philosophers. So
you have on all these seven terraces, the pleasure of the
evil or sin itself made a source of punishment and
purification; then you have, you might say, an exhor-
tation, a lure, the words of Mary and the utterances of
a beatitude. The Church has a canon of beatitudes.
They come from the sermon on the mountain. Dante is
very free and loose in this. Influenced by classical lore,
Dante does some startling things, however.

That's the general procedure; it's not at all monotonous, as Dante works it out. Purification is distrib-
uted on these seven terraces according to the canon of
the seven mortal sins. The first part of this scene of the

terrace of the proud presents us with what we might call a spiritual lure — Dante himself uses the word *logoro*. Originally it was a term in falconry. When you wanted to draw down your falcon you used a *logoro*. Here the lure is a spiritual one. You have to keep in mind in reading *Purgatorio* and *Paradiso* and in the *Inferno* too, that in addition to the essential development that is Dante's first interest, working out his subject with due consideration for the philosophical background, he often also creates an accidental emphasis that unites the canto as a whole, but which hasn't any strict connection with the theme of the canto as related to the general structure of the poem. We had one such example in the eighth canto, where he stresses a certain theme from the beginning of the canto to the end, the theme of *sensualitas*, what the Christians call *formes*, the fuel for sin. There is in us something, never silent, that reminds us to do good — a kind of voice that urges us to do what we ought to do — not conscience, although from St. Ambrose to the present it has been used in that sense. The Catholic theologians make a very clear distinction. The conscience is an act; and what you have here is not an act but a habit. A child may perform certain acts of dancing, but keeps stumbling. You say, she doesn't have the habit of dancing; for when you have acquired a habit you do things well. If a person, trying to dance, keeps stumbling, you say that he has not learned how to dance yet, or has not acquired the habit of dancing. Here we need a word for the good habit of conscience. The Catholic Church keeps the word, but except for that, the word has gone out of use. It shouldn't have. The word is *synderesis*, that voice which says: "this is wrong, this other is right." It tells you not to do something; you do it, *synderesis* goes unheeded. And immediately, that something in you, the act of conscience, tells you: alas, you did it in spite of *synderesis*, and consequently it bites you, *remordet,* you suffer remorse.

Unfortunately, as a result of original sin, we have a similar habit in the opposite direction. That is called the *formes, sensualitas.* It is a habit that always tells you to do the wrong thing, the very opposite of what *synderesis,* and reason, tell you to do. Reason can't control it. That's why you need supernatural aid to conquer it. We see this in the preceding canto, where the snake, according to St. Augustine, according to the Glosses, is sensuality. The meaning of the snake in the opening pages of Genesis is solved, not theologically, but popularly, for Vulgar Catholicism, very simply: the snake is the temptation to sexual indulgence. It is also stressed in the hymn of St. Ambrose, the hymn that prays for protection against temptation at night, when the human conscience is at its weakest. We find it also in the rather strange stress on the misdoings of that poor woman, *Giudice* Nino's wife, and of women in general, with regard to the attraction of good looks and tactile presence of a man. How short is the love of a woman, he says, when he whom she loves is out of sight and out of touch! Clearly, in addition to being what it is structurally, the eighth canto — which gives us a last description of those who are not yet ready to start purification — has this other steady emphasis on *sensualitas.*

It's even more marked in the tenth canto. From beginning to end, Dante seems to have one preoccupation which, beautiful as it is, seems to detract from the religious solemnity of the canto. It's the preoccupation with what constitutes perfection in art — particularly in sculpture. A thing is sculpturally beautiful not only when it appeals to the appropriate sense, which is sight, but also when it appeals to the other senses as well — to hearing, and the others. We will see what Dante does with it in connection with this practice, this insistence, this bearing down on some theme that seems to be peculiar to the canto itself and not connected to the other cantos or to Purgatory as a whole.

There isn't anything very original about the theme in the tenth canto. Writers in all languages in all ages have spoken of a statue that speaks; but Dante works it out systematically. To show the contrast between the outer and the inner, Dante falls back on a contrast of sound, of noise. There are harsh sounds when the gate is opened and closed and then, inside, the most beautiful music of the *Te Deum*. Even those who are not Christian or Catholics should know the *Te Deum*. It was sung when a people, when a king was victorious, when he won a battle (the other party was defeated of course). He would then order that the *Te Deum* be sung in all the churches, throughout his kingdom, to thank God for the victory. It was very common in the old culture; it was almost proverbial to say: "sing a *Te Deum*," when you had good reason to thank God. That is the music that cheers Dante as he enters Purgatory proper, at the end of the ninth canto.

In the beginning of the tenth canto, he describes the difficulty of climbing up the cleft, coming finally to the first of the terraces, that of the proud. *Dalla sua sponda, ove confina il vano, al piè dell'alta ripa, che pur sale, misurrebbe in tre volte un corpo umano.* "From the extremity where it borders on the abyss [*il vano*] to the foot of the lofty cliff, that rises sheerly [*che pur sale*], if you could measure it, the human body would be contained in it three times." That is, it is somewhat less than six yards wide, three times the height of a man, *e quanto l'occhio mio potea trar d'ale* — don't be shocked by this metaphor — "as far as the wings of my eyes should carry me," *or dal sinistro, ed or dal destro fianco*, "now on the left, now on the right side, this terrace," *questa cornice, mi parea cotale.* Here he calls it a *cornice* — it's the regular alpine term in these regions for the sheer ledges on the Alpine mountain-side. The sheer side itself is called *parate.* It's the same word in French, German, and Italian. The famous touristic by-word of one who wants it to be known that he has traveled is that he has seen, has taken a ride over the *grand cornice.* That's one of these ledges, on the Riviera, on the French side. That's the kind of *cornice* you have here.

   Lassù non eran mossi i piè nostri anco, "we had hardly there moved our feet," *quand'io conobbi quella ripa intorno,* "when I realized [recognized] that surrounding cliff." There must be a better word than cliff, for a sheer precipice; Dante is very free and loose in this, but I can't think of a better word at this moment; *che, dritto di salita aveva manco,* "which, being perpendicular, made it impossible to climb. I recalled that it was of white marble and adorned with carvings, such that not only Polycletus but nature itself would be put to shame."

   Dante, naturally, like all his contemporaries, believed that the purpose of art was to vie with nature. Of course, it was a useless task. Nature was already there; why bother, one could say. But that was the idea for a long time. Why does Dante mention Polycletus? Did he know his work? There were certain traditional names, always used as typical — a certain name that stood always for the philosopher, another that would stand for a poet, another for a painter. Dante uses these typical names; and Polycletus was the name used regularly for a sculptor. He was, in fact, one of the greatest. "So this wall" — "bank" is no better; the word *ripa* had many meanings, one of which was this, of a sheer perpendicular wall, but that meaning died out. All that the Italians know of the meaning of the word *ripa* now is "bank." That's all that is left, except in seamen's language. In seamen's language when you want to order the men to climb to the top of the mast, straight up, you say, *a ripa*. Translators no doubt look up the word in the dictionary, the worst way to find out what a word means.

This carved stone was more than naturally beautiful, therefore supernaturally beautiful. The first scene he sees carved there is the Annunciation. It's a familiar scene in a Catholic Church, even in some other Churches. In the Annunciation an angel comes to tell the Virgin Mary that she is to bear a child of the Holy Spirit, the Savior. These are the two dramatic *personae*, the Virgin Mary and the Angel. To have an annunciation, you have to have these two. Dante sees them figured on this first terrace: *l'angel che venne in terra col decreto*, "the angel who came to earth with the decree of the long wept-for peace." What war is brought to an end by the annunciation? The condition that no man can be saved until Christ came. The end of that ban was the Annunciation. So the beautiful line: *col decreto della molt'anni lagrimata pace*, that peace with God that did not exist but which had been implored for many years with tears, *che aperse il ciel dal suo lungo divieto*, "that decree which opened up again the heavens after the long prohibition," after the long ban.

This angel, *dinanzi a noi pareva si verace*, "this angel before us stood there, so true to life," *quivi intagliato in un atto suave*, "engraved, poised in a gesture of such sweetness that he seemed not an image that is silent; seemed not an image of stone; one would have sworn he was actually pronouncing the word *Ave*." *Ave* is what the Angel said to the Virgin Mary — "Hail, full of grace." In the old, primitive paintings, you often have a little arrow, with the word *Ave* pointing to the Virgin Mary. Here you don't see the word, you hear it: *perchè ivi era imaginata quella che ad aprir l'alto amor volse la chiave*, "for there was represented [that is, by the side of the angel] that one, who turned the key to disclose, to bring out, the lofty love," *ed avea in atto impressa esta favella*, "in her gesture were her words impressed, and those words were: '*Ecce ancilla Dei.*'" Those are the words with which the Virgin Mary replies to the *Ave* of the angel; words of the greatest humility, because she was the highest of all the creatures of God yet she called herself ancilla, servant. "And these words were there," *propriamente, come figura in cera si suggella*, just as one stamps an image on wax, so here one stamps sound on these sculptures. "'Don't keep your mind fixed only on one place,' said my gentle master who was by me on the side where men have their hearts. And therefore, I turned my glance and saw, behind Mary, on the side where he who moved me stood," *un'altra storia*, in the usual sense, not of history, but of a narrative, "the representation of a story fixed in the stone: I moved past Virgil and came near so that my eyes were close enough to study it." And here comes the description of David, who dances before the ark of the covenant. He forgets all his dignity, all his majesty; and his wife, who doesn't want to see his kingly majesty diminished, is indignant and enraged.

After this scene of King David comes the image of Trajan who should have been condemned but who was such a just ruler that Gregory prayed that he would be brought back to earth and allowed to live long enough to be converted and be saved.

25. THE TERRACE OF THE PROUD

The scene of the great Psalmist that Dante admires on this first terrace of Purgatory isn't set in the mountain but cut, chiseled out of it. *Era intagliato lì nel marmo stesso*, "It was cut," it was the mountain itself that was chiseled out with these representations. This is an interesting point: there are scattered in Italy, wherever there are remains of what had been quarries, where the marble is found embedded in other matter, indicating that it was about to end; in the last imbedded remains, the rude local sculptors often carved something. Some of their work has come down to us from the age of Augustus. Unfortunately, to preserve them they were dug out and brought to museums, where they don't show up very well. Dante may have seen some of these works of art cut in the mountains of the white marble of Carrara, which is that very glistening white marble that is here described.

"Cut in the marble were" *lo carro e i buoi traendo l'arca santa* "the cart and the oxen dragging, pulling the holy ark" — which reminds us that we must not perform tasks that are not asked, or required of us. You recall that the man who wanted to hold up the ark of the covenant, and could not, was struck by lightening. This is a very important line: *per che si teme officio non commesso*, "fear an office not entrusted not assigned to you." *Dinanzi parea gente*, "straight ahead people appeared, divided into seven choruses, seven groups, which to my two senses, forced one of them to say 'Yes' they sing, the other, 'No' they do not sing."

When you looked, you heard them sing, but if you tried to just listen without looking, you heard nothing. "Likewise, at the smoke of the incense which there was imaged, engraved, eyes and nose were made discordant with yes and no." Again, when you looked at them you seemed to smell the fragrance of the incense, but when you turned your eyes away from them, obviously you could smell nothing. *Lì precedeva al benedetto vaso, trescando alzato, l'umile salmista,* "preceding the blessed ark, was the humble psalmist, who was dancing with his garments lifted up."

What an artist Dante is! You can see it by comparing the original line with what people have done trying to translate it. The whole picture is masterfully chiseled: *e più e men che re era in quel caso.* "He was less than a king" because ridiculous, but more, in this instance, because, for a worthy cause, he humbly permitted himself to become ridiculous, laughable by his conduct. You can imagine, *see,* how funny he must have seemed when he pulled up his clothing and started dancing. *D'incontra effigiata ad una vista d'un gran palazzo Micol ammirava*; also represented in sculpture across from this, "at the open window of a large house, Micol looked on" — not in wonderment but in astonishment, stupor. "She looked on like a woman spiteful and dismal. I moved my feet from that place in order to be able to see, nearby, another story."

Quivi era storiata l'alta gloria del roman principato. "There was represented the lofty glory of the Roman sovereignty" — *principato,* remember, doesn't mean principality; it's a word that has to be considered with care in all languages. Today the word "prince" has been greatly reduced in significance. You call a prince the son of a king or ruler of some sort. But through the

centuries the sovereign has been called *principe*; and it
applied not only to the sovereign as a person, but even
to Parliament, if the Parliament was sovereign. The
Parliament of England could be called *principe*.
Principato, therefore, meant something much more
than what prince or its derivatives mean now, not only
in English but in all modern languages. Of course, the
Roman *principato* was always great according to Dante,
but with Trajan it is at its greatest. Why does Dante
puts such stress on Trajan? Well, he extended the
empire to limits never before reached, and which, it
was found later, could not be held. So here is Trajan,
"he whose worth," *il cui valore mosse Gregorio alla sua
gran vittoria*, "moved Gregory to his great victory" —
Gregory was able to resurrect this man, and convert
him, so that he could be saved. "I speak of Trajan."

He singles out Trajan for a number of reasons.
In the empire that Dante saw, the Holy Roman Empire,
the two figures that had always been brought forth as
the models of rule for the empire, as the ideals of the
imperial office, were Augustus and Trajan. Trajan was
a favorite of the Germans of the Holy Roman Empire.
Barbarossa got away from a tight fix, in the Alps, where
the soldiers of the Italian communes had surrounded
him and were pressing in, by ordering the unfurling of
all banners and with full fanfare his attendants announced: "Make way, the Emperor passes — the succes-
sor of Augustus and Trajan" — and the Italian soldiers
let him pass. There was a good reason for the special
significance attached to Trajan. The great legend surrounding him, which has been lost now, had long
survived, in the Balkans, Hungary and elsewhere.

Io dico di Traiano imperadore, "I speak of the
Emperor Trajan; and a poor widow who had put her

hand on his bridle, a widow all tears and sorrow" — all you could see was the sorrow that manifests itself in tears. Here is the emperor on horseback, and this little insignificant, ordinary widow. Around them *parea calcato e pieno di cavalieri*, "there was a throng all around," the army, knights, warriors on horseback, *e l'aquile nell'oro sovr'essi in vista al vento si movieno*, "and the eagles in gold" — that's not good, but it's a better phrase than golden eagles — and the eagles on the background of gold, "actually seemed to move in the wind." Again, you have this insistence on the capacity of the artist to do what seems impossible. *L'aquila nell'oro sovr'essi*, "over them the banners actually waved as the wind struck them."

The Roman eagle has had quite a success in history too. Down to recent times there was almost no ruler of any sort who didn't put an eagle on his national banners or royal emblems, in some way. *La miserella intra tutti costoro.* . . . Dante wants to be sure that you see the contrast: this poor little woman, in the midst of such people, *parea dicer*, seemed to say — you don't hear it but the expression was such that you got quite a dialogue out of it just by looking at the sculpture of this artist — "she seemed to say: *'Signor'*." Again, *Signore* doesn't mean "Sir," or "Mister," as you might think. *Signore* in Italian is the most comprehensive word to indicate political power. Think of the Palazzo della Signoria in Florence. It was the palace of the rulers, the executors of the government. *Signore* is the title of the highest political executors. Dante, for two months, was a *Signore*. Lord or anything else like that is wrong; you have to say something like Majesty, I suppose.

"*Signor, fammi vendetta del mio figliuol ch'è morto,*

ond'io m'accoro," "'do me vengeance for my son who has been killed, for whom I grieve'." *Accorare* means more than grief; it's grief that makes you break down. *Ed egli a lei risponde*, "And he seemed to answer her," "*Or aspetta tanto ch'io torni.*" "'Wait now until I return.' But she: 'My majesty,' speaking as a person whom grief causes to hurry'," in other words, grief has no patience to wait, "'what if you do not return' — and he: 'whoever will occupy my post, take my place, will do justice for you.' And she: 'the good another does, what will it be for you, if you forget your own, if you put aside yours'?" And he: "*Or ti conforta*," "'cheer up, for it behooves me that I absolve my duty, before I move; justice requires it and pity'" — not piety this time, but pity — "'pity holds me here'."

How is it possible to have this kind of sculpture? *Colui, che mai non vide cosa nuova* — *nuova* here doesn't have the ordinary meaning; there is an important philosophical sense where "new" means created in time, the opposite of eternal. That is the sense here. *Colui che mai non vide cosa nuova* — because God never saw anything start in time; he had known of it in eternity. We know things because we see them in time, but in the case of God it is otherwise: we know things because they exist, but in the case of God, they exist because he knows them. "He who never saw a new thing," that really doesn't give the true sense of the Italian, "produced this visible speech," *novello a noi, perchè qui non si trova*. It was not new to God but it was new to us because it was not to be found here below. *Mentr'io mi dilettava di guardare*, "while I was rejoicing," hardly "taking pleasure," exulting perhaps, "to see all these images of humility" — the Virgin Mary, calling herself *ancilla*, David dancing before the Ark, this Emperor Trajan who changes his imperial plans because of the pleading of a widow — these images of humility represented as examples to indicate what should be the aspiration of men, that they may not fall into the excesses of pride, "these images which are" *per lo fabbro loro a veder care,* "beautiful in themselves but dear to look upon because of their maker," *ecco di quà, ma fanno i passi radi,* in the middle of his admiration, Dante is startled by Virgil saying "'Here they come, but they are moving slowly'."

The construction is a kind of anacoluthon. Virgil was more interested in getting a guide than in admiring the sculpture. "'Here they come, but with tardy step,' said the poet, 'many are they, and they will help us to proceed to the higher terraces'." *Gli occhi miei ch'a mirar eran contenti, per veder novitadi ond' ei son vaghi,* "my eyes which were happy admiring what was before me, seeing new things, which have always attracted them. . . ." Dante here confesses that his eyes were always *vaghi per veder novitadi,* desirous to see beautiful new things. The word *vagare* originally meant what its derivations mean in English — vague, vagrancy — but has gone off on its own track in Italian and in some way or other has come to be connected with the word beautiful; and *vagare* has come to mean the act of man confronted by beauty, the act of loving. *Vagheggiare* used to be the word for love, though now it very seldom is heard. "Enamored" would fit here well. *Gli occhi miei,* "my eyes, turning toward him [at the announcement of something new] were not slow. And here's what I saw." Again you have a sort of truncated grammatical construction to show his emotion — "it was an awful thing that I saw, but reader, don't be afraid." In other words, this first sight of the punishment of Purgatory was frightful. *Non vo' però, lettor, che tu ti smaghi di buon proponimento,* "but I don't want you, my reader, to dismay yourselves"; *smagare* is the same word as dismay. *Magare, smagare* — again the language is originally from the language of love: unbewitch yourselves. *Non vo' però, lettor,* "that you lose your courage for following out your good purposes," *per udire come Dio vuol che il debito si paghi,* "because you hear how God wants you to pay your debt." *Non attender la forma del martire;* "don't look too much at the form of the punishment; think of what follows upon it, think of eternal beatitude, think that even the worst punishment here cannot be extended beyond the great judgment" — *la gran sentenza.*

Io cominciai: "Maestro, quel ch'io veggio mover a noi, non mi sembian persone; e non sò che, sì nel veder vaneggio." "I began, 'Master, that which I see coming towards us, you tell me they are persons but they don't seem to be persons, so distracted am I looking at them, I don't see persons moving toward us, but I don't know what they are.' And he to me": *"La grave condizione di lor tormento,"* "'the grievious, grave, burdensome, condition of their punishment'," *"a terra li rannicchia,"* "'makes them crouch, doubles them down to earth'," *rannicchiare* is not only to bend, but also to reduce in size. "So crushed were they to the ground, that my eyes were drawn between two possible hypotheses," *n'ebber tensione. "Ma guarda fiso là, e disviticchia col viso quel che vien sotto a quei sassi,"* "'but look fixedly there and with your eyes [*disviticchia*] unloosen'," try to discern, try to make out, "distinguish" is right, but *disviticchia* gives you a picture: just as you try to unravel something, entangled thread, branches of a tree caught in one another, or pieces of wood that have been screwed together, so here try to *disviticchiare* that man who comes under that burden of rocks.

"*Già scorger puoi come ciascun si picchia,*" "'you can see how each one beats his breast'." You beat your breast as you say *peccavi, miserere me*: I have sinned, have mercy on me. The beating of the breast corresponds to the *miserere me*. And here Dante goes off and explodes against the proud: "*O superbi cristiani,*" "O you proud Christians. . . ." Together the words jar; it's tolerable for the Romans to have been proud, but how could a Christian who has heard the teachings of Christ, the sermon on the Mount, be proud? So there is a great deal of meaning in the juxtaposition of those two words, *superbi cristiani*. The Stoics could be proud, but not Christians. "*O superbi Cristiani, miseri lassi.*"

This is addressed not necessarily to the people in Purgatory but to all people on earth. They think they are enjoying themselves as they go about, and instead they are miserable wretches, "*che della vista della mente infermi, fidanza avete ne' retrosi passi.*" In order to be proud you have to be always taking backward steps; the eye of your reason must be sick, you see things wrong, "*della vista della mente infermi,*" "'your eyes are not functioning'," "sick" is all right here but there ought to be a better word than that. Ailing, perhaps. "'Ailing in your mental sight, you put your trust in your backward steps: you think you are going forward and in reality you're going backwards. Are you not aware, you proud people that we are worms'?"

Don't be distracted by the word. We are a special kind of worm, the worm that bears the butterfly. In other words, Dante here comes out strongly with a doctrine which he doesn't always entertain — namely that human life has no meaning at all except as a passage, a preparation for the life of eternity. Of course, it is more Augustinian than the general view today. "'Are you not aware that you are born'" — every time you see *nato* in Dante or in the Latin of his day, it means "nature," you have in you by nature — *nati a formar* means intended by nature to form, not just born. Since the days of Aristotle there has been this connection between the word for "to be born" and for "nature." In Latin you have *nascer* and *natura*; φύω and φύσις in Greek have the same root also. Nature has made us worms that will produce the angelic butterflies. In other words, what counts is the spirit and not the body. Dante certainly knows that butterfly is another word for psyche.

There seems to be no concern here at this moment about the virtues that Dante had extolled and had set for life on earth. Here he is thinking only of the soul that on judgment day flies to its maker. In other words, the *angelica farfalla*, the butterfly, is the spirit. And Dante is helped to that thought by resorting to a Greek commonplace — "*l'angelica farfalla che vola alla giustizia senza schermi*," "'that flies up to the throne of justice'" *senza schermi*. That doesn't mean without defense necessarily, but with nothing to cover it, with nothing on, naked, "*di che l'animo vostro in alto galla.*"

"'That is the reason that makes your soul try to rise upward, soar upward, since, as long as you are in the flesh, you are like incomplete insects'." Life is but a transition period, not like a cocoon, but a grub. What counts is not the grub but what comes out of it. Therefore we are, like the grub, defective insects, because perfection will come when we are transformed. We are like worms, insects, in which the formation is not complete. That's a powerful *terzina* against worldly pride, and it has a great deal of truth in it. What's behind this is not the Thomistic teaching of the day but pure Augustinianism.

Now he discerns clearly these people that he wasn't able to distinguish as human beings at first. "As to support a ceiling or a roof, instead of corbels sometimes one sees a human figure which has its knees joined, or pressing his chest" — that is, sometimes when you have to support a roof or a *loggia* or something else, instead of putting a corbel under the beam you put a human figure, a man or woman in stone. Of course, to do a good job, a significant job, you don't just put a weight on the head, but you have to show the weight bearing down. Therefore the sculptor has to have the figure oppressed by the weight, bent down because of it. These are the caryatids. *Per mensola talvolta una figura si vede giunger le ginocchia al petto, la qual fa del non ver vera rancura nascere a chi la vede* — Dante is impressed by this artistic touch. His mind throughout this canto is prepossessed with art. When he sees these figures, these caryatids, he knows they're false but he feels sorry for them, *fa del non ver vera rancura nascere a chi la vede,* "makes the onlooker feel a true sorrow for something which is not true"; *così fatti vid'io color, quando posi ben cura,* "such when I looked at them, more carefully, they appeared to me."

Dante here, as in *Paradiso* and also in *Inferno,* wants to remind you that no punishment or reward is the same. Everyone has a different punishment or reward, each receiving his due. *In domo Patria mei mansione multae sunt,* "In my Father's house are many rooms." That's Biblical, of course, and Dante interprets it to mean that punishments and rewards are all different. *Ver è che più e meno eran contratti.* "The truth

is some were pressed down more, some less, according
as the weight pressed on their head;" to the extent they
had sinned, to that extent their pride was more or less.
"And one, who seemed, judging from his acts, to have
the greatest amount of patience, weeping seemed to
say: This is all I can stand." They approached, giving an
allegorical interpretation of the *Pater Noster*, which, I
must say, is not very successful. It's impossible to
change the Our Father in any way without making it
sound inferior. It can't be made more beautiful. Not
even Dante could do it.

You all know the *Pater Noster*. "Our Father who
art in heaven. . . . ." Keep it in mind. Dante first wants
us to understand more exactly what we mean when we
say, "Our Father who art in heaven." He reminds us
that it's wrong to say that, like the Platonists and many
others do, that God is everywhere. Dante explains *che
nei cieli stai,* "who art in heaven" not because you are
limited there but because of the greater love you have
for the first effects up there, *"per più amore ch' ai primi
effetti di lassù tu hai."* It may sound strange, but philosophically it's pretty clear because, when you hear the
word *effect* you immediately think of cause. And God,
who is the cause of all, loves most the first effects
because they are the things which he produced for
Paradise. He is in heaven therefore, because of His
great love for the effects in heaven.

"*Laudato sia il tuo nome.*" Here he goes off into
a sort of theological disquisition which spoils it entirely. The prayer has *sanctificetur nomen tuum. Sacti-
ficetur* is much more than *laudato.* In liturgical language *laudatur* means something else, though not too
far removed. What follows is a breaking up of God into
a trinity, a sort of dissolution. *Laudato,* "'praised be thy

name'," which is of the Father, "*e il tuo valore*," which is of the *logus*, the Second Person, "'praised be thy name, and thy power by every creature'" — not praised, but *sanctified* — "*com'è degno di render grazie al tuo dolce vapore.*" *Vapore*, it's called in Italian, and it's even worse than "vapor" in English. Today it has acquired all sorts of connotations. But it has had various meanings; and one which it had in Dante's time was *exhalation*, spiritual exhalation. Here it's the exhalation of the Holy Spirit, the Trinity — Father, Son and Holy Spirit. He uses the same expression elsewhere in connection with the Holy Spirit. "*Vegna ver noi la pace del tuo regno*," "'May the peace'" — peace means beatitude, the cessation of all desire; when you have nothing more to want, you're at peace — "'may the peace of your kingdom come to us, for we can't by ourselves attain it, unless it comes to us, whatever our wit may be. And as your angels make a sacrifice of their own will to you'" — the Latin is, *fiat voluntas tuas*, Thy will be done, "'singing Hosanna, so may men make a sacrifice of theirs'."

Dante amplifies; just as the angels refuse to have a will of their own, so too we, of ourselves, want simply what you want. Of course, the reason he introduces the angels is *sicut in cielo et in terra*, "in earth as it is in heaven." He prays for the doing of the will of God, by the abolishing of our human will, and of the angelic will. "*Panem nostrum cotidianum da nobis hodie*," "'Give us this day our daily bread'." Of course, the bread is there, but it's not just bread; there's more to it. But Dante doesn't like the literal, so daily bread becomes the comprehension that only God can give us. This was interpreted in the light of the *concursus*: we can't do anything, we could not exist if God were to disappear

— which is an impossibility of course; but if God were to disappear, we would disappear. If God ceased to think, we would not think. That is the daily *manna*, "*la cotidiana manna, senza la qual per questo aspro deserto a retro va chi più di gir s'affanna*," "'without which in this bitter desert, the more you want to proceed further, the more you slide back'." "*E come noi lo mal che avem sofferto perdoniamo a ciascuno*," "'and as we pardon everyone for all the ills we have suffered, so you kindly pardon us without regard for our merits'," *nostra virtù*. Virtue here is to be taken in its psychological sense, not in its moral sense. Do not test our power, which is so easily weakened, with the ancient adversary ("*non sperimentar con l'antico avversaro*"); that is, do not lead us into temptation, "*ma libera da lui che sì la sprona*," "'but free it from the devil that so spurs it. This last prayer is not uttered for us for we have no need'," they are beyond it, "'but for those who have remained behind'."

Does that refer to those who were in that little valley — those who were tempted, attacked by that *striscia*, that snake, which is the devil? Or does it refer to all mankind, those still on earth? *Così a sè e noi buona ramogna quell'ombre orando*, "thus those shades, souls, praying good speed for them and for us" — the word *ramogna* is very picturesque, very suggestive; good speed is as good as anything else to give the idea of it — "kept moving under their burden, like that of which we sometimes dream" — that is, the stones that were crushing them — *simile a quel che talvolta si sogna*.

The last touch in this picture is the *incubus*. There is a great deal of literature about the *incubus*, the *succubus*. It's very common, more literary than real, but there are experiences in dreams of such things as what these people called the *incubus*. We call such dreams nightmares. The *incubus*, which is on top, has to be accompanied always by something below, which is the *succubus*. There are descriptions of the *incubus* and the *succubus* causing suffocation. There are such things in our dreams. We don't know much about what suffocation is like in its final stages, but it must be something like this. No doubt the *incubus* was also connected with sexual manifestations. The ancients studied it at length, or thought they had studied it. The word has returned today, in a sense. In Italian, when you want to say, or suggest, that someone is completely under the control or influence of another man, you say he has an *incubus*. Here these people also remind Dante of someone weighed down by an *incubus*.

26. THE PAGEANT ON THE TOP OF PURGATORY; VIRGIL'S DEPARTURE; THE APPEARANCE OF BEATRICE

There are six more terraces, all full of pathos, but the punishment in all is also a source of satisfaction. Dante doesn't go as far as the modern philosopher who said there is something in the spirit of every man — a sense of justice in everyone, even the worst criminal, no matter how bad he may be — that makes him rejoice when he is justly punished; where the convicted murderer rejoices inwardly at his own execution. The innateness of the sense of justice, the *iustitia naturalis*, as the Schoolmen called it, is brought out strongly by Dante, and in a very dramatic way.

These seven terraces lead up to the plain, not of truth, but of goodness. At the top of Purgatory is Eden; which is another way of saying that when you have finally overcome all the impulses of *sensualitas* and *cupiditas* and have reached the point where you are predisposed to do what you should do, what you're supposed and expected to do, you are the perfect man, you've reached the condition man was in before the Fall. It was purely an act of disobedience that made evil come into human existence. When he says farewell to Dante, Virgil, as you know, pronounces him fit to follow the impulses of his will, as man was before the Fall. Here in this plain of nobility, as it has been called, Dante's reunion with Beatrice takes place. That occurs in connection with a pageant which is one of the most baffling things that Dante has ever written. In it, Beatrice is treated as if she were God.

This pageant starts out with a vision of seven candelabras, which seven candelabras draw out streamers of light behind themselves; Dante contemplates these seven streamers, which have the seven colors of the rainbow. How Dante came to know of the seven colors is very mysterious. Traditionally, the number of colors for the rainbow used to be given as only four. These seven candelabras, with their seven streamers are simply an image, a symbol of the divine direction of the human will before the Fall, and after the removal of the seven sins. They are the seven gifts of the Holy Spirit, which is another way of saying that God, as love, operates upon the will and inspires it to do the things that it should do. And these pennants — for that's what we should call them — these pennants of light had only ten steps separating them from the first to the last, which is a roundabout way of indicating that the inspiration of the Holy Spirit is contained within the limits set for the intellect, by natural law, which, when it was forgotten in the hearts of men, was imprinted, indelibly, in the ten commandments. After all, the ten commandments are the formulation of the first precepts that natural law commands. This pageant, this process, of course, starts off with a description of what would be innate in man, how man would properly conduct himself if he were in the original state of nature, if he were not overcome by the *formes*, by *sensualitas*. There is a division into gifts of love and gifts of reason. These banners mark the advance of the Holy Scriptures, shed light on the Holy Scriptures.

We should remember that natural law does not proceed from reason. Natural law is the stamp on the human intellect about which a man has nothing at all to do, any more than a falling body has anything to do about the law of gravity. It's of divine origin, a participation of man, inborn in him, in the eternal law. This natural law is not ratiocination, but the source of ratiocination. In men, reason can go astray, but natural law can never go astray. It is always present in man; but because it can be crusted over, hidden perhaps, it was also formulated in the laws of Moses, in the *Decalogue*. Theologians strove hard to bring back these ten commandments, to trace them back discursively, as immediate derivatives of the inspiration of natural law. Natural law in the Schoolmen, in the theologians of Dante's time, is something quite different from what you might think from your knowledge of the notion of natural law in the political development of the West. To keep this clearly in mind, all one has to remember is that politics involves only one part of the whole of natural law; it is the sphere where natural law develops into ethics and where ethics, for some reason, has to be made coercive — of social necessity — and that's how it results in the gallows. It is imprinted in us, so that, for the original act of our intellect and the original act of our will, we are not subject to fault. We can say it's in us by inspiration because it is like the inspiration of the Holy Spirit. It is sharing in a *participation*. Justice is essentially in God, but in man it is by participation.

The Scriptures are lighted up in accordance with these two great endowments of mankind: one is for the will and one is for the intellect. But the Scriptures are divided, following St. Jerome, in two parts. You have first of all those Scriptures that preceded and prophesized the birth of Christ. In the Old Testament, men were joined to Christ, not in seeing but in having faith in things not seen. They are clad in white, these men that follow immediately the streamers. In these cantos, Dante does nothing but remind you of this chromatic symbolism: white is one of the colors of the three virtues. White is for faith, green is for hope, and red for love: *caritas*, which means love in a much larger sense than we use the word today. These books of the Old Testament, following the scheme of St. Jerome, who translates them, are divided into twenty-four groups, as we are told in his famous *Prologus in libros Samuel et Malachim*. It doesn't mean there are twenty-four authors, but simply twenty-four books. Why St. Jerome adopted that division is not easy to say. After the period of anticipation, comes the period of realization. And in this canto you have that represented symbolically by the four gospels: Matthew, Mark, Luke and John. They made no distinction in those days as we do today, setting three together and one apart. To represent them, Dante predictably avails himself of the traditional symbolism. It was almost as popular as the signs of the zodiac. You find them represented everywhere, if you know what they are — not so familiarly recognized today as they were once. The symbol of St. John is the eagle. Mark is the lion. Luke is the ox, and Matthew is Man. Of course, this is again largely from St. Jerome; it is in connection with the teachings of St. Jerome that this symbolism develops.

After the four gospels you have those who followed the revelation through the gospels. The first two are the acts of the apostles, and the other, the epistles of St. Paul, represented symbolically by two men: the one interested in destruction, and the other interested in healing, in salvation. Luke, the author of the Acts is a doctor interested in salvation, in healing. St. Peter has, as his symbol, the two keys. St. Paul has the sword. St. Paul, as you know, was a man addicted to arms, to the persecution of Christians, and when he finally became converted, the sword became a spiritual sword, for cutting out the sickness of sin.

Then come the symbols of the four authors of the four so-called canonic epistles. And then, finally, one lonely man comes slowly, ending the procession: St. John. He had appeared before as author of the Gospel. St. John, in fact, comes up three times: once as the author of one of the canonic epistles; once, as we said, as the author of the Gospel, and the third time as the author of the Apocalypse, the Book of Revelation. He and the others mentioned, are not men here, but books, bringing the light of God, the Holy Spirit, to guide the natural will and the natural intellect.

Immediately before the four evangelists there is a chariot, an imperial chariot, more accurately, a *basterna*, Dante calls it. *Basterna* is not a chariot, which is the car of a warrior; *basterna* was the name given to the imperial chariot; this one drawn by a *griffon*, an animal with two natures, half eagle, half lion. It doesn't exist except in the imaginations of men — which is perhaps more important than existing in nature. You have an imperial chariot drawn by the symbol of Christ. Why should the griffon as the symbol of Christ be used here? Well, Christ has two natures: the great mystery that holds an impossible contradiction. God is man in Christ: he is man and not man, because he is God. Reason can't grasp it; only by faith are you able to accept it. So this imaginary animal serves very well as the image of Christ. And in this chariot is Beatrice. At first, this is rather shocking: you have Beatrice surrounded on the right and on the left by the whole system of virtues. She controls all the virtues, not only the four cardinal virtues, but also the three theological virtues. The chariot, which has been moving along in the procession, arrives at a tree and stops there. And with that we arrive at the beginning of canto thirty.

To understand this canto you have to draw some sort of analogy. Tossed about on the high seas of this life, how are we going to navigate? Of course, Dante did not know about the compass, although the compass was already in use. So he acts and speaks as if the only thing available here below were the stars. How do we navigate with the stars? Well, if the stars are visible, first of all you have to find the polar star; and to find the polar star you have to fall back on the *septentriones*, the seven stars. It's the word that has given us *settentrional* in Italian, *septentrional* in French and English, meaning northern. The navigator is guided to port by these *septentriones* in his sea voyages. So, spiritually, man was guided, as a navigator is, by the stars, by these seven candelabras, with their trailing lights; in other words, the seven gifts of the Holy Spirit guided man's conduct consistently until he destroyed their efficacy by disobedience. When he speaks of the halting of the chariot, Dante makes use of a simile in describing these streamers of seven lights that guided men's actions and kept them from going astray, reminding us that those lights once guided man spiritually, even as here below we are guided by the seven lights which are the lights of the *septentriones*. They are the seven stars of a constellation, four of which form a quadrant, one side of which, extended, strikes the polar star. Anyone who has watched these stars must have noticed that they are always above the horizon, at this latitude. The stars overhead, and to the south, all rise and set; they drop below the horizon into the ocean and then come up again in the east. These stars never set, never drop into the ocean, provided, of course, you always stay in the northern latitudes. If you go south, to the latitude where Dante locates Purgatory, they are no longer visible.

Quando il settentrion del primo cielo, "when the *settentriones,* when the seven stars of the first sky" — the first sky is the tenth heaven, the immaterial heaven, the unmoved heaven, and these seven stars that we see are in the second sky, counting one way, or, counting the other way, they are in the eighth sky, the heaven of the fixed stars — *che né occaso mai seppe ne orto,* this *settentrion* never knew rising or setting, nor would it ever have been clouded or veiled from man's view, except for one thing: in spite of the fact that man was originally inspired by such great gifts, there was one condition; it is the point on which all Christianity is suspended: *obedience.* After all, what is sin? It's an act of disobedience, not following God's commands. It's because of that act of disobedience that the efficacy of these stars was lost; these spiritual stars were covered over by fog, by sin. That *settentrion* never knew any veil other than the cloud of sin. These seven stars made everyone there *accorto di suo dover;* in the world of natural goodness, in Eden, they made every man aware of his duty, in the same way that the lower *settentriones* in the lower sphere, the dipper, makes man turn in his course, makes him turn the rudder correctly so as to come to port.

There is the analogy. This *settentrion,* this sevenfold constellation has come to a stop, and *la gente verace,* the truth-speaking people, that is, the people of the Old Testament, who had come before the Griffon, have turned to the chariot as if to its *pace,* rest from the turmoil of desire. Desire is a constant turmoil. You desire because you want something you don't have. When you get what you want, finally, desire stops and *pace*, happiness, beatitude follows. It's a line which may not be pleasing to the Hebrews but without which there would be no Christianity. The Hebrews felt that something had to come; there is an expectancy in their books, an expectancy about the coming of Christ. In the old days, every child was given this syllogism to learn: the Old Testament is the major premise, the New Testament is the minor premise, and the conclusion is the Holy Roman *Ecclesia*. This is very important for Dante, although often he would construct the Church after his own heart.

So they turn now toward the chariot as to their beatitude. It is a beautiful picture this, of these Hebrews looking with longing toward something they cannot have until Christ comes along to satisfy all their desires. Then, one of them, as if sent from heaven, sings out: "*Veni, sponsa de Libano*," "'Come, bride from Lebanon.'. . ." These are the words of Solomon in the Song of Songs. I doubt Solomon wrote them with holy intentions, but the Church has purified the Song of Solomon. The bride is what every good Catholic boy that read the Bible with the Glosses learned, that the bride according to the Gloss, is the bride of Christ, namely, the Holy Catholic Church. Then comes one singing: "*Veni, sponsa de Libano*." This leads you to think that Dante looks upon the woman in the chariot as the Church. Is Beatrice the Church? I don't know, I'm sure nobody knows. But I imagine she has some sort of role that had already been stated in the inspirational words of the great king and philosopher of Jerusalem. "Three times he shouted the song, and all

the others sang after him. . . ." Here again is a symbol
somewhat difficult to understand. Dante reminds us
that all those who are not going to be damned will be
blessed on Judgment Day. *Quali i beati al novissimo
bando*, "as the blessed, at the last trumpet call" —
novissimo is a pure Latinism here, meaning the last —
"Just as at the last trumpet call, the blessed will arise
spontaneously," *presto*, "from their caverns" — this is
usually the word for crypt — then comes an untranslat-
able beautiful line, *la rivestita carne alleluiando*, "singing halleluiah with the flesh, the body they will have
recovered." Before they had been mere souls, not
dressed with bodies; then, they will re-acquire their
bodies, and voices, to sing the halleluiah of the resurrection of the flesh.

The beauty of this line is that you have a double
procedure in rhetoric, as Cicero would say. The voice
stands for the flesh and flesh is considered as a garment of the soul, and this fleshy garment appears now
as a song of glory to God. "Just as they will when they
are resurrected," just as these will arise singing, so
there arose over the divine chariot — still not a good
word: chariot suggests a warrior and *basterna* suggests
imperial majesty — "so they stood up at the word of
such majesty, the word of Solomon, a hundred of
them, *ministri e messaggier di vita eterna*, "ministers and
messengers of eternal life." That's what the word angel
means, messenger. They sing too, like those who are
resurrected, and they sing *"Benedictus qui venis,"*
"'Blessed art thou that cometh'." Those are the words
that were sung in Jerusalem upon the entrance of
Christ; here they are sung because of the coming of
Beatrice. *"Benedictus qui venis," e fior gittando di sopra e
dintorno*, "casting flowers upon it and all around."

And here comes a line that is beautiful but most strange. They have just sung a phrase which is perhaps the most touching phrase of the whole Gospel, to anyone familiar with the service of Palm Sunday. Followed here by a line of Virgil, must seem strange. Dante chooses a line that was very famous in antiquity, and still is, a line that occurs in a famous passage from the sixth book of the *Aeneid*. It's the tribute to Marcellus. *Tu Marcellus eris* — Anchises points out a certain child and tells him that he will someday be the imperial child; and no sooner does he say it, but he thinks of the early death of the child. He says: "Scatter lilies by the handful," *manibus date lilia plenis* — one of the most perfect things Virgil has ever done, linking in one line the celebration of imperial birth and a death which he thinks is a great loss. It's a very beautiful tribute to Virgil, this quotation; but it is, again, one that makes us doubt the complete sincerity of Dante's attachment to the Gospel. That the angels should be made to sing a line of Virgil, beautiful as it may be, is not, surely, a manifestation of piety. Those who have studied Latin literature, may have read notes that explain that these lines of Virgil were the most highly paid lines of antiquity. In our days there is great interest in this economic side of literature.

Dante describes the aspect of this angelic apparition. *Io vidi già nel cominciar del giorno*, "toward the beginning of day on earth, I have often seen the oriental part of the sky, the east sky," *la parte oriental, tutta rosata, e l'altro ciel di bel sereno adorno*, "and the remaining part of the sky all adorned with serene blue." Serene doesn't mean, in Italian, what it means in English. It is not simply quiet, but also has the meaning of blue. A *pietra serena* is a blue stone. "So have I seen, at the beginning of day, a red zone, [let us say, in the east], while the rest of the sky is blue." And, as a result of this rosy cloud, the face of the sun was appearing — Dante says *nascere*, which is impossible to translate accurately because we lack the full conjugation of the verb "to be born" — the face of the sun was rising with shadows, so that with the tempering of the vapors, *l'occhio la sostenea lunga fiata*, the eye could look upon it, could endure the sight for a long time. And just as we sometimes have a cloud veiling the face of the sun, so here you have a cloud, a veil made up of these flowers scattered by angels.

There isn't very much religious inspiration here, but surely the beauty of the poetry makes it undoubtedly a very inspired passage. *Così dentro una nuvola di fiori*, "so within a cloudy bower of flowers," *che dalle mani angeliche saliva e ricadeva*, "which arose from the motions of angelic hands, and having risen and fallen down again within and around the chariot" — notice how suspenseful all this is — "so on a candid, white veil," *"cinta d'oliva," cinta* doesn't mean strictly, "girted"; "crowned" might be better; *cinta*, of course, can refer to any kind of cincture, not only the one in the middle, so "crowned" will do . . . "in a white veil, crowned with olive, a woman appeared, under a green mantle, clad in the color of living flame."

You have the symbolism of color again, in this first manifestation of Beatrice. To understand the lines that follow, you have to remember that Dante, while on earth, while Beatrice was still living, had but one desire; to have a glimpse of her. That was to be his greatest joy. But no sooner had he laid eyes upon her than a tremor seized him, a sort of convulsion overcame him so that he had to move away, routed by shame. So he writes: *E lo spirito mio che già cotanto tempo era stato che alla sua presenza non era di stupor, tremando, affranto*, "So my spirit that had been for so many years, or rather, for which so many years had passed since the time when, in her presence it had stood trembling in admiration." The last line describes the experience he had had ten years before on earth. In prose we would say, I haven't seen Beatrice for ten years. But, instead of saying that, he describes the experience he had in her presence on earth. "And my spirit," *senza degli occhi aver più conoscenza*, "without having further knowledge from the eyes" — He learns and feels something not because of what he saw with his eyes, but because of an occult mysterious power that moved from her; Beatrice here emanates a power, an emanation which is not perceived through the senses, *per occulta virtù che da lei mosse, d'antico amor sentì la gran potenza*.

In prose you would say, after ten years he fell in love again; but Dante says, "I felt again the great power of the old love." Here again, in this implicit quotation, we have a remainder of Virgil's power over Dante. In antiquity, in all times, Virgil was especially famous because of the episode of Dido; and that episode is crowned by a very famous line. When Dido sees Aeneas, she, who had been faithful to her dead husband for so long, forgets her vow, and falls for Aeneas. To try and justify herself she says that in the presence of Aeneas she feels the same old love; it's the same love, but not the same person. She speaks of the *antico amore*. And Dante here introduces that phrase, which we wouldn't stress so much if he hadn't elaborated this Virgilian echo later in the same canto. *Tosto che nella vista mi percosse l'alta virtù*, "As soon as my sight was struck by the great, lofty power" — *l'alta virtù* namely, the power

of the inspiration of love — *che già m'avea trafitte prima
ch'io fuor di puerizia fosse,* "that power that pierced me,
that had got hold of me when I was not yet out of
childhood.". . . Dante was nine when first pierced by
love. *Volsimi alla sinistra col rispitto col quale il fantolin
corre alla mamma, quando ha paura o quando egli è
afflitto.* He has a sense of dismay. The psychologists,
perhaps, can handle this better than we can, to make it
clear to us how this love reawakens in him, at this
distance; perhaps because of some sort of insecurity
that demands protection. Turning toward the left with
the trust with which a child runs to its mother, when it
is afraid or afflicted, "I turned to say to Virgil, 'less
than an ounce of blood is left in me that doesn't
tremble'." Then come the beautiful Virgilian lines:
"conosco i segni dell'antica fiamma" [*agnosco veteris vesti-
gia flammae*].

  With that Virgilian quotation to mark his recog-
nition of Beatrice, Dante takes leave of Virgil. He
wanted to let him know that he had recognized, had
felt again the signs of the ancient flame. We need not
again repeat here what has been said so often about the
sudden bursting out of love — that it is at once a joy and
a burning torment. *Ma Virgilio n'avea lasciati scemi di
se,* "But Virgil had left us stripped of himself," a very
pretty phrase but badly translated, *Virgilio dolcissimo
patre.* Notice the pathos of this repetition of the name.
Virgilio a cui per mia salute die' mi, "Virgil to whom I
entrusted my salvation." Then, in spite of the fact that
this is the garden of beatitude, in spite of the fact that
tears had been washed away at the beginning of Purgatory, he cries again. All the magnificence of Eden, or,
as he says here, all that the ancient mother lost, was not
able to keep the tears from flowing, could not keep my

cheeks washed with dew from becoming cloudy again with tears. Then a voice is heard: "'Do not cry because of Virgil's departure, for you will soon have to cry for another reason'."

27. THE MEETING WITH BEATRICE

Cantos thirty and thirty-one give you a clue to what Dante felt to be rectitude in life and the connection between righteous conduct and happiness. All these men built their ethics around the idea of the search for beatitude, the search for happiness. It was so for Plato and Aristotle, the Stoics, Cicero; it was so for the Christian thinkers. Dante is no exception. For the Greeks beatitude is obtained by following the natural course of reason, placing all the lower appetites under the control of reason; Christians hold that the revealed law and grace of God is necessary in addition to what the Greeks had set forth.

In canto thirty, we witness the parting, or separation of Dante from Virgil and the breaking of new ground between Dante and Beatrice. She tells him not to weep for Virgil, there will be something more serious for him to weep about in a moment. Then comes a description of Beatrice, which may strike some of us as strange, for it doesn't seem to fit in with the general picture that Dante created for us in earlier works, but which, on the other hand, does fit very well the allegorical interpretation that Dante invites us to make here.

The picture he gives us is that of Beatrice as an admiral who gives orders not only to those in his own ship, but also to other ships. "Then I saw the woman that previously had appeared to me veiled under the angelic [*festa*]" — a very beautiful picture of Beatrice coming into view through the angelic *festa*, the shower of flowers which had enveloped the *basterna* in which she is seated. "I saw this woman directing her eyes toward me on the other side of the river, even though her eyes could not be seen. The veil that fell from her head circled with the branch of Minerva, [the olive] did not allow me to see her. Like a queen [*regalmente*] in her bearing, yet stern" — *proterva* doesn't mean *stern*; the literal meaning would be *arrogant*, though stern would fit the mood here — "she spoke as one who," *come colui che dice e il più caldo parlar di retro serva,* "who speaks, holding back the worst for later." Then we have these very mysterious lines; mysterious in themselves and also because the text, the manuscripts are so uncertain: "*Guardami ben: ben son, ben son Beatrice.*" "'Look closely: I am, I am indeed Beatrice; the one that gives beatitude'." Here, Dante breaks the veil of allegory: "*ben son, ben son Beatrice. Come degnasti d'accedere al monte?*" "'How did you dare approach the mountain'?"

Of course, there is no mountain here, and no climbing; simply the passing from a world of confusion to a world of great happiness, to a world of rationality. "'Did you not know that man here is happy'?" Of course that doesn't mean that Dante doesn't believe there was a place before the fall where that happiness which men cannot attain now without a struggle was available, could be enjoyed naturally. "'Did you not know that man here is happy'?" *"non sapéi tu che qui è l'uom felice? Li occhi mi cadder giù nel chiaro fonte.*" The sound of these words, reproving and scornful at the same time, makes Dante cast his eyes down in shame. "My eyes fell down into the resplendent fount" *ma, veggendomi in esso, i trassi all'erba, tanta vergogna mi gravò la fronte*; the sight of himself

reflected in the water forced him to look away toward
the grass, "such shame was cast over my brow, [covered
my forehead]." In all this, Dante says, Beatrice appeared proud but was not, in reality. *Così la madre al
figlio par superba com'ella parve a me*, "as the mother
seems proud to the son, so she seemed to me," *perchè
d'amaro sente 'l sapor della pietade acerba*, "because he
feels that there is pity under the sternness." This pity,
however, he says, is biting, *acerba*. "For the savour of
harsh pity tasteth of bitterness." That's hardly a good
translation. What you have to stress is the pity: the
mother seems stern because the child that is reproached
sees not the pity but feels the bite of it; he feels the
reproach, but not the pity that inspired it.

Beatrice became silent; then immediately comes
the beginning of Psalm 30, a psalm of great hopeful-
ness, of great expectation, of great trust in God, and
therefore very suitable, up to a certain point, for the
occasion. "*In te Domine, speravi*," "'In Thee, O Lord, do
I hope'," *ma oltre "pedas meos" non passaro*, "but they
did not sing anything beyond the words '*pedas meos*',"
where the mood changes.

The effect of this break in the singing of the
angels — what to do with it as we pass to the allegory is
a hard nut to crack — the effect produced in Dante as
a result of this singing is described with a smile, which,
seems rather baroque. Dante says that from the scold-
ing he had received he was so hardened inwardly by
sorrow that he could not weep. But this singing melted,
thawed out his sorrow, and now he can weep. And what
happened inside him is similar to what happens, he
says, at the top of the Appeninnes, along the back of
Italy, when the cold wind from the northeast, the
Boria, has frozen the snow, made it like ice, and then

suddenly — a common enough picture — the south wind blows, and the snow that was frozen melts as though a fire had been set under it, just as a candle melts when you light it.

"As the snow amid the living rafters" — *vive travi* is rather a beautiful phrase in Italian. You have a picture which carries you from the thought of accumulated logs brought together by the sacrifice of a forest, back to the beautiful living forest itself. "As the snow amid the living rafters along Italy's back is frozen under the blast" — Dante says *si congela*, the cold snow is made fast, blown over and made solid, by the Slavonian winds — "then melted, trickles down through itself, if but the land that loseth shade do breathe," that is, the land where the sun casts no shadow, namely, the tropics. Dante must have been familiar with the Greek term for that land and he simply translates it into Italian. *Così fui senza lagrime e sospiri,* "so was I without tears or sighs" —

Not once, when he meets this situation, does Dante fail to fall back on the physics and psychology of his time, to account for the phenomena: namely, that sorrow pressing inside you can make you turn solid; the air and liquid compressed by sorrow, become ice. When finally the pressure is released, the sorrow comes out in two ways. Again, that's rather awkward and baroque in poetry but there it is: the elementary reduction to air and water, and a flow from the mouth and eyes in the form of sighs and tears. Whenever the situation comes up, Dante gives this account, and here again he does not fail to do so: *lo gel che m'era intorno al cor ristretto, spirito ed acqua féssi, e con angoscia per la bocca e per gli occhi uscì del petto.* "The ice which had been compressed about my heart became air and water,

and in anguish came out from my breast through my
eyes, and mouth." Dante cries bitterly, happy to be able
to cry. "She, still fixed firm on the side of the carriage,
turned toward the [*sustanzie pie*]."

Sostanzia is a very generic term; it applies to
angels, it applies to men, to horses, and everything
else. Everything that is, is either a substance or an
accident; and every accident exists only because it
subsists in a substance. So you see how general in its
applications this word *sostanzia*, "substance," is. The
qualifying word is important; these were angelic substances. Beatrice turns and says to them: "*Voi vigilate
nell'eterno die*." One must be careful not to change the
significance here. "'Ye watch in the everlasting day'";
doesn't give the idea. Dante wants to say that the angels
are in eternity, and in eternity there is no cessation of
activity such as we experience, being conscious part of
the time, unconscious at other times. There is no day
and night in eternity, just a continuous day; you are
awake, cogitation goes on, without interruption.
Vigilare means to be awake, that's how the word *vigil*
gets its meaning.

"'You who are awake in the eternal day'," "*sì che
notte né sonno a voi non fura passo che faccia il secol per
sue vie*," "'so that neither night nor sleep steals from
you any step that the world, the world of time, takes
along its way'" — In the phrases *terno die* and *il secol*,
eternity and time are contrasted; very often you contrast eternity with century. That's how you get the
meaning of the term secular in contrast with spiritual.
Nothing, no words I have said, nothing that happens
in time escapes you, Beatrice seems to be saying: I'm
talking to you about these things only so that *he* will
understand. My answer is precisely put in order that he

may understand me, he who is there weeping, so that sin and sorrow may be of equal measure; so that, through weeping he may expiate his sin. This attack is in reality a great self-exaltation by Dante. Beatrice goes on to say that Dante's great endowments, whatever they may have been, had not been given to him solely through nature, but through God's inscrutable grace. In other words, Dante was a great poet not only through nature but through the grace of God, *gratia Dei*. I have repeatedly stressed, in the course of these lectures, that for Dante and his contemporaries, the principle of causality rests in the stars, that if you would understand the ultimate causes of things here below, all must be traced back, all must be brought back to the revolutions of the stars. The only thing that is not controlled by the stars is the spirit. Everything else is under them. This astral determinism, this astrology, is a well-known fact, and it's pretty general.

So Beatrice says, your talent is not solely the result of the *rote magne* — you will see in a moment that the great revolutions must be those of the planets that direct each seed to its appropriate end. There's grace in addition to nature; but when he gets to the sky of Gemini, which is the sky of the constellation which presided over his birth, Dante utters a prayer which is the most solemn prayer of thanks which we have from him, a prayer he addresses to the stars. He tells the Gemini that they are the cause of everything that has made him great as a poet. It is a beautiful prayer as poetry, but quite a dangerous prayer from the point of view of Christian piety. He tells us that these great revolutions are the causes that direct each seed to its end, *secondo che le stelle son compagne* — according to the stars that accompany the movement. In other words, the effect of the planets is not in itself perfect; it acquires perfection as it passes and is conjoined with one of the constellations of the third heaven. For example, Mars becomes much stronger in its efficacy when it approaches and passes through the constellation of the Lion.

"'According to the stars'" — the fixed stars, we should say — but in addition to the stars and planets, Dante was gifted also by divine generosity. *Non pur,* Dante writes, but also *per larghezza di grazie divine.* Someone might ask: why did God single you out? So he adds, by way of explanation, *che sì alti vapori hanno a lor piova, che nostra viste là non van vicine,* the help of grace comes from vapor so high that we can't see it, it's mysteriously given. "*Questi fù tal nella sua vita nuova,*" "'This man was such in his *vita nuova'*—" what are we to make of *vita nuova* here? It seems to mean the life approaching holiness which is described in the book called the *Vita Nuova;* that is, not simply his life as a youth, but his life when it was to have been properly oriented. "He was such [in his *vita nuova*]," not actually, but *virtualmente* — potentially — that is, he was such on account of what was in him as a seed, potentially, "*ch'ogni abito destro fatto averebbe in lui mirabil prova.*" We cannot translate that *abito* otherwise than as *habit*; *abito destro* means a right habit, or good habit. When you speak of the faculties of the potentialities of man — the apprehensive and appetitive faculties and so on — they are free to go in any direction they please; but you can make them go in the right direction by developing a *habitus,* and you can also make them go in the wrong direction by developing a *habitus.* The habit which makes them go in the right direction is called a good habit, or virtue. The habit which makes them go in the wrong direction is called a bad habit, or vice. Here one has to use the word *habit*, not talent. "*Ch'ogni abito destro fatto averebbe in lui mirabil prova.*" "'Every good habit would have had a marvelous [a supernatural] actualization in him'."

Prova is the coming out, the actualization of the *abito destro*. It's hard to translate that literally. To translate it as "'that every good talent would have made wondrous increase in him'" completely destroys the notion. Dante systematically uses *mirabile, ammirare,* and other derivates, to indicate what is beyond the possibility of nature. In other words, he would have been a very extraordinary, unusually moral man; but the better the soil, when not well cultivated, the worse the crop. "*Ma tanto più maligno e più silvestro si fa il terren,*" "'So much more rank and wild the ground becomes',," that is, if you let the land lay fallow, *mal seme,* weeds will grow on it. The more it has of good strength of soil, the richer the soil was to begin with, the wilder the growth. That's what happened to him. Of course, Dante entrusts the utterance to Beatrice, and she applies it to him. She says: "'For some time I sustained him with my countenance [with my face]'." That takes us back to the *Vita Nuova.* Just by showing him her face that was supernaturally beautiful, she rectified his course: "*Mostrando li occhi giovinetti a lui, meco il menava in dritta parte volto.*" This is philosophically and lyrically very beautiful. "'Showing my beautiful, youthful eyes to him, I led him in the direction of righteousness'." "*Si tosto come in sù la soglia fui di mia seconda etade, e mutai vita,*" "'as soon as I was on the threshold of my second age, and I changed life',," when I passed from materiality to immateriality, "'when I died, this one removed himself from me, forsook me and gave himself to others. When I was risen from flesh to spirit, and beauty and virtue were increased within me, I became less dear and less pleasing to him'."

The whole purpose of her beauty had been to lead Dante to beatitude; that, of course, necessitated her death, because the bodily beauty of a living person is far inferior to the beauty of the spirit. Again, we go back to Plato. The body is an evil-smelling *sema*, or sepulcher. She became more beautiful and more powerful after death; but he could not see the increased beauty and power, and he turned his steps along a way which is not the true one. Dante never once forgets the *via veritas*, the true way; here it is the *via non vera*, "*imagini di ben seguendo false*," "'pursuing images of good which are false'." All these things are false goods, in this world of senses, when they are considered as ends in themselves and not as stepping stones to a higher end. And that they are false, Dante says, can be shown by the fact that they never keep their promises. In other words, those of you who trust the things of the senses for their promises of happiness, whether in pleasures of sensuality or in any other way, will be disappointed. "*Nulla promission rendono intera. Ne l'impetrare ispirazion mi valse, con le quali ed in sogno ed altrimenti lo rivocai; si poco a lui ne calse.*" This brings us back to the time when Dante was having visions and dreams, visions that were brought about by Beatrice. But all in vain. "'Nor did it serve any use for me'" to *impetrare spirazion* — *impetrare* means to obtain by request, that's what the Italian word here means — it in no way availed, "*si poco a lui ne calse*," "'so indifferent was he to me'." "*Tanto giù cadde, che tutti argomenti alla salute sua eran già corti, fuor che mostrarli le perdute genti.*" "'He fell so low'," the only remedy was to show him the damned.

What the depths were we don't know. Of course, we have to remove here any idea that this refers to infidelity in love. The reference is no doubt to some heinous doctrine he took up, which was probably Epicureanism. "'So low sank he that all arguments for his salvation were insufficient, except to bring him within sight of lost mankind. For this reason I forced the portal, the gate of the dead. And to this one who has lead him up to this high point, I directed my request'" — namely, Virgil. That tearful request always comes back. She smiled and wept to persuade Virgil to help Dante reach this point. You see, he has something important in mind here. "'A lofty decree of God would be broken if Lethe were to be crossed, and such foods, such nourishment tasted, without the proper scot [*scotto*] of penitence being paid'." We do say *scot-free*, but we don't use the word *scot* by itself, in English. Penalty won't do; it's a payment. What does that payment consist in? Tears.

Dante now has to go through a two-fold sacramental purification by immersion. One is by immersion in the waters of Lethe, that makes him forget all the bad that he has ever done; the other by immersion in Eonoe, which restores the knowledge of all good deeds. But before that, he must do penance, and here is the penance of tears. In the next canto, comes the development of this confession, and purification by contrition. "*O tu, che sei di là dal fiume sacro,*" "'O you who are on the other side of the sacred stream,' she said, now directing her word with the point toward me, which even when the edge only touched me felt sharp" — until then, she had spoken to the angels and not directly to Dante; that is, when the sword was not turned toward Dante, he had already felt the sharpness of the blade; now he is about to feel the point — *ricominciò, seguendo senza cunta, "dì, dì, se questo è vero;"* "'she began again, continuing without a pause, tell me, tell me if this is true';" *"a tanta accusa tua confession conviene esser congiunta,"* "'your confession must be brought face to face with such an accusation'." *Era la mia virtù tanto confusa, che la voce si mosse e pria si spense che da li organi sui fosse dischiusa.* "My powers, [his psychological power] here were so overcome, that my voice would not come forth, quenched before it could be brought out by the speaking organs." You have here an intense emotion trying to find utterance. "A short time she bore with me, and then said: 'what are you thinking?'" *"rispondi a me,"* "'answer me'," *"ché le memorie triste in te non sono ancor dall'acqua offense,"* "'for Lethe has not yet destroyed the memory of all your evil deeds; the dismal memories are not yet blurred out'." *Confusione e paura insieme miste mi pinsero un tal "sì" fuor della bocca, al quale intender fur mestier le viste.* "Confusion and fear together, confounded brought out of my mouth a 'yes,' to understand which, sight was necessary." Hearing was not sufficient apparently, because the utterance was so faint.

"As a cross-bow breaks itself — both string and bow — when it is shot with over-drawn tension, and weakly misses the mark," that is, when you are over-charged with emotional tension and you try to speak, you don't get very far, you break down in the same way that, if you pull the cord of a bow too tightly, you break the bow and the cord, and the arrow can go but a short distance, *sì scoppia' io sott'esso grave carco fuori sgorgando lagrime e sospiri,* "so did I burst under the heavy charge, pouring forth, bringing forth a torrent of tears and sighs, and my voice died away in the passage."

Beatrice apparently was satisfied when the weeping had taken place; his weeping had been enough to accord in some way with the gravity of the sin; *ond'ella a me,* "and she said to me," *"per entro i miei disiri, che ti menavano ad amar lo bene di là dal qual non è a che s'aspiri,"* "'within my desire'" — really it says: "'the desires you had of me, your longing for me'" — *entro i miei desiri,* by the desire that you had of me, or better, by the love you had of me which led you to love the good, that is, in loving me you loved the good, *"lo bene di là dal qual non è a che s'aspiri,"* that good which we call the *summum bonum,* beyond which there is nothing which you might possibly desire — every desire you have leads you to another and another and another until you reach one beyond which there is nothing more to desire — in other words, in loving me you were oriented toward love of God.

"'Within that love you had of me'," *"quai fossi attraversati o quai catene trovasti"* — the picture is supported here by an image of reality; you were moving along the way, what ditch or chains stopped you? What the ditch is can easily be imagined; but the *catene* perhaps cannot so easily be imagined. For a long time, in Italy, roads, for one reason or another, were closed off with chains, usually to facilitate the collection of tolls. "'What chains did you find stretched across the highway, or what ditches did you find that prevented you from moving on?'" What did you encounter that should have made you lose hope of following in my wake? Was it that, or was it the allurement of some other kind of happiness, a desire for some other attractive thing? "'And what allurements or what advantages were displayed to you in the aspect of others, that you had to stray, go after them?'"

This is not quite precise. Up to the last line it follows the text, but then, "*per che dovessi lor passeggiare anzi?*" What was so attractive that made you follow *their* direction, rather than the direction in which I was leading you? *Dopo la tratta d'un sospiro amaro, a pena ebbi la voce che rispose, e le labbra a fatica la formaro.* He is still insisting on the double process of speech, the formation of the speaking organs and the utterance. "After the heaving of a bitter sigh, I hardly had the voice to answer and my lips with difficulty took the necessary form. But presently weeping, I said": *"Le presenti cose"* [things present to the senses] "'things which you see with the senses'" *"col false lor piacer,"* "'with their disappointing false pleasures, lured me, they turned away my steps','" *"tosto che il vostro viso si nascose,"* "'as soon as your countenance was concealed from me'.'" That is, he fell back from the desire of spiritual things to the desire for material things as soon as she died. "And she to me: 'Were you to be silent, or were you to deny that which you confess'," *"non fora men nota la colpa tua: da tal giudice sassi,"* "'your guilt would not be less known; such is the judge who knows it'.'" You did well to confess everything; to try to conceal it would be of no avail. *"Ma quando scoppia dalla propria gota l'accusa del peccato, in nostra corte rivolge sé contra il taglio la rota."* "'But when the accusation of one's own sin comes from one's own lips, when one pours out the confession of one's own sin, in our court, the blade of the sword blunts itself against the wheel','" the blade blunts itself against the grindstone. *"Tuttavia, perchè mo vergogna porte del tuo errore, e perchè altra volta, udendo le sirene sie più forte"* — "'however, in order that you may now bear shame for the transgression and that another time you may be stronger hearing the sirens'" — the sirens, of course, are what bewitched him to love false things — "'put away your weeping, and listen; so you will hear how my buried flesh [my death] should have moved you to a contrary goal; that is, along the right road'."

"*Mai non t'appresentò natura o arte piacer, quanto le belle membra in ch'io rinchiusa fui, e sono in terra sparte.*" "'Never did nature or art, present to you anything so pleasing, never was there a living woman, or a piece of sculpture so beautiful, that showed itself so desirable, as the members of the body in which I was enclosed'" — again the Platonic conception of the body as a sepulcher which encloses the soul — "'and which are now scattered about the earth, buried and decayed. I was the most beautiful thing you ever saw, and yet as a material thing, I failed you'." The argument is: if the most beautiful material thing so failed you, why should you go on to look for joy in other material things? "*Se il sommo piacer sì ti fallio per la mia morte, qual cosa mortale dovea poi trarre te nel suo disio?*" "'If the highest joy so failed you by my death, I, who was more beautiful than anything — what material thing, what thing destined to die, should ever have moved you to desire it'?" "*Ben ti dovevi, per lo primo strale delle cose fallaci, levar suso di retro a me che non era più tale.*" "'After this first blow of disappointing things, of fallacious things, you should have lifted yourself and followed me who was no longer a disappointing thing, a fallacious thing'." And so, Beatrice goes on to explain why she had to die in order to bring Dante to God along the line of love, that moves through beauty.

———————